Printed in the U.S.A.

ISBN 978-0-544-57881-4

2 3 4 5 6 7 8 9 10   0868   24 23 22 21 20 19 18 17 16 15

4500544309   A B C D E F G

Cover, Title Page Photo Credits: Escalator ©Rodrigo Apolaya/APU Imagenes/Getty Images. All Other Photos ©HMH

Houghton Mifflin Harcourt

Escalate  English

5

What is

Dear Student,

Welcome to *Escalate English*! This program is designed to help you take the final steps to becoming fully proficient in English. You will practice and master the skills you need to listen, speak, read, and write English at home, in your community, and at school. This is your opportunity to fine tune your skills so that your English is great in both social and academic situations. You will be ready to conquer the next phase of your education.

Escalate English and your teachers will help you, but you also have a job to do. As you work through this program, ask questions, share what you are learning, and discuss your ideas. The more you practice, the faster your skills will improve. Being an active partner in your learning will ensure that you reach your goals—one step at a time!

Escalate English is a program designed to help you quickly increase your English skills so that you can fully participate in all of your classes. You will master the academic language you need to excel—now and in the future.

escalate *verb*
1. to increase rapidly
2. to rise quickly
synonyms: soar, climb, accelerate

Escalate English?

You are ready.

Ready to increase your English skills.

Ready to achieve more in school, in life, in a career.

Ready to tackle the language you need to succeed.

You are ready to Escalate!

UNIT 1

Meet the
Challenge

Wild Encounters

UNIT 3 Revolution!

UNIT 4

The Power of Storytelling

Under Western Skies

UNIT 6

Journey
to Discovery

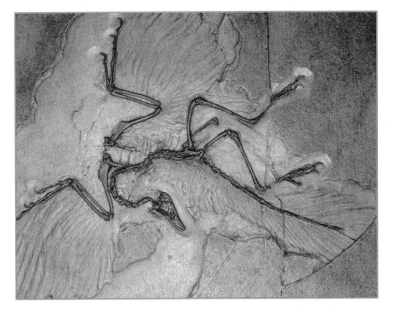

Student Resources

Connecting to Your World

Every time you read something, view something, write to someone, or react to what you've read or seen, you're participating in a world of ideas. You do this every day, inside the classroom and out. These skills will serve you not only at home and at school, but eventually (if you can think that far ahead!), in your career.

The digital tools in this program will tap into the skills you already use and help you sharpen those skills for the future.

Start your exploration at my.hrw.com.

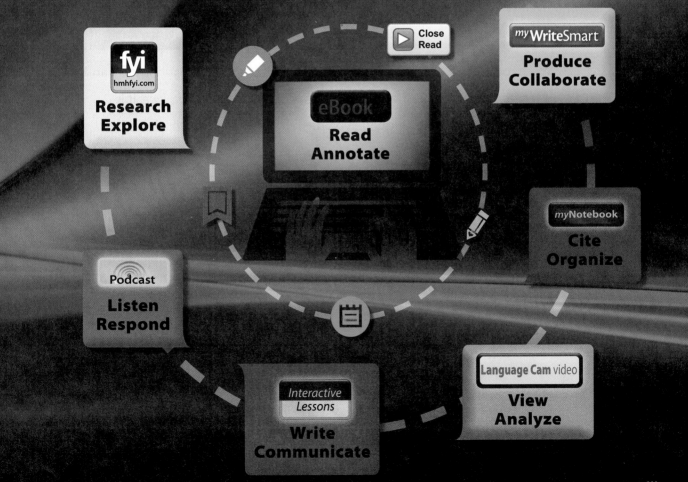

Interacting in Meaningful Ways

Every day you interact with people in many different situations. You text with friends, make plans with family, give directions to your siblings, talk with people in your community, and participate in discussions at school. You have probably noticed that the language you use in one situation might not work in another. In *Escalate English*, you will see and hear examples of English used in meaningful ways. You will have opportunities to practice using words, phrases, and structures so that you are able to successfully interact in every situation.

Collaborating

You have a lot of knowledge to share with others and there is a lot you can learn from others. Whether at home, at school, or in the workplace, it is important to learn the language you need to participate in collaborative discussions. You will be successful if you are prepared for discussions, listen carefully to what others say, and can ask questions and provide feedback.

It is also important to pay attention to the rules of conversation, such as knowing when to take your turn.

Sometimes your interactions are spoken and sometimes they are written. Either way, it is important to understand your purpose and your audience. It is different to exchange social texts and emails with friends than it is to exchange information for school or work. In *Escalate English*, you will practice writing and responding to blogs as well as collaborating with your classmates on a variety of academic topics. The more you practice, the more you will be able to express what you know.

In *Escalate English,* you will learn about many topics and you will have an opinion about what you hear, view, and read. You may need to support your opinion and persuade others. It is important to provide facts and examples to support your opinion. In *Escalate English*, you will learn the language you need to clearly make claims and to persuade others. You will know what language to use in every situation.

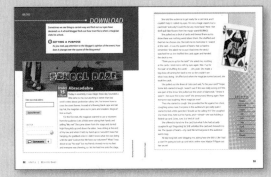

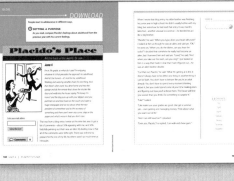

Interacting in Meaningful Ways

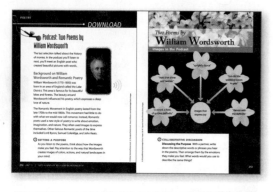

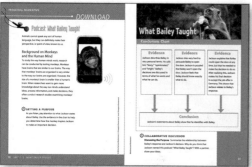

To effectively communicate, it is important to listen and read as carefully as you speak and write. Sometimes it is easy to understand what we hear and read and other times the language and the topic may be less familiar and more challenging. In *Escalate English*, you will learn many strategies for listening, viewing, and reading.

Interpreting

It is important to know how to ask questions when you do not understand or when you want more information. In *Escalate English*, you will learn when and how to ask questions effectively.

Even when what you are viewing or reading seems difficult, it is important not to give up. In *Escalate English*, you will learn to view and read closely. The skills you learn will help you figure out what unfamiliar words and phrases mean and explain what you understand.

You will see that some words and phrases have different meanings in different contexts. As you learn more about language choices, you will be able to impress people with your ability to use language accurately.

Language Cam video
Watch the video to find out more about ways people can reach out and help others.

Language Cam video
Watch the video to find out more about kids making discoveries.

Language Cam video
Want to learn more about revolution? Watch the video.

Language Cam video
Watch this video to learn about nature at work.

Producing the Right Language

One of the most important skills you will develop in school is the ability to talk to a group of people in a formal situation. You will be asked to do this frequently in *Escalate English*. At first, it can be frightening to prepare and present to a group of people, but, with practice, you will find it gets easier. Learning to present formal oral presentations on a variety of topics is a skill you will need throughout your life.

Producing

Sometimes, instead of expressing your ideas orally, you will be asked to write them. You will learn a variety of formats and will practice using different technology tools to organize your thoughts and to write. Being able to explain your ideas and opinions, to present your argument, and to share information with others clearly will prepare you for college and for your future career.

at the Right Time

In *Escalate English,* you will learn that "one size does
not fit all." The way you write will change if you are
communicating with friends via social media, completing
homework or a test, or doing a writing assignment
for class. You will learn to select the most appropriate
vocabulary and language structures to effectively
convey ideas depending on the situation.

Understanding How English Works

Have you ever noticed that texts look different depending upon where you see them? Some texts might be easier for you to read and some might be more difficult. Is it easier for you to read a magazine, a story, or something from your science or social studies text? That is because texts are put together differently for different purposes. In *Escalate English,* you will practice reading varied texts. As you do, you will also learn how these texts are put together and why. You will practice writing using these texts as models. Soon, you will be able to write accurately for multiple purposes.

Some texts are harder to follow than others. Sometimes readers get lost in a story or article and have to use strategies to find their way. In *Escalate English,* you will learn how to identify words and phrases that help you, as a reader, understand how the text is glued together. This will help you read more fluently and, with practice, reading and understanding will become much easier.

You will also learn to watch for language that tells you the important details in a text. You will begin to notice language that indicates when something happened. You will begin to tune into the language that describes what is going on in the text. You may be surprised how exciting it can be when you understand all the details.

Understanding How English Works

The more you read and listen to English for different purposes, the more you will be able to express yourself in many ways. As you prepare for your future college and career experiences, you will want to be sure you are able to write and speak fluently and efficiently.

In *Escalate English*, you will learn the language you need to connect your thoughts together. You will practice this orally and, with enough practice, you will be able to use the language in writing. The people who listen to what you say and read what you write will be able to understand exactly what you mean.

You will also learn words and phrases that will help you become more efficient with your language. Learning how to condense your ideas will enable you to say what you mean and mean what you say!

This is your opportunity to become academically proficient in English. Work hard, practice, and prepare for your successful future!

Meet the Challenge

" . . . true progress is to know more, and be more, and be able to do more."

— **Sir John Lubbock, scientist**

Essential Question

What kinds of challenges do people face?

The Language of Challenges

People face challenges in many of the things they do.
A challenge is anything that poses difficulty, or is not immediately easy to solve. Learning a new language, lifting a heavy weight, and solving a complex problem are things many people find challenging. Overcoming a challenge may require strength, work, intelligence, creativity—or some combination of all of these.

Some challenges are individual. What's easy for you might be difficult for someone else. You may be great at math, but a friend might struggle with it. Each of us experiences things that are not easy for us, and each person struggles with different things.

Societal challenges involve groups of people. How to deal with waste or pollution in our community is a societal challenge. Learning to live together even when our ideas differ is a societal challenge, too. People often work together to solve these kinds of problems. Justice leaders, like Martin Luther King Jr. and Mahatma Ghandi, are needed to lead the way to finding solutions to difficult social problems.

Facing challenges helps us learn about ourselves. Whether dealing with personal challenges or working to solve societal problems, we can discover something new about our own strengths and weaknesses. Facing challenges is important to our individual growth and for our collective growth as citizens of the world.

> **How do people grow and learn by facing challenges?**

Say **What?** Difficult Words

Sometimes when we read, we come across hard words. We might not know the meaning of a word, or we might not know how to pronounce it. Working through difficult words can be challenging, but this process helps us to learn new things. Here are a few tips you can use when you come across new words.

To find the meaning of a word	To pronounce a word
• **Use context clues** The sentences before and after an unfamiliar word often give hints that can help you figure out the word's meaning.	• **Identify syllables** Break up long words into smaller parts. Then try saying the parts one at a time. Syllables usually have just one vowel sound, so look for the vowels to help you.
• **Identify word parts you recognize** Look at the unfamiliar word for parts, like prefixes or root words, that you know. This can help you figure out the meaning.	• **Find pronunciation guides in the dictionary** These tools show you all the sounds in a word, and show which sounds are stressed.
• **Look up the word in a glossary or dictionary** After looking up a word, use it in a sentence. This can often help you remember the word and its definition.	• **Look up the word online, and listen to it said out loud** Online dictionaries often include recordings of words so you can hear them pronounced correctly.

↻ Performance Task

Choose an example of something that can be challenging. It may be one of the examples listed on page 4, one in **Browse** magazine, or something else that interests you. Write a short speech about your chosen example. Why might others find this topic challenging? How might someone face this challenge and how will facing it help him or her to grow? Use the supports in your **Activity Book** as a guide.

➜ *Browse* *magazine*

DOWNLOAD

You just read about different kinds of challenges. Read ahead to find out what challenge GamerGuy faces.

⏻ **SETTING A PURPOSE**

As you read, think about the problem GamerGuy faces, and how he solves it.

GamerGuy

Enter your email address:

Subscribe me!

SEARCH

💬 **Comments** 10

March 15, 3:00 pm

I'm having the worst time in math class. No matter how hard I try to pay attention or how many times I ask my teacher for help, I just don't get it. We're working on fractions and I barely understand how to add and subtract them. Now I'm supposed to be able to multiply and divide them? Dream on! I'm supposed to be working on my homework now, but all I can think about is how hard it is. I'm going to play video games instead.

March 15, 3:35 pm

My mom told me to work on my math assignment. I did the easy ones first. Now my older brother is in here bothering me. That should help me concentrate. Who needs math, anyway? It's not like I'm going to be a math teacher. I'm going to make video games. Plus, can't we just use calculators? They're right there on our phones!

March 15, 4:24 pm

Turns out my brother didn't come into my room to bug me. Mom told him I was working on fractions and he came to help me. He said he hated fractions at first too, which I can hardly believe. The guy is like a math genius. I felt better knowing that he had trouble with them, too. He wanted to sit down and see what I find so hard about fractions. He said I probably wanted to give up, which I did.

He showed me some tricks to remember for working with fractions, and somehow explained the same things my teacher tried to explain, only he made sense. I think it helped that he could sit next to me and watch me work. Sometimes I get lost when we work as a class and I can't catch up. He was able to see where I was messing up. I was still frustrated, but he was making it better.

Then he showed me something even cooler! Online there are games for learning math. Would you ever think there were video games created to teach kids fractions? You know what else my brother said? He said making video games is pretty much all about doing math. Maybe I'll need math after all! Yikes!

March 22, 4:02 pm

Just got done with my math homework in record time! I don't think fractions are easy yet, but my brother has worked with me every day for the past week and I'm determined to master them. Plus, playing a video game about math doesn't feel like homework. Now that I know I'll actually need to use math, I'm ready to put in the extra effort to learn this stuff. If something's hard, stick with it, guys! If I can learn fractions, you can do anything!

UPLOAD

⏻ COLLABORATIVE DISCUSSION

Discussing the Purpose How did GamerGuy meet the challenge of math? What was the solution to his problem?

Talk About It With a partner, discuss how GamerGuy tells how he feels about math. Which words and phrases show that he dislikes math? Which words and phrases show that his feelings about math are changing?

Staying Safe What are the possible risks of communication online? How can bloggers stay safe? Work in a group. Make a list of rules that bloggers should follow to help limit risks.

Write On! Add a comment to GamerGuy. Tell about a challenge you faced. Then exchange your comment with a classmate and write something in reaction to his or her comment. | 💬 Comments | 0 |

⟳ Performance Task

Writing Activity: Start a Blog People write blogs about many different things. Some blogs are written as many entries about a blogger's daily life. Other blogs might be about one subject, such as sports.

1 Start a blog that you will continue to write as you complete this unit. The first thing to decide on is what you want to write about. Pick a topic you care about.

2 Next, pick a website to host your blog. There are many sites that have free blog hosting. You don't have to pay anything to get started!

3 Then, think about how you want your blog to look. Some free blogging websites come with many themes that you can choose from. Pick a unique title for your blog. Make it fun! You can even add an image at the top of your blog or in the background. Be safe! Use a nickname when blogging.

4 Finally, start writing! Share your blog posts with people you know. If you use a free blogging website, you can often follow other users on that website. They might follow you back! You can keep a "blogroll" that lists other blogs you enjoy reading. It's common for bloggers you add to your blogroll to add you back. Then you'll reach even more readers.

Language Cam video

Watch the video to learn more about meeting challenges.

DOWNLOAD

Athlete vs. Mathlete

GamerGuy challenged himself by practicing his math skills so that he could one day make video games. In *Athlete vs. Mathlete*, Russell and Owen are both taking on the challenge of trying out for the school basketball team.

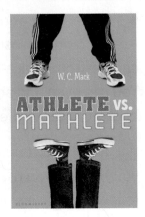

Know Before You Go

In *Athlete vs. Mathlete*, Russell and Owen are fraternal twin brothers ("fraternal" means that they don't look exactly alike.) Russell is the mathlete, and the team leader of the Masters of the Mind club. Owen is the athlete, and plays for the school's basketball team. That is, until a new coach requires tryouts for all players, even those already on the team. He makes Russell try out because he is tall. Owen and his dad help Russell practice for the tryout, but Owen doesn't think Russell will make the team. And that's okay by Owen, because each twin has his own activity that he is good at doing. . . .

⏻ SETTING A PURPOSE

As you read, compare and contrast how Owen and Russell approach the basketball tryout.

from Athlete vs. Mathlete

by W.C. Mack

Russell tucked his shirt into his shorts and moved away from the wall. He swallowed hard and walked to the line.

I gave him a thumbs-up as he went by, and I watched him get into starting position, his awesome Nikes **toeing** the line. He was all alone. With a crowd staring at him, waiting for him to fail. I took a deep breath, wishing I didn't have to watch.

> **toeing:** touching with your toes

And then it hit me. I *didn't* have to.

10   When I stood up and walked toward my brother, everyone started whispering, but I ignored them.

Russ jumped when I stepped onto the line next to him.

"What are you doing?" he asked.

I cleared my throat and told Coach, "I'll run with him."

"You're sure, Owen?" Coach asked.

"Yeah," I said, nodding.

"Okay, then." Coach blew the whistle.

20   As soon as we took off, I knew I'd done the right thing.

Russell was *super slow,* and if he'd run with anyone else, he would have been **left in the dust** in two seconds. I tried to forget that Coach was timing us and kept pace with Russ, so he wouldn't look bad.

> The idiom **left in the dust** means "to be quickly left behind."

The **prefix *re-*** means "again." What does it mean to retie shoelaces?

What two words make up **stopwatch**? How does this help you determine the meaning of the word?

But of course he looked bad.

He fell over twice when he bent to touch the lines, *and* he tripped over his shoelaces on the way back. He even stopped to **retie** them about halfway through, like
30   Coach's stopwatch didn't even exist.

"Double knots," I hissed, then heard some of the guys laughing.

I had to keep reminding myself that Coach had already recorded my time, so I wasn't risking anything by helping my brother.

When we were finally finished, the **stopwatch** clicked, and Russell slid down the wall until he was sitting on the floor, with his head on his knees.

Coach Baxter growled, "Nice teamwork, Owen."
40   That felt good.

"Man," Chris said, shaking his head when I walked back to the guys. "It's like Russ was in slow motion."

"Yeah," Paul said, "like a replay on ESPN."

"And he doesn't mean a **highlight**," Nicky Chu added.

I glared at them and they dropped it.

Dribbling was next. Coach told us he wanted to check out our ball-handling skills, but he was looking for control, not speed.

Lucky for Russ.

50   Coach split us into two groups, and we stood in front of the rows of orange cones Mr. Webster had put out.

"I want you to dribble through the cones and go in for a layup at the end," Coach explained. "Got it?"

I was near the end of the line, which was fine with me. When each of the guys ahead of me ran the drill, I watched closely to see what mistakes they made so I wouldn't make them, too.

Russell's turn was right before mine, and I heard more **snickering**.

60   *Come on, Russ. Do it for us.*

Coach blew the whistle and my twin took off. He managed to keep control of the ball, but barely. He knocked over three of his cones, but made it to the end.

When he went in for the layup, he totally missed the hoop.

"Air ball," Nicky Chu sang quietly, and a couple of guys laughed.

I didn't have time to worry about it, though, because I was up next.

70   When the whistle blew, I dribbled through the cones and made a perfect shot, off the backboard and through the net.

Yes!

> **highlight:** draw attention to

> What does **dribbling** mean? Keep reading to find out.

> **snickering:** quiet laughing, in a mean or unkind way

What two words make up **tryout**? How does this help you understand its meaning?

We ran the same drill four more times, and I shot 100 percent. Seriously awesome!

Russell only made one basket, but he *did* leave all the cones standing on his last run. His **tryout** had started out stinking like old cheese, but it was getting better. Kind of.

"Okay," Coach said. "We know basketball is about 80 scoring points, but it's also about defense."

I was relieved when he put me and Russ together for one-on-one.

"You ready?" I asked my brother.

"I missed every basket on that last drill," he said, and sighed.

"So what? *This* is what you do best. Remember what I told you the other day, about just standing there?"

Russ nodded.

"That's all you have to do. Just stand there and block 90 my shots."

"But then you won't score, Owen."

Whoa! I hadn't thought of that. "Okay, let me make a couple of them."

For the next few minutes, I made Russell look like he had some idea what he was doing, which was good enough. With my help, he blocked about 75 percent of my shots.

Then it was my turn to defend the net against Russell. He slowly dribbled toward me, biting his lip. He checked 100 the net, then looked back at me and came closer.

Just stay calm, Russ.

I bent my knees, ready.

He dribbled for a couple more seconds, and just when I thought he was going to go right, he lifted the ball in front of him and jumped straight up in the air.

He let the ball fly.

Stunned, I turned to watch it drop right into the net.

What?

110 The guys on the sidelines went nuts.

"Beautiful," Coach said, grinning. "Great form, kid. Give it another try."

Russell and I lined up face-to-face again.

"I can't believe I made that," he whispered to me, smiling.

"Me neither," I told him. What were the chances?

"I mean, that was a jump shot!"

"Yeah," I muttered, ticked off. How did he know that's what it was called? And weren't we supposed to be

120 showing off *my* defense, not *his* shooting? "You made a jump shot."

And then, right in my face, he made seven more.

By the time my defensive "showcase" was over, I hadn't touched the ball once, and the rest of the guys were staring at Russ like he was a superhero.

No one said anything until Coach let out a quiet, "Wow."

Russ smiled, but he didn't look like he understood what had just happened.

130 I didn't either.

"Who taught you to shoot like that?" Mr. Webster asked.

I waited for Russ to say my name or point to me. I probably didn't wow anybody during the drill, but I could get some brownie points for teaching him everything he knew.

"No one," Russ said, shrugging.

What?

Of course, he was right. I couldn't do a jump shot
140 myself, so there's no way I could have taught the most
uncoordinated kid on the planet how to do one.

Or eight.

But still.

"You've just been practicing by yourself?"
Coach asked.

"No," Russ said. He cleared his throat and I could tell
he was embarrassed that everyone was staring at him.
"That was my first try."

Coach's whistle fell out of his mouth. "Really?"
150 Russ shrugged.

Coach kept staring at my brother, like he couldn't
believe it, then he shook his head. "Okay, everybody line
up at center court."

We groaned, since we were way too tired for
more drills.

But drills weren't what Coach had in mind.

"If you hear your name, you're on the team," he said,
then waited for us to calm down before he announced,
"Nicky Chu."

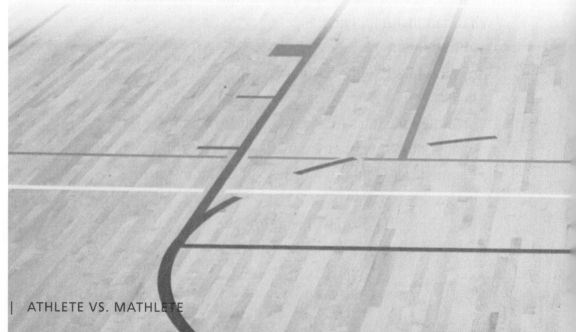

160　　My old **teammate** waved his fist in the air and grinned.

　　Coach kept listing names and guys high-fived each other when they were called. Most of the players had been on the team last year.

　　But not all of them.

　　I was just starting to get worried when Coach said, "Owen Evans."

　　''Yes!'' I bumped fists with Chris, who'd already made it. We both jumped about four feet off the ground.

170　　"Russell Evans," Coach said.

　　What?

　　If I could have frozen in **midair**, I would have. Instead, my second-class shoes hit the floor with a thud. I turned to stare at my brother, who looked as shocked as I was.

　　Russ made the team?

　　How was that even possible?

> Think about other compound words that end in -*mate*. How do those words help you understand what **teammate** means?

> The prefix *mid-* means "in the middle." How does this help you understand what **midair** means?

UPLOAD •

⏻ COLLABORATIVE DISCUSSION

Discussing the Purpose Think about how Owen feels about Russell's tryout and how he feels about his own tryout. With a partner, discuss how the twins' experience is similar, and how it is different.

READING TOOLBOX

Compare and Contrast

When you **compare**, you show how two things are alike. When you **contrast**, you show how two things are different. Think about what characters say, do, and think to help you determine how they are the same, or how they are different.

It can be helpful to organize the different characteristics, or traits, of a character to figure out how he is similar to, or different from, another character. Think about Russell and Owen. How are they similar? How are they different? Use a graphic organizer like this one to help you.

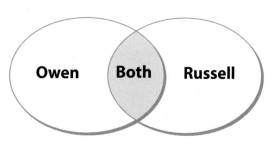

Analyzing the Text [Cite Text Evidence]

1. **Restate** What is the central idea of this selection?

2. **Analyze** How does Owen feel about Russell's tryout? Do his feelings change from the beginning of the selection?

Vocabulary Strategy: Specialized Vocabulary

This story includes some words about basketball that may not be familiar to you. Specialized vocabulary means the words and terms that are particular to a job, activity, or area of study. For example, you may know the meaning of the word *defense* (lines 80 and 120), but context will help you determine the meaning of the word as it is used in the selection. Use the other words in a sentence to help you determine a word's meaning.

Term	Guessed Meaning	Dictionary Meaning
layup (line 53)	dribbling and shooting a basketball	an often one-handed shot made close to the basket, usually bounced off the backboard
drill (line 55)	exercise, practice	a repeated exercise meant to help teach or practice a skill
air ball (line 66)		
backboard (line 71)		
jump shot (line 117)		

Practice and Apply Finish filling in the chart above to find out the meaning of the specialized vocabulary in this selection. Use context to first guess at the meaning. Then use a dictionary to find the meaning of the word or term.

The Sun Dance

Think about Russell and Owen's basketball team tryout, and how it was a challenge for each of them. Read the following selection to learn about how young men meet a challenge in their culture.

Background on Rituals

Cultures throughout the world have rituals to mark what they consider important. From religious rites to celebrations of history, people's traditions shape their lives. In some cultures, an important ritual is an initiation, or coming of age, required for young people to enter adulthood. These take many forms, often requiring training and skill, but these rituals are not considered a competition.

READING TOOLBOX

Main Idea and Details

The most important idea of a selection is called the **main idea**. A selection might have one main idea. It could also have a main idea in each paragraph. When you read a selection, ask yourself, "What is the most important idea that the author wants me to know?"

The phrases, words, and sentences that give more information about the main idea are the **details**.

⏻ SETTING A PURPOSE

As you read, think about the main idea of the selection.

The Sun Dance

by Reda Ali

One by one the young men stood quietly in front of the elder. Taking a fold of skin on each man's chest, the elder pierced the skin with a knife. Then he threaded a sharp bone **skewer** through the skin. Attached to the bone was a long rope made of buffalo skin, which was tied to the top of a tall pole. Soon the young men would begin to dance to **drumbeats**. As they gazed up at the sun, they pulled until the skewers tore through their skin.

The shocked observer who reported this saw the Sun Dance in the 1800s, but it was a tradition of the Plains Indians long before then. To explorer Frederick Schwatka, the Sun Dance looked like ritual torture. But the participants saw it very differently. The challenge of the Sun Dance did not **intimidate** them. Instead, they considered it an honor to dance.

skewer: a long pin inserted through food while cooking

The compound word **drumbeats** is made up of the words *drum* and *beats*. Can you guess what it means?

intimidate: Spanish cognate, meaning "to fill with fear"

10

shone: the past tense of the verb *shine*, which means "to give off light"

gazing: looking steadily

teepees

Each of the Plains peoples had its own tradition for the Sun Dance. The dance that Frederick Schwatka saw was a Sioux dance. Many Sioux people had come together for the ceremony. It was held at the time of the summer solstice, when the sun **shone** the longest. For days before the ceremony began, Sioux men and women had been preparing a ritual circle. In the middle they put up a sacred pole, which represented the center of the world.

As the dancers looked up at the top of the pole, they were **gazing** at the sun. They believed that the sun embodied divine power. The dancers were seeking spiritual insight from the sun—knowledge and power they could use for the well-being of their people.

Two animals, the buffalo and the eagle, played an important role in the Sun Dance. Many of the Plains peoples used a buffalo skull as an altar during the dance. The Plains Indians depended on the buffalo for their lives— for everything from their food to their **tepees** to their clothes. But in order to use the buffalo, they had to kill it. So the buffalo represented both life and death.

The eagle had different significance for the Plains peoples. Eagles were sacred animals because, 40 flying high in the sky, they were closer to the sun than humans could be. They also had many traits humans value, such as courage and speed. Because eagles were sacred, their feathers were used in the ceremony.

The Sun Dance usually lasted for about four days. During that time, the dancers took no food or water. After all of the dancers had **torn themselves free**, the dance ended. The dancers were "reborn."

torn themselves free: pulled themselves away

COLLABORATIVE DISCUSSION

Discussing the Purpose With a small group, discuss the main idea of the selection. Was there more than one main idea in "The Sun Dance"? Cite evidence to support your answer.

READING TOOLBOX

Main Idea and Details

There can be one **main idea** in a selection. Sometimes, there can be more than one main idea. The main idea can be stated directly. When the main idea is stated directly, it is easy to find. When the main idea is not stated directly, it might be hard to find. If the main idea is hard to find, look at information in the selection to guess the main idea.

Details can come in different forms. Sometimes, the details in a text are examples, which are experiences or stories that support the main idea.

To keep track of the main idea and supporting details in a selection, use a graphic organizer like the one below.

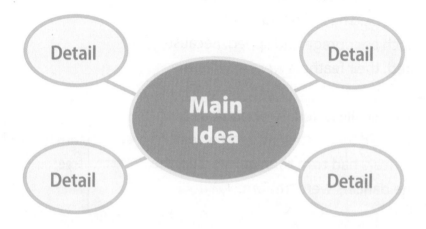

Analyzing the Text `Cite Text Evidence`

Summarize Explain how the details in the selection support the main idea.

Vocabulary Strategy: Making Nouns into Adjectives

A suffix is a series of letters added to the end of a word to change its meaning.

Read this sentence from the text: "They also had many traits humans value, such as courage and speed." (lines 41–42) In this sentence, *courage* and *speed* are nouns. They can be made into adjectives by adding a suffix.

To make *courage* into an adjective, add the suffix –*ous*. To make *speed* into an adjective, add the suffix –*y*. You can use a chart like the one below to help you make nouns into adjectives.

noun	+ suffix	=	adjective
courage	+ *ous*	=	courageous
speed	+ *y*	=	speedy

Practice and Apply Make adjectives from the nouns *mess, advantage, rain, posi*, and *danger*. Decide if you should add –*ous* or –*y* to the end. If you do not know the meaning of these words, you can look them up in a dictionary.

Speak Out! What is a tradition that you know about from another culture? Tell a partner about the tradition. Ask your partner to explain anything that is not clear.

Useful Words

▷ mess   ▷ advantage
▷ poison   ▷ rain
▷ dirt   ▷ danger

Podcast: East of the Sun and West of the Moon

The sun is a common subject of rituals and stories for many cultures around the world. For the Sioux, the sun is a symbol of divine power. In this podcast, a folktale from Norway, it shows the way to a far-off castle.

Background on Norwegian Folktales

In the 1800s, two writers named Peter Christen Asbjørnsen (PEH-ter KRIS-ten ahs-BYERN-sen) and Jørgen Moe (YER-gen MOH) published a collection of folktales called *Norwegian Folktales*. It was based on their research into stories that people in Norway told each other about fairies, trolls, magic, and adventure. Asbjørnsen and Moe were inspired by the Brothers Grimm, who had done the same kind of research into German folktales.

East of the Sun and West of the Moon is one of the stories published in *Norwegian Folktales*.

⏻ **SETTING A PURPOSE**

As you listen, pay attention to the story as it unfolds. Use the timeline to follow along with the main events of the narrative. Think about the decisions Elsa makes. Do you agree with her decisions?

East of the Sun and West of the Moon

The Podcast Timeline

Elsa leaves her family to live with the bear in his castle.

The bear changes into a prince at night. He sleeps in Elsa's bedroom, but leaves before Elsa wakes up.

Elsa's mother thinks that the person in Elsa's bedroom might be a troll.

Elsa uses a candle to look at the person sleeping in her room. She realizes that the bear is actually a prince.

Elsa drips candlewax on the Prince's shirt and wakes him up. The Prince explains that his stepmother bewitched him, and now he must go to her castle far away.

Elsa asks the Winds how to get to the stepmother's castle.

At the stepmother's castle, Elsa meets the Prince. He explains his plan to free himself from his stepmother's spell.

Princess Longnose tries to wash the Prince's magic shirt, but she fails. Elsa is able to wash it, and she frees the Prince from the spell.

⏻ COLLABORATIVE DISCUSSION

With a partner, write down all of the choices Elsa made during the story. Pretend you are in Elsa's shoes. Would you have done things differently? Why, or why not?

DOWNLOAD

You listened to a podcast about the challenge Elsa faced in freeing her husband from a spell. Read ahead to find out how some animals have adapted to live in challenging environments.

⏻ SETTING A PURPOSE

As you read, think about why these animals developed their adaptations.

EXTREME ADAPTATIONS

Shiraz Lall

Every environment has different challenges. Living things have developed strategies to meet the challenges that they face.

1 The Portia spider uses its intelligence to hunt other spiders, including species that are much larger. Most spiders forget about anything they can't see, but the Portia doesn't forget. It can follow difficult paths to get to its prey. The Portia breaks down tasks into

10 small parts and thinks about them one at a time. Its brain is the size of a **pinhead**, so it can't think as fast as big animals can. But with enough time to think, it can notice details and solve some mazes.

> Break the compound word **pinhead** into the two words that form it, for clues to its meaning.

2 Ice worms are closely related to the common earthworm. However, they are much smaller. And they live in ice! In fact, they can only survive at low temperatures. Ice worms **burrow**
20 below the surface of the glaciers they live in during the day to avoid overheating in sunlight. Their diet is a mix of pollen and snow algae. When the temperature drops, ice worms can increase their cells' energy production.

burrow: to dig into the ground

3 You wouldn't expect a fish to live in a desert. But the Death Valley pupfish lives in the hottest, driest desert in America. 50,000 years ago, this valley
30 was a lake as deep as 590 feet! All that's left of the lake is a tiny creek, twice as salty as the sea. That's much too salty for most fish to live in. But the pupfish adapted to these harsh conditions.

4 The fennec fox lives in the Sahara desert. The secret to its success is its enormous ears. The fennec fox uses

40 its ears to listen for the sound of **prey** moving underground. Like other desert animals, the fennec fox has to avoid getting too hot. Its ears help solve that problem, too. Their great surface area allows the fennec fox's body heat to be released through its ears!

5 The silversword plant grows on the tops of volcanoes in Hawaii. While you might think of volcanoes as hot, their slopes can be very cold. The

50 silversword has adapted to this cold. Its shiny leaves are curved so that much of the light that hits them reflects off the leaf to the center of the plant. By concentrating light on its center, the silversword raises its temperature enough to grow from the center outward.

6 Polar bears live in the far north. Up there, few large animals can 60 survive on land. So polar bears go into the water to hunt. They are so well-adapted to the cold that they risk **overheating**, even in the freezing Arctic! On days that are hot for polar bears, the bears jump into the icy water to cool off.

How does breaking the compound word **overheating** into two words help you understand its meaning?

UPLOAD

⏻ **COLLABORATIVE DISCUSSION**

Discussing the Purpose What is the cause of the animals and plants in this selection developing extreme adaptations?

READING TOOLBOX

Cause-and-Effect

A cause is an action that makes an event happen. A cause has an effect, which is the result of the cause.

To find the effect of a cause, ask yourself, "What happened?"

▶ To find the cause, ask yourself, "Why did this event or action happen?"

▶ Look for phrases and words such as *as a result, due to, because, since, therefore,* and *since.* These words and phrases show a direct relationship between a cause and its effect.

A selection that is organized with a cause-and-effect structure may directly state the order in which events occurred. Sometimes this information is stated indirectly. If you are having trouble identifying cause-and-effect relationships, use a graphic organizer such as the one below to help you record the information as you read.

| Cause | ⟹ | Effect |

↻ Performance Task

Writing Activity: Informative Essay When writing an informative essay, the first step is to think about how the essay is organized. With a partner, think about other ways the information in this informational text could be organized.

- Look at the facts and details in this selection.

- Think back to the organizational structures you have already learned about in this unit—main idea-and-details and compare-and-contrast.

- Use a graphic organizer to arrange the facts and details. Which graphic organizer works best?

- Present your graphic organizer to the class. Did any other pair choose the same graphic organizer as you?

Write On! Which animal's adaptation would you like to learn more about? Write a short paragraph that tells why you want to learn more about that adaptation.

Speak Out! Can you think of ways that humans have adapted to their environments? With a small group, discuss how humans handle cold and hot temperatures.

DOWNLOAD

What's Up?

The animals in "Extreme Adaptations" had to adjust their bodies to survive in their surroundings. The astronauts in this article have to adjust to life without gravity.

Background on Space

Space is a unique place. It is a place where few humans have gone. Astronauts train for years to go into space. To travel to space, astronauts have to ride immense rockets. Once they arrive, everything in space is different from on Earth. Things we take for granted, like air, have to be carefully managed. Even basic directions, like *up* and *down*, cease to have meaning in orbit.

⏻ SETTING A PURPOSE

As you read, think about what problem the astronauts face, and how they find a way to solve it.

What's Up?

by Ernesto Borraz

In space, astronaut Ed Lu explained, anything eaten with a utensil has to have sauce. Otherwise, the food flies all over the place. "You have to move fairly slowly when eating," he added, "or the food will **literally** fly right off your spoon (and onto the wall)." Astronauts eat at a table, Lu said. But there are no chairs. "We . . . float around the table while we prepare our meals and eat," he said. They use **bungee cords** to keep utensils and food from floating away. And when they do want
10 to sit at the table, the astronauts have to slide their feet under railings on the floor to stay in one spot.

Floating food and floating astronauts! What's up? It's all about gravity. Actually, Ed Lu was describing what is called "zero gravity." The force of gravity that allows us to walk on our two feet, or to sit at a table, or to drop a ball expecting it to bounce, is not experienced in space. Zero gravity presents many challenges for astronauts, for scientists, and for others who design for life in space.
20 Zero gravity is another term for **weightlessness**. Floating food is just one of its effects. Changes in the human body can be more important. Astronauts have to adjust their sense of balance in zero gravity.

In this sentence, the word **literally** is an adverb used to modify the verb *fly*. It means "in the real sense" or "truly."

bungee cords: strong, stretchy ropes with hooks on either end

The word *weightlessness* has **two suffixes**: *-less*, meaning "lack of," and *-ness*, meaning "state of."

35

At first, many have what they call Space Adaptation Syndrome (otherwise known as "throwing up"). After a few days in space, though, astronauts begin to understand directions as they relate to body position. *Up* is wherever your head is. And *down* is wherever your feet are.

30 Many other physical changes take place in zero gravity. Astronauts' hearts beat more slowly. Muscles that we use to stand upright on Earth shrink in space. Bone density is lost. Some of these changes are reversed when the astronauts return to Earth and its gravity. Others, such as bone density, are more problematic.

Because of the differences between zero gravity and Earth's gravity force, scientists use the International Space Station as a research laboratory.
40 ISS astronauts have tested the effects of exercise on bone loss (it helps prevent it). Experiments with robot

About 10 years ago, Ed Lu spent six months on the International Space Station. The ISS is the largest human-made object in space. It has been in space since November 2000. Fifteen nations participate in the ISS program. Ed Lu was part of Expedition 7. Expedition 47 takes off in 2016.

technology on the space station have led to advances in brain surgery and cancer research on Earth. These are just some of the results.

Dr. Alan Hargens, whose specialty is **orthopedics**, worked with NASA. He studied bone loss in astronauts. Hargens points out that one day astronauts will travel to Mars. That is a six-month trip in zero gravity. And once on Mars, they would experience only 38% of the gravity 50 on Earth. The astronauts will have to be in top shape to function on Mars, Hargens notes. So the challenge is how to ensure their good health on the trip. Scientists like Hargens don't have all the answers yet. But they are working hard to meet the challenge.

orthopedics: branch of medicine that tries to prevent and cure problems that affect bones and muscles

UPLOAD

⏻ COLLABORATIVE DISCUSSION

Discussing the Purpose How are astronauts meeting the challenge of living in space? With a small group, discuss how life in space is different from life on Earth.

READING TOOLBOX

Problem and Solution

When you are trying to determine what the problem of the selection is, follow these steps:

1. Find the cause of the problem. This may appear in the first or second paragraph of a story or article.
2. Look for words such as *challenge* and *reason*. These words can signal an explanation of the problem.
3. To find a solution, ask yourself, "What facts and details does the author give to solve the problem?"
4. Look for words such as *conclude*, *answer*, and *propose*. These words can signal where to find the solution.

Presenting a problem and offering a solution is one way to organize an informational essay. Sometimes, the solution can be presented first, as a way of showing how a problem was solved. If you are having trouble identifying a problem-and-solution relationship, use a graphic organizer such as the one below to help you record the information as you read.

Problem	→	Solution

Vocabulary Strategy: Suffix –ly

You know that a suffix is attached to the end of a word to change its meaning. The suffix –ly means "like" or "resembling." For example, you can say that someone is a *quick* walker, or that he walks *quickly*.

Practice and Apply Find two examples of words that contain the suffix –ly in the reading "What's Up?"

LISTENING TOOLBOX

Active Listening
Always be respectful of others when they are talking.

▶ Wait for your turn. As excited as you may be to add to the conversation, don't interrupt.
▶ Ask if you don't understand what's been said.
▶ Let the speaker know that you understood the point, even if you disagree.

Speak Out! Would you want to be an astronaut? With a partner, share your opinion. Cite evidence from the text to support your opinion.

Around the World in 80 Days

You've read how astronauts in space meet the challenge of living far away from Earth in zero gravity. In *Around the World in 80 Days*, you will read about Phileas Fogg, who takes on the challenge of traveling the earth in only 80 days.

Know Before You Go

GENRES The selection you will read is based on a book by the same name. The book is an adventure novel that was written by Jules Verne in 1873.

ABOUT ADVENTURE BOOKS In books like this, the characters leave everyday life behind. They take risks. Things happen fast. Adventures from early times were often about knights. This one is about a gentleman and his servant.

Around the World in 80 Days is one of many adventures in a series that Verne wrote called *Les Voyages Extraordinaires*. This is French for "The Extraordinary Journeys."

The characters in this story are:

Phileas Fogg

Detective Fix

Jean Passepartout

Aouda

⏻ SETTING A PURPOSE

As you read, think about the way the characters react to their challenges.

Jules Verne's
Around the World in 80 Days

retold by Jessica E. Cohn

MR. PHILEAS FOGG IS AN ENGLISH GENTLEMAN. HE HAS JUST TWO PASTIMES: READING THE PAPER AND PLAYING CARDS AT HIS CLUB IN LONDON. EACH DAY, HE GOES TO THE CLUB AT THE SAME TIME.

ONE DAY, HOWEVER, TWO EVENTS CHANGE EVERYTHING. HIS NEW SERVANT ARRIVES . . .

The new servant.

Passepartout at your service, sir.

. . . AND A BET IS MADE.

Did you read about the bank robbery? The thief is on the run.

The world is big enough.

It was, once.

No country is safe for him!

He could be half way around the world by now!

Impossible!

The newspaper says it's now possible to circle the world in 80 days.

FOGG HAS HEARD ENOUGH.

I will bet 20,000 pounds. I will make the tour of the world in 80 days or less!

We accept!

LONDON, ENGLAND: EVENING OF DEPARTURE

FOR THE VERY FIRST TIME FOGG RETURNS HOME FROM THE CLUB BEFORE MIDNIGHT.

But, sir . . .

Passepartout, we start for Dover in ten minutes!

We are going around the world in 80 days!

THEY ARE NOW IN COMPETITION WITH THE CLOCK. THEY WILL TRAVEL FROM EUROPE TO ASIA, FROM THERE TO AMERICA, AND BACK HOME AGAIN.

We haven't a moment to lose! We'll buy our clothes along the way.

'Round the world!

BUT THE POLICE ARE ALSO MOVING QUICKLY — THEY ARE LOOKING FOR THE BANK THIEF, WHO IS STILL ON THE RUN.

IN A FEW DAYS, FOGG AND PASSEPARTOUT REACH EGYPT. AN OFFICER IS CHECKING THE SHIP FOR THE THIEF. HIS NAME IS DETECTIVE FIX.

SUEZ HARBOR, EGYPT

Ah! So Mr. Fogg is an eccentric man, making a last minute trip like this. Is he rich?

No doubt, for he is carrying a huge sum. And he may make more if he wins his bet!

Fogg must be the thief!

FIX IS EXCITED WHEN HE ADDS UP WHAT HE HEARS. A FAST EXIT, A LARGE SUM OF MONEY, THE STORY OF THE BET . . .

FIX SENDS A REQUEST FOR THE PAPERS HE NEEDS TO ARREST FOGG. THEN, HE BOARDS THE SHIP. HE MAKES FRIENDS WITH PASSEPARTOUT, TO KEEP AN EYE ON FOGG.

I am pleased to meet you. Where are you bound?

Like you, to Bombay. The bank thief might be there!

IN INDIA, THEY TAKE A TRAIN. BUT THE TRACKS ARE NOT FINISHED. THEY NEED TRANSPORT TO GO ON.

Two thousand pounds for an elephant? We'll take it!

EN ROUTE TO ALLAHABAD, INDIA

THEY ALSO SAVE A WOMAN'S LIFE.

Take me with you!

My pleasure!

Let us be off!

HER NAME IS AOUDA. SHE HAS A RELATIVE IN HONG KONG. FOGG WILL BRING HER TO HIM.

ONCE AGAIN, THEY HEAD EAST BY TRAIN.

FIX NEEDS TO DELAY THEM. HE STILL NEEDS HIS PAPERS. SO IN CALCUTTA, FIX HAS THEM ARRESTED FOR HELPING *AOUDA*. BUT PHILEAS FOGG BUYS THEIR FREEDOM.

CALCUTTA, INDIA

A SHIP TAKES THEM TO SINGAPORE. FIX FOLLOWS, HOPING TO GET THE PAPERS HE NEEDS THERE.

It's clear! He's a spy sent by Mr. Fogg's friends!

PASSEPARTOUT NOW WONDERS WHY FIX IS STILL AROUND. MAYBE SOMEONE DOESN'T WANT THEM TO WIN THE BET.

STORMS DELAY THEIR TRAVELS.

Don't worry, my dear! It will be ok.

Poor Mr. Fogg . . . your bet . . .

THEY MISS THE SHIP THEY ARE SUPPOSED TO TAKE. BUT ANOTHER TAKES THEM TO HONG KONG. THERE, THEY DISCOVER THAT AOUDA'S RELATIVE HAS LEFT—FOR EUROPE.

What should I do, Mr. Fogg?

Come with us to America, and from there, to Europe.

HONG KONG

PASSEPARTOUT RUNS INTO FIX WHEN GETTING TICKETS FOR A SHIP TO JAPAN. THE PAPERS FIX NEEDS STILL HAVE NOT SHOWN UP. SO HE CONFESSES . . .

What nonsense!

Mr. Phileas Fogg is a thief. Help me delay him.

PASSEPARTOUT NOW KNOWS FIX'S SECRET.

I can't risk you telling Fogg that I'm after him!

FOGG AND AOUDA BOARD A LATER SHIP.

But where can Passepartout be?

I'll leave people searching for him, but you and I must go on. We cannot miss another ship.

IN HIS ZEAL TO FOLLOW FOGG, FIX BOARDS THE SAME SHIP.

I guess I'm off to America!

AND PASSEPARTOUT? HE WAKES UP ON THE SHIP. SOME SAILORS FOUND HIM WITH HIS TICKETS AND PUT HIM ON BOARD. THIS WAS THE SHIP THAT AOUDA AND FOGG HAD MISSED.

I must find Fogg. I'll try to find him in America.

EN ROUTE TO YOKOMAHA, JAPAN

IN THE MIDDLE OF A STORM, FOGG'S SHIP NEEDS TO BE RESCUED. LUCKILY ENOUGH, PASSEPARTOUT'S SHIP FOUND THEM.

FIX FINALLY GETS THE PAPERS HE NEEDS TO ARREST FOGG. HE MAKES AN AGREEMENT WITH PASSEPARTOUT, SO THERE WON'T BE ANY MORE DELAYS.

I won't delay you anymore. I will help you. And the truth will come out in England.

THEY REACH SAN FRANCISCO, WHERE THEY BOARD A TRAIN. THERE IS A SEVEN-DAY RIDE AHEAD.

THERE IS NO TIME TO LOSE.

EAST HUMBOLDT MOUNTAINS, NEVADA

TERRITORY OF IDAHO

Mr. Fogg, the bridge is broken!

If we go fast enough we can jump it!

Ooohh!

DAYS LATER, THEY MUST ESCAPE ATTACKERS.

FORT KEARNY STATION, NEBRASKA

THEY ARRIVE IN NEW YORK BEHIND SCHEDULE.

And we still must cross the Atlantic. We must board a ship to Liverpool immediately.

THE SHIP IS SLOW.

Sorry, mister. We are low on coal.

Burn wood instead. Your ship is made of it.

Burn my vessel?!

Sell me your vessel. I shall have to burn the wooden parts of her.

FINALLY, THEY ARE BACK IN ENGLAND, BUT THEN . . .

Mr. Fogg, you are under arrest for robbing a bank.

!!!??

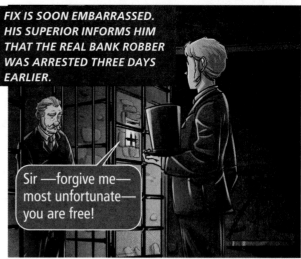

FIX IS SOON EMBARRASSED. HIS SUPERIOR INFORMS HIM THAT THE REAL BANK ROBBER WAS ARRESTED THREE DAYS EARLIER.

Sir —forgive me— most unfortunate— you are free!

THE TRAIN TO LONDON HAD LEFT THE STATION. THERE MAY STILL BE TIME, BUT FOGG NEEDS TO FIND ANOTHER WAY . . .

. . . BUT FOGG'S WATCH TELLS HIM IT'S TOO LATE.

One day late, after all! Tomorrow, Monday, I'll go to the club, to pay my debt.

BUT ALL HOPE IS NOT LOST.

But, sir, look! Today is Saturday, not Sunday. . .

Of course! We traveled East and arrived 24 hours ahead. But now, we only have 10 minutes to get to the club.

AS THE CLOCK STRIKES THE HOUR. . .

Here I am!

I say!

Congratulations! You won the bet.

Better yet, I found my bride!

47

UPLOAD

⏻ COLLABORATIVE DISCUSSION

Discussing the Purpose With a small group, discuss the characters in "Around the World in 80 Days." Respond to the following questions. Cite evidence from the story.

1. How does Phileas Fogg respond to the challenge of traveling around the world in 80 days?

2. How does Passepartout react to the challenges he faces with Fogg while traveling?

3. How does Detective Fix deal with tracking down the bank thief?

4. Do the characters act in a uniform way when meeting these challenges?

SPEAKING TOOLBOX

Formal and Informal Language

When you need to speak to an adult or someone you do not know, it is important to speak in a way that is respectful.

▶ **Formal language** is a polite way to speak to someone. You use this kind of language when you speak to someone such as your teacher, or an adult of authority such as a school principal.

▶ **Informal language** is the casual form of expression that you use with your friends. When you are in a group setting, it is natural to speak in a familiar, or informal way. Examples of informal language are slang and idioms. Slang is used by a specific group. Idioms are expressions whose meanings are different from their literal meanings.

Speak Out! Phileas Fogg encounters many problems on his adventure in "Around the World in 80 Days." Which problem was hardest to solve? With a partner, share your opinion. Cite evidence from the text to support why you think that problem was the hardest one that Fogg faced.

↻ Performance Task

Writing Activity: Short Response Phileas Fogg is called "an English gentleman" at the beginning of the story. Detective Fix is on the hunt for a bank robber. Write a short response to compare and contrast Fogg and Fix.

1. Explain how Fogg and Fix are similar.

2. Explain how Fogg and Fix are different.

3. Cite evidence from the story to support your reasons.

Here are some Useful Words to help you in your writing. You can look them up in a dictionary if you do not know their meaning.

Useful Words

▷ gentleman   ▷ competition
▷ thief   ▷ eccentric
▷ excited   ▷ zeal

Performance Task

Writing Activity: Informative Essay

You have been reading informational texts and stories about meeting different kinds of challenges. Now it's your turn to write an informational essay about it!

Planning and Prewriting

Connect to the Theme

Living things—whether plant, animal, or human—meet the challenges of survival by adapting to their surroundings. Some of these adaptations occur slowly over time. Others are temporary. Sometimes the environment can be changed to increase a living thing's chance of survival. Sometimes the changes occur within the bodies and systems of the living organism itself.

In this activity you will write an informative essay about meeting a challenge. But first you need a main idea. What will it be?

Write Down Your Main Idea

Your main idea is the most important idea about your topic. It is a statement that expresses and summarizes your thoughts. Write down several possible main ideas using the information you learned in the selections you've read. Choose the one that seems most promising. You can use an idea from the list below or one you've thought of.

Here are examples of main ideas taken from the selections you read:

- Plants and animals have developed unique adaptations that help them deal with extremes of heat and cold.
- Sometimes it takes nerves of steel to be accepted by a community.
- Astronauts must adjust their habits in order to survive in deep space.

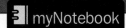

Decide the Basics

Now that you have a main idea that reflects the theme of the unit, you'll need to figure out how to support your idea with examples and details from the selections.

Main Idea

- Write your main idea in the form of a sentence.
- Think about the most important point you're making.
- Present your main idea early, in the first sentence. Hook your reader's interest with a fact that will surprise them or make them curious; or by asking a question that readers can relate to.

Supporting Details

Supporting details are facts or examples that support the main idea.

- Find details in the selections that tell more about your main idea.
- Use enough details to support your main idea.
- Include only evidence that is relevant to the topic.
- Include details from a variety of sources.

Vocabulary

- Use a formal and objective tone. (But don't lecture the reader!)
- Explain any proper nouns that a reader may not be familiar with.
- Include transitional words and phrases (*first/next; for example; however*) to help readers connect one idea to the next, and to clarify the relationships between ideas.

Text Features

Text features organize information.

- **Title:** The title of your essay should identify the topic in a way that encourages the reader's interest.
- **Subheadings:** If your supporting details can be grouped together, use a subheading for each grouping.

Performance Task

Finalize Your Plan

You know the basics of your essay. You have a main idea based on the theme of meeting a challenge. You know which facts, examples, and details from the selections you'll use to support this main idea. You may even have your title picked out.

Now you need to decide how you will present your information. Follow the structure in the Writing Toolbox.

WRITING TOOLBOX

Elements of an Informative Essay

Opening Paragraph	Present your main idea. "Hook" your audience with an interesting detail, question, or quotation that relates to your main idea. The first sentence in your essay should refer to the overall main idea.
Supporting Details	Each of these paragraphs should include a supporting detail for your main idea, or a group of examples that have a common thread.

If your main idea has several parts, you may want to use subheadings to introduce paragraphs that deal with each part. Each new paragraph can begin with a sentence that refers to the main idea of the paragraph. |
| **Conclusion** | The conclusion should follow and sum up how the details support your main idea. You may want to include an insight about the topic or pose a question that will make the reader think. |

Draft Your Essay

You have the basics of your informational essay. Start writing! As you write, think about:

- **Purpose and Audience** What effect do you want your essay to have on readers? Try to present your information in such a way that your audience understands and learns from what you've written.

- **Point of View** Establish your main idea reasonably quickly, so that the reader can follow the points you are making.

- **Structure** Use the diagram to help you organize the information you are presenting. Use subheadings where necessary. Be sure to link your ideas together in a way that makes sense.

- **Conclusion** Use a concluding paragraph to tie your ideas together. You may want to restate your main idea, which will have more weight now that you have supported it with examples. You may want to come to your own conclusion based on evidence you find in the selections.

Revise

Self Evaluation

Use the checklist and rubric to guide your analysis.

Peer Review

Exchange your essay with a classmate. Use the checklist to comment on your classmate's essay.

Edit

Edit your essay to correct spelling, grammar, and punctuation errors.

Publish

Finalize your essay and choose a way to share it with your audience.

Wild Encounters

Climb the mountains and get their good tidings. Nature's peace will flow into you as sunshine flows into trees. The winds will blow their own freshness into you, and the storms their energy while cares will drop away from you like the leaves of Autumn.

— John Muir, naturalist

Essential Question

How do people interact with nature?

The Language of Nature

Plants, animals, and all features of the earth are part of nature. From the tallest mountains to the smallest bacteria, the earth is covered with many types of natural things, both living and nonliving.

Nature can be both beautiful and useful to humans. Most of the foods we eat, like fish, vegetables, and grains, come from nature. Many of the resources we use, such as minerals, water, and oil, come from nature, too. Nature provides us with many things we need, but its beauty also enriches our lives.

Humans can impact nature. People change natural environments when they build towns, cities, and farms. Many kinds of plants and animals have become extinct or endangered as a result of people and their actions.

Nature deserves our respect. It is important to take care of Earth's wilderness. People can pass laws that protect our natural resources. We can preserve natural areas and protect wild habitats by setting aside land for national parks. People can keep natural areas clean by using trash bins for garbage.

In this unit, you will discover ways in which people have impacted nature by introducing foreign species into new environments, and how choices like this have had long-term effects on nature. You will also learn about people who work to protect nature, like Jane Goodall, a scientist who studied gorillas.

> **Why is it important for people to respect and care for nature?**

In a **Jam**: Idiomatic Expressions

Quick, would you help me out? I'm in a jam!

The expression *in a jam* is an idiom. An **idiom** is a phrase in which words put together have a meaning that is different from the dictionary definition of each word individually. *In a jam* doesn't mean someone is in a pot of jelly; it means someone is in trouble. The English language is filled with idioms that can be interesting and fun to learn. Here are a few that play on things from nature.

Idiom	Meaning
heard it through the grapevine	to find out about something in an informal way
let sleeping dogs lie	to let something be, usually because it would result in complications
under the weather	sick
raining cats and dogs	pouring down rain
every cloud has a silver lining	even difficult situations have positive aspects
once in a blue moon	happening very infrequently
till the cows come home	a very long time

↻ Performance Task

Explain why it is important to respect nature. Use the information on page 56 to help organize your thoughts. You can also use information from **Browse** magazine. Write a short speech to communicate your thoughts. Why is nature important? Why should we protect it? Use the **Activity Book**.

➡ *Browse magazine*

DOWNLOAD

Read the blog below to find out what one fifth-grader learned about animals and conservation.

⏻ **SETTING A PURPOSE**

As you read, pay attention to the problems of garbage and their solutions that this blogger learns about.

BaseballFan01

April 22, 4:30 p.m.

Today is Earth Day. Our class cleaned up the fields near our school. Our teacher gave us rubber gloves and garbage bags. I thought we might find a few pieces of garbage. Boy, was I wrong! You would not believe how much garbage we picked up.

We found soda bottles, yogurt cups, fast food wrappers, plastic shopping bags, pieces of newspaper, and batteries. We even found an old bandage and a diaper! Gross! Our teacher asked us where we thought they came from. Some of my classmates said that people throw things out of their car windows. Others said the wind can carry trash away accidentally. We wondered if animals carried garbage here from other places.

In class, one of the worst things we learned about litter is how it can harm animals. If a container isn't

Enter your email address:

Subscribe me!

SEARCH

💬 **Comments** 11

rinsed out, an animal might stick its head into the container to lick any remaining food and get stuck. The batteries we found could poison an animal if it ate them. Animals could get cut on broken glass. Plastic rings for soda-can six-packs could get wrapped around an animal's neck. Animals might climb inside of plastic bags and suffocate, or eat the bag and choke on it. They might get trapped in the handles of the bag. Most often it's wild animals that are hurt. It's pretty unlikely that anyone will find them and take them to the vet for help.

April 23, 4:45 p.m.

My teacher gave us a handout with some simple ways to make our garbage safer for animals. Easy things to do include putting lids back on jars and bottles, crushing yogurt containers, and clipping plastic rings. Tying plastic bags into knots before getting rid of them can also help. And, of course, we can always recycle!

He reminded us that even throwing out food isn't a good idea. Human food could make animals sick or even give them food poisoning. We should drop our food off at composting sites instead.

I still can't believe how much litter we found yesterday! Our school is going to make some changes to lower its amount of litter. We will get bigger trash cans with lids. All of the classes are getting the handout about getting rid of garbage properly. We're even organizing a group to clean around our school once a month. Hopefully, now that people know more about how bad litter can be for animals, they will start to make better choices!

ARCHIVES

April

March

February

January

December

November

October

September

August

👍 Like   👎 Dislike

⏻ COLLABORATIVE DISCUSSION

Discussing the Purpose What are some of the problems related to garbage that are discussed in the blog?

Share Your Opinion With a partner, discuss some of the solutions the blogger learns about garbage and animals. Could these solutions be used where you live? Support your opinions with reasons.

Staying Safe Avoid specific details in your blog that would allow a stranger to be able to identify you. Do not share personal information with the people you interact with through your blog (like people who make comments). Staying anonymous is a good way to stay safe. In a small group, make a list of the kinds of personal details to avoid sharing on your blog.

Write On! The blogger wrote about his class's experience on Earth Day. Write a summary of what he learned from his experience, or write a paragraph about an experience you had that was similar. Then exchange what you have written with a classmate. Write something in reaction to his or her paragraph.

↻ Performance Task

Writing Activity: Brainstorming Topics for Your Blog
Now that you have started a blog, what do you write about when you are stuck for ideas? If you don't blog about your experiences, coming up with topics for your blog might be a challenge. You can write about things that interest you, hobbies, or your favorite subject at school. Use your imagination!

1. Maybe you are interested in giraffes. If you are knowledgeable about them, you can share new and exciting facts that your friends may not know. If you don't know much about giraffes, you can do research and share what you learn.

2. You can write about a place that you have visited. You can also write about a location that you want to visit in the future.

3. You may wish to talk about one of your favorite bands. If so, you can upload audio files or links to music videos.

4. Other ideas for topics can include writing a review about a book you read, a movie you saw, or food you ate. Maybe you want to share instructions for a craft project, or present your opinion about a current event at school or in your town.

Language Cam video
Watch the video to learn more about how people interact with the environment.

DOWNLOAD

You have read about how people can impact animals and their environment, but how can animals impact humans?

⏻ SETTING A PURPOSE

As you read, think about the problems invasive species introduce to their new environments.

Invasive Species

by Brittany Adelman

> Can you guess the meaning of **invasive**? Keep reading to find clues.

> **funguses:** the group of species related to mushrooms and molds

Non-native species (also known as *exotic*, *alien*, and *non-indigenous*) show up in new places all the time. Usually, nothing bad happens: just because something is new to the area doesn't mean it's going to cause a problem. But some new arrivals become **invasive**: they adapt and spread quickly and end up causing real damage to their new environment. This can hurt the local economy; it can even have harmful effects on human health. Invasive species can be plants, insects, animals, or **funguses** and
10 other diseases. Governments spend millions every year fighting to keep these invaders in check.

Newly Arrived Species Are Often Invasive

Maybe the new arrivals have an edge in their new location. Perhaps there are no predators to keep them in check; maybe they crowd out local competitors by growing faster, hogging all the food, or reproducing more quickly. They might even get ahead by feasting on local species. As they

◀ *the cane toad*

spread, they alter the ecosystem to their own advantage, making it harder for native plants and animals to survive and compete.

Where Do Invasive Species Come From?

20 Each invasive species has a story about how it ended up in its new home. Many of the stories involve people—things they did by mistake, and things they did on purpose.

Take, for example, the cane toad. Introduced into Australia in 1935 to kill pests in the sugarcane fields, the toad killed no pests and became a far worse problem itself. With no natural predators outside its original home in Central America, the poisonous toad kills anything that tries to eat it.

Fur farmers introduced the nutria to the
30 U.S. in the early 1900s. The plan was to farm these small, beaver-like mammals for their fur. But the plan **never panned out**. The nutria escaped or were released into the wild, where they thrived and multiplied. Now they are causing serious damage to wetlands and marshes in 22 states.

never panned out:
never succeeded

the nutria ▶

the zebra mussel ▶

Can you guess the meaning of the compound word **out-compete**?

intake valves: mechanical devices that control the flow of water by opening and closing

The arrival of the zebra mussel was an accident. The mollusk most likely hitched a ride on a boat traveling from Europe to U.S. waters. Today, zebra mussels grow and spread quickly, **out-compete** local species for food, and clog up the water **intake valves** of power plants and other factories.

40

Rethinking Our Attitudes

No matter what we do, it is impossible to stop all invasive species from spreading, even if they endanger local plants and animals. Some scientists wonder if we should even try. Of course, there are situations where an invasive species is causing terrible damage and has to be dealt with. But these scientists argue that some invasive species have become a valuable part of their new ecosystems. Removing them would hurt native species and would be a waste of time and money. Instead of "invasives," they suggest we call these species "recent arrivals." It certainly sounds less threatening!

50

One lesson we have learned: humans have a responsibility to think carefully before introducing a species into an area. All our smarts and technology may be of little help if the new arrivals act in unpredictable—and uncontrollable—ways.

Not all invasive species are bad

Honeybees were brought to the U.S. in the 1600s, and they have been restocked several times since. Today, people are more worried about what would happen if the bees died out than about their spread.

⏻ COLLABORATIVE DISCUSSION

Discussing the Purpose What problems do invasive species cause? What is one solution to dealing with invasive species? Discuss these questions with a small group.

READING TOOLBOX

Analyze Structure: Text Features

Text features are the parts of a text that help organize and call attention to important information. Informational texts often contain one or more text features such as those found in the chart.

Text Features in Informational Texts	
title, subheadings	The title is the name that is attached to a text. It often identifies the topic of the whole article. Subheadings appear at the beginning of sections in the text and identify the focus of that section.
sidebar	A sidebar is a box alongside or within an article that gives more information related to the article's main text.
boldface type	Boldface type is dark, heavy print that is used to draw attention to unfamiliar vocabulary.

Speak Out! With a partner, find two text features in this selection. How do these features help you better understand the selection?

DOWNLOAD

The presence of invasive species can impact humans and the environment. Read the article below to learn how smallpox impacted humans in the 1500s and 1700s.

⏻ **SETTING A PURPOSE**
As you read, think about the effect smallpox had on early Americans.

A Deadly Traveler

by Tony Alemán

No one knows exactly how many people lived in the Americas in 1492. Historians and archeologists think the population could have been as high as 30–50 million at that time. The original Americans lived throughout the continents, from Alaska to the tip of South America. Their lives were rich with traditions and agriculture, communities, and tribal alliances. They had lived in the Americas for thousands

10 of years. A great change happened when the Native Americans encountered Europeans, however. Within just a few generations, Native Americans died off in enormous numbers. Some say that 95 percent of their population died within the first half of the 1500s.

What Happened?

What caused this terrible loss? The answer is disease, mainly **smallpox**. Smallpox is a deadly virus. It is passed from one person to another through contact. The smallpox virus had existed in Europe for thousands of years. Over time
20 more and more Europeans survived smallpox epidemics. They passed on their immunity, or resistance, to the next generations. European explorers and colonists could be exposed to smallpox or carry the virus but not become sick with the disease. And about 70 percent of Europeans who got smallpox survived it. This was not the case with the **native population** of the Americas.

Where Did Smallpox Come from?

One **theory** is that the first appearance of the smallpox virus in the Americas happened in 1520. Some think a Spanish soldier with smallpox landed in Mexico. The
30 disease quickly devastated the population and swept across North and South America.

Smallpox in Wartime

As Europeans took control of the Americas, they sometimes used smallpox deliberately. In the British colonies, settlers and soldiers battled the surviving Native Americans. Both sides were willing to fight to the death. One weapon the British used was smallpox. For example, in 1763, Native Americans attacked Fort Pitt on the Pennsylvania frontier. Nearby settlers crowded into the fort for protection. Smallpox **broke out**. The British then gave Native
40 Americans blankets infected with smallpox.

Keep on reading to learn about the meaning of **smallpox**.

The **native population** was the people living in the Americas before European explorers arrived.

theory: an idea or set of ideas that is intended to explain facts or events

broke out: a phrasal verb that means "to have started suddenly"

A Lasting Effect

The huge population loss had a profound effect. No one knows what the relationship between Native Americans and settlers would have been if the native population had not been so radically reduced. Surely it would have been different. Population loss was also responsible for deep cultural changes for Native Americans. So many **elders** died, for example, that oral traditions were lost. Whole villages were abandoned. Survivors had to join forces with other groups. Native Americans were less able to defend 50 themselves and their land. But more than any other factor, smallpox changed the story of the encounter between Europeans and Native Americans.

elders: people of age and experience

⏻ COLLABORATIVE DISCUSSION

Discussing the Purpose What effect did smallpox have on the Americas? Discuss this question with a small group. Cite evidence from the text to support your answer.

Analyzing the Text [Cite Text Evidence]

1. **Details** How did smallpox come to the Americas?

2. **Details** How did the British use smallpox?

3. **Text Features** How do the headings help you understand the selection?

4. **Headings** Which section of the text tells about the attack on Fort Pitt?

5. **Headings** Which section of the text tells about the impact smallpox had on Native American populations?

Speak Out! What are some ways that we protect ourselves from illness today? Share your ideas with a partner. Remember to follow the rules for classroom discussion. You may want to use some of the Useful Phrases from the box below in your discussion.

Useful Phrases

▷ I'm not sure what you mean by ____.

▷ I understand what you mean, but ____.

▷ That sounds right, but I still think ____.

Podcast: Website Warrior: Blogging for the Animals' Benefit

You read about an encounter between people in "A Deadly Traveler." The podcast you'll hear describes an encounter between a girl and an opossum, and how that encounter helps both of them.

Background on Wildlife Conservation

Wildlife conservation means protecting animals, plants, and their homes. Human activity like hunting and construction can make the environment unsafe for many creatures. Conservationists do many kinds of work to help wildlife live healthy lives. They may fight to make it illegal to hunt animals that are endangered, or at risk of dying out completely. They might also teach people about the animals in the community or ways to save energy and natural resources.

Conservation is important to humans and wildlife. Plants, animals, and people are part of a giant ecosystem. Protecting wildlife helps make the whole planet healthier.

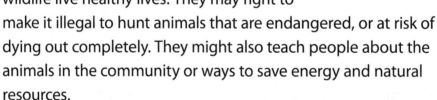

⏻ SETTING A PURPOSE

As you listen, pay attention to the story as it unfolds. Use the sequence of events to follow the narrative. Think about what the speaker, Cynthia, does to protect animals in her community. How does she advocate for them?

Website Warrior: Blogging for the Animals' Benefit

Sequence of Events in the Podcast

Cynthia grows up in Chicago and visits the Lincoln Park Zoo.

↓

Cynthia starts a blog with pictures and videos from the zoo.

↓

The animals and blog keep her active even though she is shy.

↓

Cynthia realizes that habitat destruction harms animals. She wants to help these animals.

↓

Cynthia moves to a small town in Indiana.

→

Cynthia realizes that she can still see wild animals even though there are no zoos.

↓

Cynthia and her mother find an injured opossum.

↓

Cynthia and her mother take the opossum to a wildlife rehabilitation center.

↓

Cynthia becomes the center's official blogger to help with donations and publicity.

⏻ COLLABORATIVE DISCUSSION

Discussing the Purpose In a small group, talk about how Cynthia's experiences with animals in Chicago and Indiana helped her become a conservationist and blogger.

Inside or Outside: Where Do Pet Cats Belong?

The opossums in the podcast were wild animals that are not kept as pets. Continue reading to learn more about domestic cats.

READING TOOLBOX

Fact and Opinion

An opinion piece presents facts and opinions about a topic. A **fact** is a true statement. The date or time that something happened is a fact. How you feel about something is an **opinion**.

Fact	Opinion
Apples are a fruit.	Apples are delicious.
Great Danes are very large dogs.	Great Danes are the best-looking dogs.

Background on Opinion

When you read an opinion, look for facts that support the author's position. A strong opinion will be backed up by reasons. A strong opinion will also tell about an opposing opinion. The author thinks about what someone who disagrees with his or her opinion might say, and then counters that viewpoint.

⏻ SETTING A PURPOSE

As you read, pay attention to how the author supports her opinion with facts.

Inside or Outside:
Where Do Pet Cats Belong?

by Talanie Gooding

As the leader of my town's Bird Watching Club, I want to share my opinion about cats. Pet cats should never be allowed outside. Everyone knows that cats are cute and cuddly, but it seems that no one knows they are also a danger to other living things. Outdoor cats kill more than a billion birds every year. Most of these birds are extremely important to the environment. Also, birds are much prettier to look at than cats. By killing these beautiful birds, cats put our ecosystem at risk.

10   Cats don't just kill a few birds. Sometimes, they kill entire species. Since the 1800s, cats have caused 33 species of birds, reptiles, and small mammals to become **extinct**. Other species remain at risk from cats that go outdoors.

> **extinct:** an adjective that means "no longer existing"

Domestic cats share the same instinct to hunt for prey that large cats in the wild have. But pet cats do not need to hunt for food, like their distant relatives—which include mountain lions. Pet cats hunt

20   for fun, which is why their owners need to take action.

stray cats: cats that live on their own outdoors, with no one to take care of them

In the United States, there are about 84 million cats that people own. It is up to the owners to decide whether or not to keep their pet cats indoors. However, this doesn't solve the problem of **stray cats**, which live outdoors. There are between 30 and 80 million stray cats in the U.S. Stray cats kill much more wildlife than pet cats do, because they have no other source of food. Outdoor pet cats are still part of the problem, but that problem
30 can be solved.

On a farm, outdoor cats might help their owners. They hunt ugly mice and annoying sparrows that would eat the crops in the fields. And, of course, anyone can see that cats feel freer when they get to go outside. But who can really say that cats are happier inside or outside?

Indoor cats can still use their hunting skills. A pet cat that does not go outside is still very happy because it can catch gross insects that may come inside. They can get exercise and practice "hunting" when their owners play
40 with them, which makes cats happier than anything in the entire world.

It's wrong to continue letting pet cats kill wildlife. It's easy to make them stop. All cats should be indoor cats.

⏻ COLLABORATIVE DISCUSSION

Discussing the Purpose How does the author support her opinion? With a small group, discuss how facts help make an opinion stronger.

Analyzing the Text `Cite Text Evidence`

1. **Stating Opinions** Which sentences in this selection are opinions? Find three.

2. **Finding Facts** Which sentences in this selection are facts? Find three.

SPEAKING TOOLBOX

Persuasive Speaking

Present your opinion without lecturing or bullying the listeners.

▶ **State your opinion.** Make it plain what position you take and state your points clearly.

▶ **Support your opinion.** Give facts and details that support your position.

▶ **Be convincing.** Explain your opinion evenly but with enthusiasm.

Speak Out! The author of this opinion concludes that all pet cats should be indoor cats. Do you agree? Why, or why not? Share your opinion with a partner.

Write On! Think about the opposing opinion to the author's opinion. Write a short paragraph that states the opposing opinion. Support this opinion with two facts.

Island of the Blue Dolphins

People can keep indoor pet cats almost anywhere. In *Island of the Blue Dolphins*, a girl living on an island cares for some wild animals she considers pets.

Know Before You Go

Karana has lived alone on an island for many years. She has learned to find her own food, build her own shelter, and make a life as the only human on her island. She befriends a wild dog she calls Rontu, and cares for many other animals she finds on the island.

Island of the Blue Dolphins is based on the true story of a girl who lived alone for 18 years on an island in the Pacific Ocean.

⏻ **SETTING A PURPOSE**

As you read, pay attention to the specific language Karana uses to talk about the animals on the island.

from

Island of the Blue Dolphins

by Scott O'Dell

Spring again was a time of flowers, and water ran in the **ravines** and flowed down to the sea. Many birds came back to the island.

Tainor and Lurai built a nest in the tree where they were born. They built it of dry seaweed and leaves and also with hairs off Rontu's back. Whenever he was in the yard while it was being made, they would swoop down if he was not looking and snatch a **beakful** of fur and fly away. This he did not like and he finally hid from them until the nest was finished.

I had been right in giving a girl's name to Lurai, for she laid speckled eggs and, with some help from her mate, hatched two ugly **fledglings** which soon became beautiful. I made up names for them and clipped their wings and before long they were as tame as their parents.

ravines: narrow, steep-sided valleys usually created by the effects of running water on soil over a long period of time.

The suffix *-ful* means "full of." What does the word **beakful** mean?

fledglings: baby birds

Which words in the sentence help you understand the meaning of the word **teetering**?

sinew: tough tissue that connects muscle to bone

reef: a chain of rocks or coral at or near the surface of a body of water

I also found a young gull that had fallen from its nest to the beach below. Gulls make their nests high on the cliffs, in hollow places on the rocks. These places are usually small and often I had watched a young one

20 **teetering** on the edge of the nest and wondered why it did not fall. They seldom did.

This one, which was white with a yellow beak, was not badly hurt, but he had a broken leg. I took him back to the house and bound the bones together with two small sticks and **sinew**. For a while he did not try to walk. Then, because he was not old enough to fly, he began to hobble around the yard.

With the young birds and the old ones, the white gull and Rontu, who was always trotting at my heels, the

30 yard seemed a happy place. If only I had not remembered Tutok. If only I had not wondered about my sister Ulape, where she was, and if the marks she had drawn upon her cheeks had proved magical. If they had, she was now married to Nanko and was the mother of many children. She would have smiled to see all of mine, which were so different from the ones I always wished to have.

Early that spring I started to gather

40 **abalones** and I gathered many, taking them to the headland to dry. I wanted to have a good supply ready if the Aleuts came again.

One day when I was on the **reef** filling my canoe, I saw a herd of otter in the kelp nearby. They were chasing each

Gull ▶

▲ *Otter*

other, putting their heads through the kelp and then going under and coming up again in a different place. It was like a game we used to play in the brush when there
50 were children on the island. I looked for Mon-a-nee, but each of them was like the other.

I filled my canoe with abalones and paddled toward the shore, one of the otter following me. As I stopped he dived and came up in front of me. He was far away, yet even then I knew who it was. I never thought that I would be able to tell him from the others, but I was so sure it was Mon-a-nee that I held up one of the fish I had caught.

Otter swim very fast and before I could take a breath,
60 he had snatched it from my hand.

For two moons I did not see him and then one morning while I was fishing he came suddenly out of the kelp. Behind him were two baby otter. They were about the size of puppies and they moved along so slowly that from time to time Mon-a-nee had to urge them on.

flippers:

Sea otter cannot swim when they are first born, and have to hold on to their mother. Little by little she teaches her babies by brushing them away with her **flippers**, then swimming around them in circles until they learn
70 to follow.

Mon-a-nee came close to the reef and I threw a fish into the water. He did not snatch it as he usually did, but waited to see what the young otter would do. When they seemed more interested in me than in food, and the fish started to swim away, he seized it with his sharp teeth and tossed it in front of them.

I threw another fish into the water for Mon-a-nee, but he did the same things as before. Still the babies would not take the food, and at last, tired of playing with it,
80 swam over and began to nuzzle him.

Only then did I know that Mon-a-nee was their mother. Otter mate for life and if the mother dies the father will often raise the babies as best he can. This is what I thought had happened to Mon-a-nee.

I looked down at the little family swimming beside the reef. "Mon-a-nee," I said, "I am going to give you a new name. It is Won-a-nee, which fits you because it means Girl with the Large Eyes."

The young otter grew fast and soon were taking fish
90 from my hand, but Won-a-nee liked abalones better. She would let the abalone I tossed to her sink to the bottom and then dive and come up holding it against her body, with the rock held in her mouth. Then she would float on

her back and put the abalone on her breast and strike it again and again with the rock until the shell was broken.

She taught her young to do this and sometimes I sat on the reef all the morning and watched the three of them pounding the hard shells against their breasts. If all otters did not eat abalones this way I would have thought it was a game played by Won-a-nee just to please me. But they all did and I always wondered about it, and I wonder to this time.

After that summer, after being friends with Won-a-nee and her **young**, I never killed another otter. I had an otter cape for my shoulders, which I used until it wore out, but never again did I make a new one. Nor did I ever kill another cormorant for its beautiful feathers, though they have long, thin necks and make ugly sounds when they talk to each other. Nor did I kill seals for their sinews, using instead kelp to bind the things that needed it. Nor did I kill another wild dog, nor did I try to spear another sea elephant.

Ulape would have laughed at me, and others would have laughed, too—my father most of all. Yet this is the way I felt about the animals who had become my friends and those who were not, but in time could be. If Ulape and my father had come back and laughed, and all the others had come back and laughed, still I would have felt the same way, for animals and birds are like people, too, though they do not talk the same or do the same things. Without them the earth would be an unhappy place.

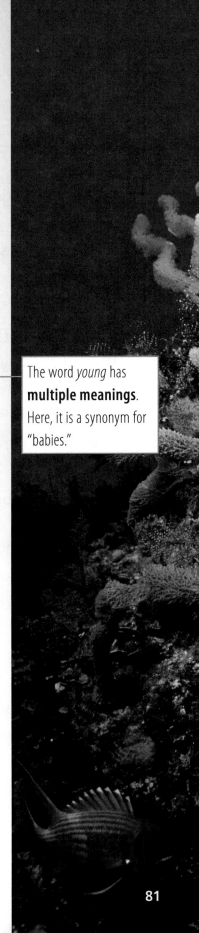

The word *young* has **multiple meanings**. Here, it is a synonym for "babies."

UPLOAD

⏻ COLLABORATIVE DISCUSSION

Discussing the Purpose What words and phrases does Karana use to talk about the animals on the island? With a small group, find examples that show how Karana feels about the animals she cares for.

↻ Performance Task

√ my WriteSmart

Writing Activity: Opinion Essay Write a short response to answer the following question: Do you think that "animals and birds are like people"?

- When writing an opinion essay, think about your position on the topic.

- Next, think about the reasons for your opinion. How can you support your opinion? Make note of examples from the text to support your position.

- Include an opposing opinion in your essay. Then give examples to counter that opinion.

- Restate your opinion in your conclusion.

Speak Out! Would you like to live alone on an island? With a partner, share your opinion. Provide reasons to support your opinion. Remember to follow the rules for classroom discussion.

Vocabulary Strategy: Similes

A simile is a sentence or phrase that compares two different things using the word **like** or **as**. Writers use similes to help them express ideas in imaginative ways.

In this selection, the author uses a simile to describe the way the otters move. Read the following sentence:

It was like a game we used to play in the brush when there were children on the island. (lines 48–50)

The author uses *like* to show how the movements of the otters is similar to a game of chase. This simile helps us understand what the main character is seeing.

Practice and Apply You can make your writing stronger by using similes. For example, instead of writing "I ran fast," you could use a simile to help you express this idea in a more interesting way:

I ran **as fast as** a hungry cheetah chasing an antelope.

Identify the correct simile from the box below to complete each sentence.

as cold as	**as tall as**
like a painting	**like a blanket**

1. I am growing ___ a tree.

2. I am ___ a block of ice.

3. The house was brightly colored, ___.

4. The kitten was soft, ___.

Jane Goodall

Much like Karana in *Island of the Blue Dolphins*, Jane Goodall cares about the well-being of animals.

Know Before You Go

Jane Goodall studies chimps to better understand them—and us. Goodall is famous for finding new facts. Here are four facts that she was the first to observe.

Chimps adopt chimps without mothers.

Groups of chimps sometimes go to war.

Chimps use plants for medicine.

The animals teach one another how to make tools.

⏻ **SETTING A PURPOSE**

As you read, think about the effect of Jane Goodall's work.

Jane Goodall

by Mercedes Roffe

WHEN JANE WAS A LITTLE GIRL, HER FATHER GAVE HER A VERY SPECIAL GIFT.

Jane, this is for you.

Daddy, she's so cute! I'll love her all my life!

JANE CARRIED HER TOY CHIMP WITH HER EVERYWHERE.

Heavens! What's that awful thing you carry? Doesn't it give you bad dreams?

This is my friend Jubilee! I love her very much!!

BUT JANE DIDN'T JUST LOVE TOY CHIMPS. SHE LOVED REAL ANIMALS, TOO.

Mom, can a girl go to the jungle?

Honey, I promise you, if that's what you want, you'll go.

WHEN JANE WAS OLDER, SHE WENT TO VISIT A FRIEND'S FARM IN KENYA.

I'd love to study the life of animals, their habits, the way they . . .

You should meet my friend, Professor Louis Leakey, an archaeologist. He studies human history, but also works on animal conservation.

85

SO JANE CALLED PROFESSOR LEAKEY AND A FEW DAYS LATER, SHE WENT TO MEET HIM.

What do you think, my dear? Wouldn't it be fantastic if Jane accepted the offer to be my assistant?

HER FIRST MISSION WAS TO VISIT A NATIONAL PARK IN TANZANIA.

"Professor Leakey thinks that studying the behavior of chimpanzees could teach us more about the past of humans."

BUT JANE NOTICED MORE THAN JUST CHIMPS IN GOMBE PARK. SOON JANE MET A YOUNG PHOTOGRAPHER AS INTERESTED IN ANIMALS AS SHE WAS.

Look at them, Hugo. Aren't they lovely?

SOON AFTER THAT, JANE AND HUGO WERE MARRIED.

I do.

Who are you, handsome? I'll call you David. David Graybeard.

SHE STARTED NAMING THE CHIMPS, AND BEGAN TO STUDY THE WAYS THEY LIVED AND BEHAVED IN THEIR HABITAT.

But . . .

Jane, I'm very proud of everything you're doing, but it's not enough.

If you really want to become a scientist, you must go to the university and get a degree.

JANE WAS ACCEPTED TO STUDY AT CAMBRIDGE UNIVERSITY.

I think we'll learn a lot here! Don't you think so, Jubilee?

FIVE YEARS LATER, SHE GRADUATED. HER THESIS WAS ABOUT ALL SHE HAD LEARNED IN THE JUNGLE . . . AND AT SCHOOL!

SOON AFTER HER THESIS SHE WROTE HER FIRST BOOK.

Thank you!

Thank you! It looks fascinating!

JANE DIVORCED HUGO AND LATER SHE MARRIED DEREK BRYCESON. HE WAS THE DIRECTOR OF TANZANIA'S NATIONAL PARKS, AND HELPED PROTECT JANE'S RESEARCH PROJECT.

SHE ALSO DARED TO CONTRADICT SOME OLD SCIENTIFIC BELIEFS—LIKE ONLY HUMANS CONSTRUCT AND USE TOOLS.

And they are not vegetarians as many books say! I saw them fishing termites for food.

SO JANE LEARNED THAT NOT EVERYTHING WAS PEACEFUL AMONG CHIMPS . . . NOR AMONG PEOPLE.

Goodall's methods are not serious. She involves herself too much with her object of study!

She is too emotional!

AFTER SO MANY YEARS OBSERVING THE CHIMPS, JANE HAD SOME IMPORTANT CONCLUSIONS TO SHARE.

"Human beings are not the only ones to have a personality, nor are they the only ones capable of thoughts, and emotions such as joy and sorrow . . . "

JANE FOUND THAT CHIMPS COULD BE VERY AGGRESSIVE.

"They can form groups to isolate smaller primates, such as the colobus monkey, and even kill them and eat them."

BUT JANE HAD ALREADY BECOME AN ADMIRED AND FAMOUS SCIENTIST.

Our mission is to create conservation programs around the world.

Chimpanzees can teach us many things . . .

SHE WAS INVITED TO GIVE LECTURES WORLDWIDE . . .

. . . AND PUBLISHED MANY BOOKS. SOME HAVE EVEN BEEN TRANSLATED INTO OTHER LANGUAGES!

SHE ALSO CREATED CONSERVATION PROGRAMS FOR CHILDREN AND TEENAGERS.

Our Roots and Shoots program has over 10,000 groups in over 100 countries.

BUT, AFTER SO MUCH TRAVELING, JANE KNOWS THAT WHEN SHE GETS BACK TO HER STUDIO IN LONDON, JUBILEE WILL BE THERE, WAITING FOR HER.

UPLOAD

⏻ **COLLABORATIVE DISCUSSION**

Discussing the Purpose What was the effect of Jane Goodall's unique work? With a partner, find one example.

- How did Jane's study of animals change our thinking about chimps?

LISTENING TOOLBOX

Active Listening
Always be respectful of others when they are talking.

▶ **Wait for your turn.** As excited as you may be to add to the conversation, don't interrupt.

▶ **Ask if you don't understand** what has been said.

▶ **Let the speaker know that you understood** the point, even if you disagree.

Useful Phrases

▷ Would you please repeat that? I'm not sure what you mean.

▷ I agree with most of what you say, but ____.

▷ I heard Lila say ____, and Courivan just pointed out ____.

Speak Out! Would you like to study chimpanzees? Share your opinion with a partner. Remember to take turns when speaking and listening.

↻ Performance Task

Writing Activity: Write a Letter You have read about the work that Jane Goodall did with chimps and people. Write a letter to Jane, including any questions you would like to ask her.

- When you write a letter, think about the person you are writing to. What kind of language should you use?

- Begin your letter with a greeting, such as "Dear Jane," or "Greetings, Jane."

- Close your letter with "Sincerely," "Your friend," or "Best," followed by your name.

- Read your letter aloud to a partner to check that it is written clearly.

- Revise your letter if necessary.

Vocabulary Strategy: Using Context Clues

When you read an unfamiliar word in a text, use context clues to figure out the meaning. **Context clues** are the words and pictures that surround an unfamiliar word. Read this sentence:

Jane carried her toy chimp with her everywhere.

The sentence says that Jane carried her "chimp." In the picture, Jane is carrying a small ape, so "chimp" must mean "a kind of ape." The dictionary definition of "chimp" is "a type of ape that lives in Africa."

Practice and Apply Reread "Jane Goodall" and find the words *lecture, aggressive,* and *conservation.* Look at the surrounding words and pictures for clues to each word's meaning. Then check your guess using a dictionary.

Performance Task

Writing Activity: Opinion Piece

In this unit, you have read about how a place's natural wildlife is affected by people and other animals. Your task is to write an opinion piece about the importance of respecting the natural world.

Planning and Prewriting

Connect to the Theme

When something gets into an ecosystem that doesn't belong there, it can affect wildlife in that area. Scientists sometimes introduce a new species into an ecosystem to help the ecosystem survive. But that often causes even greater imbalance in the environment. In this activity you will be writing an opinion piece stating your views about respecting the natural world. But first you need a topic. What will it be?

Write Down Some Possible Topics

In an opinion piece, you give your feeling and beliefs about a topic. Think about the topics covered in the selections you read. Jot down several statements that express your opinion on one of these topics. Choose the one that's most promising to write about. Here are some examples:

- Small changes in the natural world can change history.

- Humans are the biggest threat to the environment.

- Respect for nature is essential to human survival.

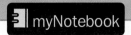

Decide the Basics

Once you have chosen a topic you have a definite opinion about, you'll have to back up your opinion with reasons from the selections. You'll need to organize your thoughts and decide how to express yourself.

State Your Opinion

In an opinion piece you take a position on an issue.

- Write your opinion in the form of a statement.
- Make sure your opinion is clearly stated at the beginning of your piece.
- Begin your opinion piece with a fact or a question that will make readers curious.

Find Reasons

Reasons are examples from texts that back up your opinion.

- Use only those examples that relate to your position.
- Look for examples in more than one selection. This makes your case stronger!
- Make sure your reasons are factual and not just the author's opinion.
- Present your reasons in logical order.

Vocabulary

Think about vocabulary and word choice.

- Use a formal tone. (But don't lecture the reader!)
- Explain words that a reader may not be familiar with.
- Include enough connecting words, phrases, and clauses (*first/next; for example; however*) to link opinion and reasons and ensure a smooth flow of ideas.

Performance Task

Present the Information

You've got the basics down. You have an opinion based on the selections you read; you know which facts, examples, and details you'll use to support your position on the issue. All you need is a way to present the information.

Use the Writing Toolbox to help you.

WRITING TOOLBOX

Elements of an Opinion Piece

Introduction	The **introduction** should state the topic and give your opinion about it. Try to grab the reader's attention in the first sentence.
Reasons	Give **reasons** for your opinion. Use information from the selections to support your opinion. (Using more than one selection gives it more weight.) You may also want to use this section to respond to opposing viewpoints. Just make sure you can back up your ideas with information from the text.
Conclusion	The **conclusion** sums up your ideas. Write a concluding section that restates your opinion and summarizes the information you used to support it. You can also make a comment of your own, or offer a thought-provoking question.

Draft Your Opinion Piece

You have your topic and opinion. You have a way to organize your ideas. Now it's time to start writing! As you write, ask yourself:

- **What's my point?** Make sure you state your topic and opinion at the beginning so that readers can follow the rest of what you have to say.

- **Can I come up with good examples?** Make sure you include only meaningful examples from the texts, and that you have enough of them to make your case.

- **Is my opinion my own?** Not everyone sees things the same way. Your opinion doesn't have to be shared by everyone—it just has to be supported by the facts. It might be a good idea to mention a viewpoint you don't agree with, and tell why you disagree.

- **Do my ideas flow?** Make sure that your ideas are linked together in a way that makes sense, and that they appear in logical order.

- **Does the conclusion tie my ideas together?** The conclusion should summarize and unite your ideas. Remember to refer to the opinion statement you made in the introduction.

Revise

Self Evaluation

Use the checklist and rubric to guide your analysis.

Peer Review

Exchange your opinion piece with a classmate. Use the checklist to comment on your classmate's work.

Edit

Edit your opinion piece to correct spelling, grammar, and punctuation errors.

Publish

Finalize your opinion piece and choose a way to share it with your audience.

JULY 4, 1776

States of

dissolve the political bands which have

entitle them, a decent respect to the o

all men are created equal

ts are in

Revolution!

Every revolution was first a thought in one man's mind.

— **Ralph Waldo Emerson, writer**

Essential Question

What is a revolution?

The Language of Revolution

Sometimes a discovery or invention is so important that
we call it *revolutionary.* The discovery of electricity as a form
of energy is one example of a revolutionary change. It changed
our lives in innumerable ways. The discovery of penicillin to cure
disease and infection is another example. It saved countless lives
and changed the way we practice medicine. These discoveries
were so significant that they changed the way we think and act.

In government and politics, *revolutionary* has a different
meaning. A *revolution* is an attempt by many people to
change the rule of the land. After fighting and winning
the Revolutionary War, American settlers gained
independence from British rule. They chose a new kind
of rule, democracy, in which people vote for their
leaders. We are still a democracy today.

Whether in science, government, or life, revolutions
are a sign of big and sudden changes. Change often helps
people grow. When change is sudden, however, it can be
difficult for some people to get used to new ideas or new
ways of thinking.

In this unit, you will find out about a revolutionary discovery
that changed the way we think about matter. You will also read
about revolution in governments and how different sides may
see things differently.

> **Do all revolutions bring about change?**

Change It Up: Etymology

Prefixes and suffixes are the revolutionaries of language. They cause the meaning of words to change. A **prefix** is a word part added to the beginning of a base word. A **suffix** is a word part added to the end of a base word. The charts below show some common prefixes and suffixes and how they change words.

Prefix	How It Changes a Word	Examples
in- *dis-* *un-*	changes a word to mean its opposite	infrequent, incorrect, disadvantage, disapprove unfriendly, unhappy
anti-	changes a word to mean "against"	antifreeze, antihero
re-	changes a word to mean "again"	refreeze, redo

Suffix	How It Changes a Word	Examples
-ly	changes an adjective to an adverb	quickly, happily
-ful	changes a verb or noun to an adjective, meaning "full of"	wonderful, helpful
-less	changes a verb or noun to an adjective, meaning "without"	fearless, hopeless

↻ Performance Task

Describe an invention or discovery you think was revolutionary.
Use the information on page 98 and in **Browse** magazine to help organize your thoughts. Write a short speech to communicate why you think this invention was revolutionary. Be sure to include facts and examples to support your ideas. Use the **Activity Book** as a guide.

DOWNLOAD

Revolution is a word that means different things to different people. Read ahead to find out what the Revolutionary War means to this blogger.

⏻ **SETTING A PURPOSE**

As you read, pay attention to the specific facts and details in DrummerGuy617's blog.

DRUMMERGUY617

BACK IN TIME

April 21, 8:00 p.m.

I just spent the weekend hanging out in the year 1775 . . . No, I don't have a time machine. Every year, my family participates in a reenactment of a famous Revolutionary War battle. The American Revolution really started with the Battles of Lexington and Concord. We live in Concord, Massachusetts, which is where the ammunition and weapons were stored in April 1775. Each year, people reenact these battles. It's a really big deal. There's more to the reenactment than just the fighting, though.

The main question people ask me is if I have to wear funny-looking clothes. Yes! Reenactments are all about historical authenticity, which definitely includes clothing. We can't have cell phones, watches, or even modern-looking glasses. Clothing must look like it did in 1775.

Enter your email address:

Subscribe me!

SEARCH

💬 Comments 14

A reenactment includes many activities and demonstrations by both military members and civilians. You might see how artillery from this time worked, or how minutemen were armed and trained. One popular thing to see is a session on battle tactics from that time period. There are presentations about food and other things from 1775. There's even a fashion show! Many people like to watch demonstrations of skills and crafts. My dad worked this year as a blacksmith, someone who makes things from iron or steel. But there are many different historic occupations represented. If you're taking part in the reenactment, you could be one of the town's residents. That's what my mom did this year. She talked about what it would have been like to see the fighting, and answered questions people had about daily life at that time. My sister and I took part in the fife-and-drum concert. My sister played the fife, which looks like a little flute, and I played the drum. When I'm older, I'll be able to act as a soldier. I can't wait!

The battle is one of the main things people come to see. The 21-gun, musket-and-cannon salute signals the start of the battle. The people playing the part of the British soldiers reenact the search for the militia's weapons, and while they're doing that, the number of Americans ready to fight grows as men from Concord and other neighboring areas show up. The American patriots fight the British at the North Bridge, forcing the British troops to retreat. When you watch the battles, it's easy to forget that it's just a reenactment.

My parents talk about how educational reenactments are, which is true; but I like them because they're fun. It's cool to see what it was like for the colonists in America who fought so hard to get independence from the British. But for now, I'm glad to be back in the 21st century and able to blog again!

ARCHIVES

April

March

February

January

December

November

October

September

August

UPLOAD

COLLABORATIVE DISCUSSION

Discussing the Purpose With a partner, find two facts in the blog. How does this help you better understand what a reenactment is?

What Would You Do? Discuss the jobs that the blogger writes about. Which job would you want if you had a part in reenacting Concord, Massachusetts, 1775? Tell your partner why you would want to have that job.

Staying Safe Think carefully about uploading pictures of yourself. Once you've posted a picture of yourself online, anyone can see it. People also may be able to download it.

Write On! What other facts do you want to know about the reenactments or the Revolutionary War? Write a comment to DrummerGuy617 asking for more information about one of these topics. Then exchange your comment with a classmate.

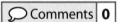 Comments **0**

↻ Performance Task

Writing Activity: Designing Your Blog Your blog design shows readers your personality. Your blog software should have a feature for designing its appearance. You can choose from a number of different templates or themes. These range in color and style. They also allow you to design your layout. You can choose the number and size of your columns. You might have a sidebar column where you can keep a list of website links that you often visit. You can also upload photographs and art images into your template.

Note: If you are using a photo or an image that is not yours, you must give proper credit. You can do this by giving the person or organization's name and the date of the photo or image.

1 Write a blog post describing why you chose your template and art images. You can use a bulleted or numbered list to organize your thoughts. This might be a good place to insert a link to your design inspiration or upload an image. Adding links to your posts gives your readers more information about a subject.

2 Preview your draft. Spell check and fix any grammatical errors. If you have added a link, check that it is correct and does not load to an incorrect site.

3 Publish your post.

Language Cam video
Want to learn more about revolution? Watch the video.

DOWNLOAD

Revolutionary Air

The Revolutionary War changed the lives of the new Americans and how they thought about "freedom." In this selection, you will read about how a revolutionary discovery changed the way people thought about **matter**.

> **matter:** anything that has mass and takes up space

READING TOOLBOX

Reading Hard Words

This selection contains scientific terms. You may not know their meaning.

▶ **Read the selection once** to see what it's mainly about. Decide how much you need to know about the technical terms.

▶ **Use the resources provided** to understand the terms. Is there a diagram that gives information about them? Does the context help? Do you need to use a dictionary or look up the terms online?

⏻ SETTING A PURPOSE

As you read, think about the main idea and supporting details of the selection.

Revolutionary Air

by Minh Pham

In a candlelit room, *a scientist bends over a glass jar. He is pumping the air out of it to create a completely empty space. It is the middle of the seventeenth century. Until this time European* **scholars** *believed it to be impossible to create airless empty space. They thought air itself was empty space. Contrary to that belief, the air pump experiment worked.*

scholars: educated specialists in a branch of knowledge

▲ *Robert Boyle*

chemistry: the science that studies the composition, properties and activities of substances and forms of matter.

We know now that air is made up of tiny particles, not attached to each other, bouncing around in empty space. You cannot shape air, and it doesn't have any patterns. Air is so light that it seems like it doesn't weigh anything, but it is a kind of matter. Anything you can touch is made of matter, and all matter behaves in certain ways. The air pump experiment, first done by Robert Boyle in the 1650s, led to a revolution
10 in how we think about matter. This was the beginning of **chemistry**. It was a new discovery, a revolutionary kind of matter. It was the discovery of a gas.

The word *gas* was invented around the middle of the seventeenth century. It was based on the Greek word *kaos*, which means "disorder and empty space." The new word was needed to describe a new idea. Scientists discovered that air was not empty. They discovered something
20 revolutionary. Everything, even air, is made up of tiny invisible particles, which they called *atoms*.

These scientists did not invent the word *atom*. Over a thousand years before, philosophers in Greece, India, and the Middle East believed in atoms. Different thinkers talked about tiny unseen particles that made up matter. Ancient Greek philosophers first used the word *atom* to describe these particles. The word *atom* means "something that cannot be cut smaller." They thought there had to be something smaller

30 than everything else. Atoms were these smallest things, which made up everything else.

The Same Amount of Gas Can Take Up Different Amounts of Space

Empty space between atoms

The same gas can fit into a smaller volume due to the empty space between atoms

Atoms in a gas bounce around freely

Boyle's Law states that a fixed amount of gas can fill any space. The pressure gets higher as the space gets smaller.

However, because nobody could see or prove the existence of atoms, the ancient philosophers could not persuade most people to believe in them, and philosophical atomism died out.

Over a thousand years later, scientists had new equipment and new methods. They could experiment on the world, and while they still could not see atoms or examine individual ones, 40 they had devices like the air pump. Through experimentation they could show that atoms exist. Since that scientific revolution, scientists have discovered far more about the atom, and we now know what the particles that air is made of actually are. But we've known since Boyle's revolutionary air pump experiment that they were there.

What scientists in the past called atoms weren't always what we would call atoms today. Another kind of particle is a *molecule*, which is a number of atoms bound together. Unlike atoms, molecules can be broken up easily or put together, which is called a "chemical reaction." The study of molecules is the science of chemistry.

⏻ COLLABORATIVE DISCUSSION

Discussing the Purpose With a small group, discuss the main idea of the selection. Find two details that support the main idea.

Vocabulary Strategy: Word Origins

This selection contained some unfamiliar words that you may not have recognized. Often, knowing the origin of a word can help us understand a word's meaning. For example, in "Revolutionary Air," the author tells us that the word *gas* comes from the Greek word *kaos*, meaning "disorder and empty space." A gas is a kind of matter with a lot of empty space between atoms.

The following chart shows words from the story. Notice how the origin of the word gives us a clue to the word meaning.

Words	Language of Origin	Word of Origin	Definition
atom (line 23)	Greek	atomos	indivisible
particles (line 1)	Latin	particula	small part

Practice and Apply What is the language and origin of the word *molecule*? You can use a dictionary to help you. How does this information help you understand the word's meaning?

RESEARCH TOOLBOX

Gathering Information

When you have to give information about a topic you don't know much about, you have to do your research. You can go to the library or use a search engine online to learn about what you are going to talk or write about. But . . . be careful where you get your information from!

▶ **Check your sources.** Whether you are getting information from a book or from the Internet, it is important to verify that the authors of the information are reliable. Are they experts in that topic? Have they studied in that field? Have they worked in that field for many years? Or are they just interested in the topic as a hobby?

▶ **Check your facts.** It is helpful to check different sources about each fact to make sure that the information is the same. For instance, if you are trying to write about an event in history, check two or more sources to verify that the date of the event is the same in each source.

▶ **Double-check your work.** Once you have information you can trust, organize it in a clear way. Then, go over it again to make sure you have included the information correctly. The clearer it is, the better your audience will understand it.

↻ Performance Task

Writing Activity: Search Terms When you research a topic, you may use the internet to help you find information. You use **search terms** to find the information you want. Search terms are the words and phrases you use to find out more about your topic. For example, if you wanted to learn more about what a panda eats, you might search for "panda, food, and diet," or "What does a panda eat?"

- Once you have decided on the search terms you need for your topic, type them into a search engine.

- Next, review the search results. Think about the websites you visited for information. Are they reliable sources? Don't forget to keep a list of the sources you use.

- Think about which search terms you might use to find out more about the discovery of gas. Write down at least three terms, and then share your terms with a partner.

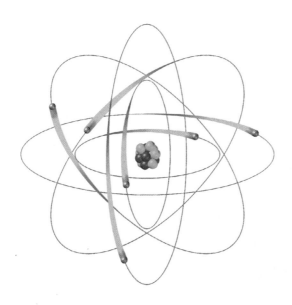

Who Rules the Trees?

You just read about a revolutionary scientific discovery. Now read a poem about a revolutionary symbol of the American Revolution.

Know Before You Go

Before the Revolutionary War even began, American colonists rebelled against the British in what became known as the Pine Tree Riot. The British Navy needed trees to build ships. A law was passed that made it illegal for colonists to cut down pine trees of a certain size. Some colonists snuck into the place where British officials were sleeping and attacked them. Pine trees became a symbol of the American Revolution.

READING TOOLBOX

Understanding Poetic Style

A poem's **style** focuses on *how* something is said instead of *what* is said. The following elements are part of a poem's style:

▶ **structure** or **form** line length, rhyme, punctuation
▶ **figurative language** words and phrases that express ideas in an imaginative way
▶ **sound devices** ways of using words for the sound qualities they create

⏻ **SETTING A PURPOSE**

As you read, pay attention to the rhyming words used in the poem.

Who Rules the Trees?

By Felicia Gonzalez

The king's men would make three cuts on a tree
that **claimed** the tree trunk for the Royal Navy.
A **brand** of a crown on each tree that was stripped
marked it as the mast for a new British ship.

> **claimed:** demanded, required

> **brand:** mark or label

5 The tallest trees fell, the wood shipped away,
and the Colonists wondered "Don't we have a say?"
The mark of the king on the trees in their land
Was a slap in the face—hard as any strong hand.

The crown of a tree is its shape in the sky,

10 its glory of greenery stretching so high,

and the crown of a ruler (from far away, yet)

is more than a hat, it's a powerful threat.

And the **wounds** on the trunks of American pines

Became more than just marks, they became hated signs.

15 Just three **blows** from an axe became one contribution

to an anger that led to a great revolution.

What do you think the word **wounds** is referring to?

blows: powerful cuts

⏻ **COLLABORATIVE DISCUSSION**

Discussing the Purpose With a partner, find two examples of rhyming words in the poem. How do the rhyming words add to your understanding of the poem?

SPEAKING TOOLBOX

Reading Aloud with Expression

When reading poetry and other text out loud, it is important to use your voice to convey and enhance the meaning of the words you are saying. Pay attention to the meanings of the particular words in the poem, the way the words are written on the page, and the punctuation used to show the best way of communicating what you are reading. Control your voice for different effects. Read words carefully, picking which syllables in words to emphasize.

To control your voice, speak:		
fast or slow	high or low	loud or soft
	with emotion or without emotion	

Speak Out! Memorize a section of "Who Rules the Trees?" Then, recite it to a small group. Remember to speak slowly and clearly.

DOWNLOAD

Our Declaration of Independence

The poem you just read described an early symbol of the American Revolution. In this podcast, you'll listen to people read the document that made American independence official.

Background on The Declaration of Independence

The Declaration of Independence is a very important document in the history of the United States. On July 4, 1776, representatives from all the American colonies met in Philadelphia. There, they signed The Declaration of Independence. This document stated why the colonies were breaking off from England and starting a new country. Today, people consider the Declaration to be an inspirational description of why the United States was founded.

⏻ SETTING A PURPOSE

The language in The Declaration of Independence can be difficult because it is a formal document written hundreds of years ago. If you hear something you don't understand, think about the context and keep listening. Use the chart to help you understand some of the more difficult sentences in the podcast.

Our Declaration of Independence

Original Text	Meaning
" . . . Governments are instituted among men, deriving their just powers from the consent of the governed . . . "	Governments can do things because the people who are being governed agree that they have that power.
" . . . it is the right of the people to alter or abolish it, and to institute new government, laying its foundation on such principles and organizing its powers in such form as to them shall seem most likely to effect their safety and happiness."	If a government is not doing its job, the people have the right to change it and make a new one that can keep them safe and make them happy.
"The history of the present king of Great Britain is a history of repeated injuries and usurpations, all having in direct object the establishment of an absolute tyranny over these states."	The King of Great Britain has harmed the American people over and over again. He wants to rule them completely, in a cruel and unfair way.
"We have appealed to their native justice and magnanimity. And we have conjured them by the ties of our common kindred to disavow these usurpations, which would inevitably interrupt our connections and correspondence."	We asked Great Britain to stop being unfair to us because it is damaging our relationship.

⏻ COLLABORATIVE DISCUSSION

In small groups, talk about the problems that The Declaration of Independence describes between Great Britain and the American colonies. Does declaring independence seem like a good response to these problems?

Princess Academy: Palace of Stone

The Declaration of Independence was written by a group of men working together and states the rights of all people to equal liberties. In *Princess Academy: Palace of Stone*, Miri sees how powerful people working together can be.

Know Before You Go

The people in Miri's village, Mount Eskel, are at odds with the palace royalty. Despite the unfriendly relationship between the palace and the villagers, it is decided that the prince will marry a girl from Miri's village. All of the girls from the village are required to attend the new princess academy. One of the girls from the academy will one day marry the prince.

After the prince has chosen his princess, Miri travels with her to the city. There, Miri attends school at Queen's Castle, where she makes some new friends. These friends are making big plans, and revolution is in the air. . . .

⏻ **SETTING A PURPOSE**
As you read, think about what effect Timon's words and actions have on Miri and the crowd.

from

Princess Academy
PALACE OF STONE

SHANNON HALE

He shrugged. "We pay tribute to the noble who owns the land we live on, the same as all commoners. Still, the wealth of the sea has been good to my family. My father is determined to make so much money the king will be forced to offer him a noble title. He thinks I'm a fool to fight for change."

"He's wrong," Miri said, feeling certain of the words.

10 Timon's smile seemed grateful. "Last year I tried to sell one of his ships and use the money to help families whose **tenement** was destroyed in a fire. He sent me back to the Queen's Castle because he didn't know what else to do with me. If I don't turn into a reformed, obedient boy, he'll ship me off to the **far-flung** territories to see how much I like the poor once I become one." He laughed. "But I don't care, Miri. Some things are more important than one person. Lady Sisela showed me that. I don't want to live a comfortable, 20 small life. I want to change the world."

tenement: apartment house

The **compound word** *far-flung* means "distant" or "remote."

119

amassed: gathered together

They were returning, sails down. A group of people had **amassed** on the dock, and even from the ship's deck, Miri could hear angry voices.

As soon as the gangplank hit the deck, Timon said, "Come on." He grabbed Miri's hand and pulled her along.

affixing: sticking

Merchants mobbed together, grumbling. An official in green clothes was **affixing** pieces of paper to large earthenware jugs. One paper blew free and stuck to Miri's boot. She picked it up. It read: *Claimed in tribute for the king.*

30

"Now he's taking cooking oil," Timon said, shaking his head.

"The attempt on his life spooked the old boy, that's what I think," said a nearby merchant, nearly as short as Miri and with a fuzzy brown beard. "He keeps enlarging the royal guard—and claiming more tribute to afford them."

"He can take whatever he wants?" said Miri.

40 "He's the king," the merchant said.

"Why, he's nothing more than a bandit," she said.

"They're bandits and robbers, the lot of them," the merchant agreed.

"The king already claims a portion of all grain and meat brought into Asland," said Timon. "If he takes oil too, the oil merchants will raise the price of what's left over. The rich can afford to pay more for oil, much as they'll resent it. It's the **shoeless** who can barely afford bread as it is. I doubt the king even

50 cares that his greed causes starvation."

> The **compound word** *shoeless* is used to label and describe the very poor.

"If anyone stole something on Mount Eskel— even the head of our village council—my pa and his friends would tell him to give it back or else."

"The king has his own army," said Timon.

"Well, it's time someone told him to stop being a bandit."

Timon's eyes lightened. "You're right, Miri. It's time."

60 He ripped the paper off the nearest jar and crumpled it into a ball.

Miri held her breath. She had not meant he should get himself arrested. What of Sisela's husband? Instinctively, she tried to quarry-speak.

linder: a stone that is used as a means of communication

Stop. A common warning, but there was no **linder** underfoot to carry her message, and anyway his lowlander ears would not hear it.

Timon ripped off another paper. "No," he said.

70

Two soldiers stood with the official, their silver breastplates and tall stiff hats marking them as members of the royal guard. One had noticed Timon. Frowning, he approached. Miri covered her mouth with her hands.

Timon grabbed at all the tribute notices he could reach, saying "No! No!"

Both soldiers were nearly upon Timon. One was **drawing his sword**.

to draw a sword: to take a sword out of its cover

Then the short, bearded merchant said, "No."

Another joined. Another. The soldier hesitated.

80

"No!" Timon said again, and with that, the general **despondency** flashed into anger. The merchants moved closer to Timon and began to chant "No, no," as they ripped the notices. The soldiers took a step back.

despondency: being disheartened, lacking hope or courage

To Miri, never had any word seemed so powerful. And dangerous too. What would happen if she joined in? Would the official recognize her from the palace?

"No," Miri breathed, not moving her lips.

90

The chant was nearly a song, a "Shoeless March" kind of thrumming music that got inside her head, slid down into her muscles, and made her want to *do* something.

"No," Miri whispered, thinking of two gold coins in a shawl and five goats that lifted their heads at the sound of her voice. "No," she said, imagining how the tributes would impoverish her entire village. "No!" she said, because never had she felt so **powerful**. She was not one person; she was a crowd.

100 She belonged to the mass of bodies and voices, strong in number, united in purpose. Two soldiers were **insignificant** compared to thirty merchants, and the scholars and sailors now lending their voices too. Who could stop such a force? And what outcome would not be worth joining in?

"No!" Miri shouted. "No!"

The official and his soldiers were backing away. The crowd closed in, tossing papers and shouting. The official ran as if afraid for his life, the soldiers on

110 his heels.

The mob's shouts turned joyous, and still they called out, pumping their fists and chanting that powerful word. Miri did not want the moment to end. She felt tall and strong, as if she and this mob could move together like a giant, striking down any obstacles, remaking the whole world.

> Identify the **suffix *-ful*** in the word *powerful* to figure out its meaning.

> **insignificant:** not important

As soon as the official disappeared around a corner, the chanting broke into cheers, and merchants and sailors and scholars alike thumped one another on backs and shook hands. Timon pulled Miri into his arms, spinning around. The world seemed so large, and yet Miri felt so much a part of it.

Trade resumed, with merchants buying the oil and loading it onto their carts to sell across the kingdom. Master Filippus could not rally the scholars into any semblance of a group and released them for the day.

Miri found herself walking on her toes as if the wind were **tugging her up**, up into the sky. Timon laughed with delight.

"It's begun!" he said. "When one voice shouts, dozens will join. Thousands! Real change comes soon, Miri. So soon."

tugging her up: pulling her up

120

130

⏻ **COLLABORATIVE DISCUSSION**

Discussing the Purpose What effect do Timon's words and actions have on Miri? What effect do his words and actions have on the crowd? Discuss these questions with a small group. Then, find words and phrases from the story that support your answer. Follow the classroom rules for discussion.

READING TOOLBOX

Making Inferences

As you read, look for clues about characters. Authors don't always tell you everything you need to know about a character. You can use what you already know about people to find out more. Ask yourself, "If a friend did what this character just did, what would I learn about my friend?"

Analyzing the Text [Cite Text Evidence]

1. **Main Idea** What is the main idea of this story?

2. **Making Inferences** How does Miri feel when Timon pulls the paper off of the first jar?

3. **Making Inferences** What is Timon's opinion of the king?

4. **Compare and Contrast** How are Miri and Timon similar? How are they different?

Write On! Do Miri's feelings change from the beginning of the story to the end? Write a short summary of the events in this story to help you answer the question.

DOWNLOAD

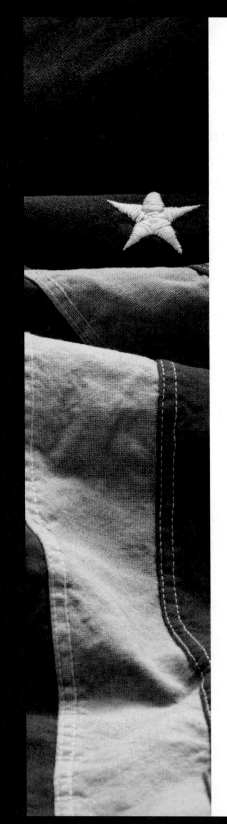

Who Is a Hero?
Who Is a Traitor?

In *Princess Academy: Palace of Stone*, Miri was part of a small act of revolution. Benedict Arnold was involved in one of the most famous acts of revolution in history, the American Revolution.

Background on the American Revolution

For most of the 1700s, the British Empire included thirteen colonies in North America. Toward the end of the 1700s, the people of those colonies rose up against British rule. They fought to become a new country, the United States of America. Not everyone in the American colonies supported the Revolution, however. The people who wanted to remain part of the British Empire were called Loyalists. The people who wanted to become part of the United States of America were called "patriots" or Americans.

⏻ SETTING A PURPOSE

As you read, pay attention to how the events in the text are related.

Who Is a Hero?

Who Is a Traitor?

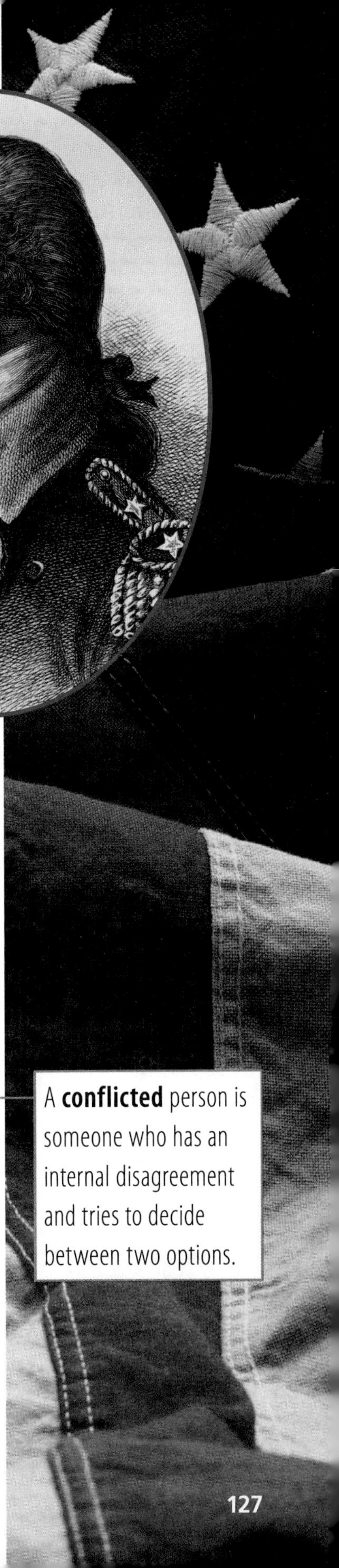

by Susan Buckley

"Benedict Arnold, hero of the American Revolution."
"Benedict Arnold, traitor."

Benedict Arnold is a study in opposites. He was a brave and patriotic soldier who played a key role in helping the American cause in the Revolution, as well as a **conflicted** and resentful soldier who turned against his country and plotted its defeat.

Arnold's great-great-grandfather was one of the first settlers in Rhode Island in the 1600s. When the British defended their American colonies in the French and Indian War, 15-year-old Benedict Arnold ran away
10 and enlisted to defeat the French. He soon deserted and went home, however. Arnold was a loyal soldier who then changed his mind: it was a pattern he would repeat—disastrously.

A **conflicted** person is someone who has an internal disagreement and tries to decide between two options.

127

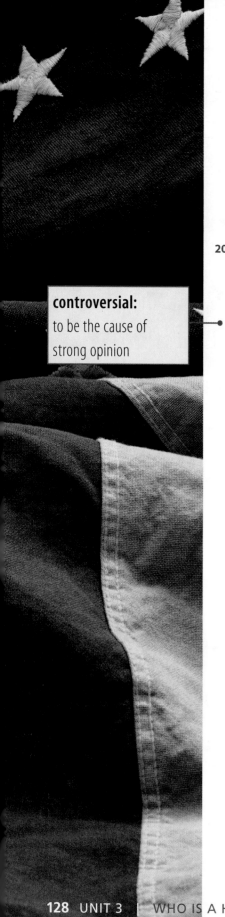

As an adult, Arnold became a successful international merchant. From his viewpoint, British taxes were unfair, so he joined the patriot group the Sons of Liberty. When he heard about the battles at Lexington and Concord in April 1775, Arnold immediately led a group of volunteer soldiers to Boston. There, Benedict Arnold worked with General George Washington to plan American strategy. It was

20 Arnold's idea to capture the British fort at Ticonderoga, an early victory which gave the Continental forces confidence.

Even in victory, though, Benedict Arnold was **controversial**. After Ticonderoga, a fellow officer accused Arnold of misconduct. The charges were dismissed. But Arnold gained a reputation as a troublemaker. Soon

controversial:
to be the cause of strong opinion

▲ General George Washington

▲ Fort Ticonderoga

afterwards, he was passed over for promotion. Then
came the crucial Battle of Saratoga in 1777. Leading the
American armies was General Horatio Gates, who disliked
Arnold intensely and tried to ruin him. In a brilliant charge,
30 however, Benedict Arnold disobeyed Gates's orders. On
horseback he broke through enemy lines and defeated the
British. But General Gates took full credit for the important
victory. Benedict Arnold was a bitter man.

Next, General Washington put Arnold in charge of the
Continental Army forces in Philadelphia. There, he was once
again accused of misconduct. Although the key charges
against him were **dismissed**, Arnold was disillusioned.
Along with his Loyalist wife, he came to believe that the
American cause was lost. As the war dragged on, Arnold
40 decided it would be better for America if the British won,
and committed his betrayal.

> Identify the **prefix**
> **dis-** to figure out the
> meaning of the word
> *dismissed.*

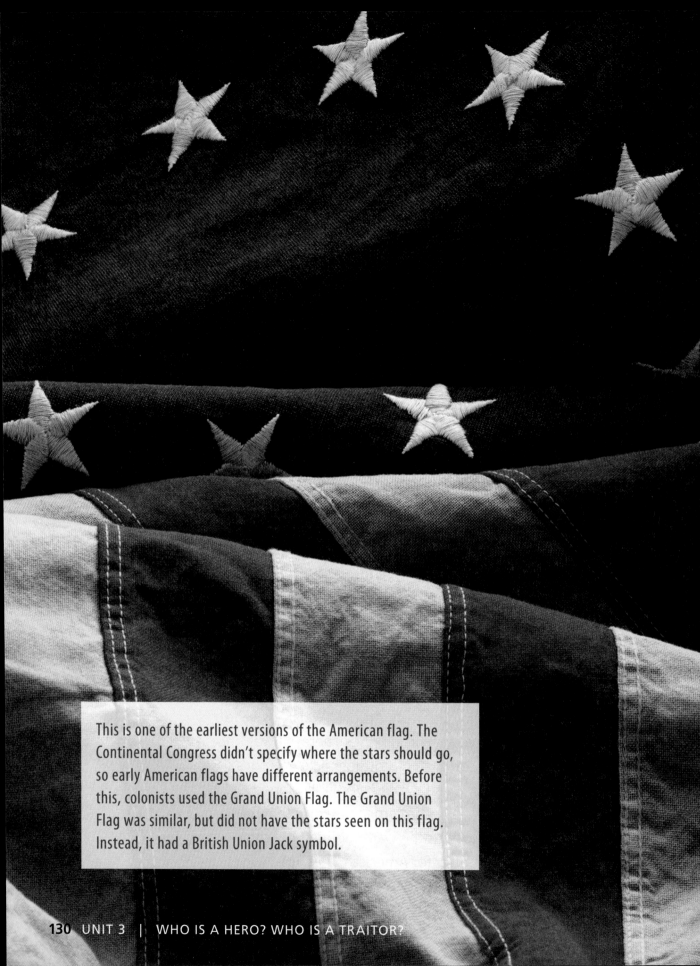

This is one of the earliest versions of the American flag. The Continental Congress didn't specify where the stars should go, so early American flags have different arrangements. Before this, colonists used the Grand Union Flag. The Grand Union Flag was similar, but did not have the stars seen on this flag. Instead, it had a British Union Jack symbol.

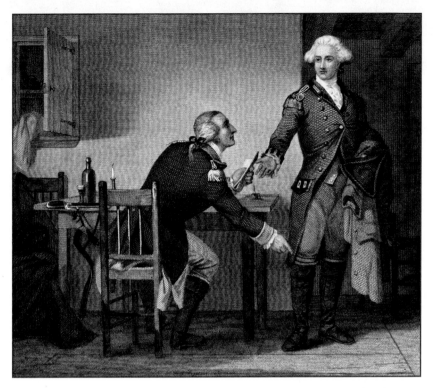

▲ Benedict Arnold persuades Andre to conceal papers in his boot.

Through his wife, Arnold had made contact with a British officer, Major John Andre. Arnold began to give Major Andre secret information about American strategies. Then, in 1780, he managed to get himself appointed head of the American fort at West Point. Contrary to what he was supposed to do, Arnold began weakening the fort. He exchanged letters and papers with Major Andre, a fatal error. When American soldiers captured Major Andre, they found the correspondence between the two men. Arnold's treason was exposed.

Major Andre was hanged as an enemy spy, but Arnold escaped to fight **alongside** the British, against his own countrymen, until the end of the war. Then he was allowed to go to England with other defeated British troops.

To use the name "Benedict Arnold" today is to call someone a traitor. But, during much of the war, Benedict Arnold was known as an American hero.

The word **alongside** is a compound word. Can you guess what it means?

⏻ COLLABORATIVE DISCUSSION

Discussing the Purpose How are the events in this selection related? Discuss your ideas with a partner. Cite evidence from the text in your response.

RESEARCH TOOLBOX

Paraphrasing

When you paraphrase, you do not change the author's meaning. You restate the author's ideas using your own words. Paraphrasing helps you check your understanding of a text and better remember what you have read. It will also help you cite evidence from a text in your own words.

▶ **Identify the main idea** of the selection or paragraph. Ask yourself, "What is the author trying to tell me?"

▶ **Look up words and phrases unfamiliar to you.** Use a dictionary or online source.

▶ **Restate ideas and details using your own words.** Don't just rewrite the words in a different way. Ask yourself, "How can I use my own words to restate what the author is saying?"

Paraphrasing will also stop you from accidentally copying or taking credit for another person's ideas.

Practice and Apply Paraphrase the first three paragraphs of the selection.

↻ Performance Task

Writing Activity: Take Notes When you take notes, you record the main ideas in a text. You can go back to these notes later to help you remember and understand what you've read.

- Record the date of your notes.

- If you are reading a book or article, write down the title and the author's name. If you are reading something on the Internet, copy the complete url and name of the website.

- Write down the main ideas and the important points. Include the page numbers of where you found key information. That way you can easily find the information again later on.

- Do not copy sections of the text word for word. Instead, summarize the main ideas. When you summarize, you retell the main idea and details of a text. A summary is shorter than the original text.

- Make notes as you re-read the selection.

The Legend of Robin Hood

Much like Benedict Arnold, Robin Hood has been considered both a traitor and a hero. To the rich, he was a traitor to the crown and a thief. But to the poor, he was a hero.

Know Before You Go

SETTING Sherwood Forest is a real place. English kings set the land aside so royals could hunt there. Today, this land is a park for people to visit.

The forest is home to a big tree called Major Oak. People say that Robin Hood and the Merry Men used it for shelter.

Major Oak weighs about 23 tons.

The tree is 800 to 1,000 years old.

Some years, it produces 150,000 acorns.

⏻ SETTING A PURPOSE

As you read, think about how Robin Hood responds to challenges.

THE LEGEND OF Robin Hood

retold by Jessica Cohn

PERHAPS YOU'VE HEARD OF ROBIN HOOD, A HERO FROM LONG AGO.

HE AND HIS MEN LIVED IN SHERWOOD FOREST.

THEY TOOK FROM THE RICH, AND GAVE TO THE POOR . . .

. . . WHICH MADE THEM UNPOPULAR WITH SOME.

LONG AGO, IN ENGLAND, THERE LIVED A BAND OF FRIENDS CALLED THE MERRY MEN.

THEY WERE KNOWN FOR THEIR DARING AND LAUGHTER.

THEY WERE CELEBRATED THROUGHOUT THE LAND.

THEIR LEADER WAS THE MAN THEY CALLED ROBIN HOOD. HIS VIEWPOINT WAS QUITE UNIQUE.

SOME THOUGHT OF HIM AS A GENTLEMAN . . . OTHERS, A NO-GOOD THIEF.

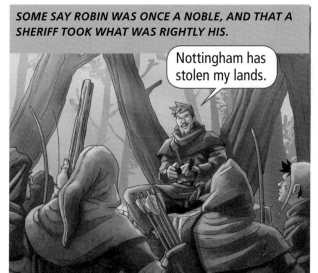

SOME SAY ROBIN WAS ONCE A NOBLE, AND THAT A SHERIFF TOOK WHAT WAS RIGHTLY HIS.

Nottingham has stolen my lands.

THEY SAY THE SHERIFF WAS CRUEL AND EVIL —AS WERE MANY OF THE POWERFUL THEN.

Personally, I vow, he will not rest as long as I live!

Nor I!

ROBIN BECAME AN OUTLAW. TALES ABOUT HIM WERE SHARED FAR AND WIDE. THE MANY ADVENTURES OF ROBIN HOOD BECAME LEGEND OVER TIME.

He robs from the rich and gives to the poor!

IN EACH TELLING, THE FACTS ARE DIFFERENT. YET, SOME PARTS OF THE LEGEND REPEAT. ROBIN LIVES DEEP IN THE FOREST. HE IS SKILLED AT FIGHTING AND FAST ON HIS FEET.

See there, how remarkable!

Hail, Robin Hood!

Hail, Robin Hood!

AT ROBIN'S RIGHT HAND IS THE MAN THEY CALL "LITTLE JOHN."

THEY LEAD HUNDREDS OF MEN IN THE WOODS.

EACH BOWS TO THEIR LEADER, AND ADMIRE THEIR CHIEF THIEF. THEY LAUGH IN THE FACE OF THE LAW.

Nottingham is nothing!

Huzzah!

TIMES ARE VERY HARD, AND THE PEOPLE GO HUNGRY. YET, THE ROYALS TAKE ALL THAT THEY CAN.

Halt!

SO, THE MERRY MEN BAND TOGETHER. THEY IMPOSE JUSTICE THAT HELPS THEIR FANS.

Contrary to your orders, sir, I know the rightful owner of this wheat!

SOME STORIES FEATURE A LADY. THEY CALL HER MAID MARIAN.

SHE IS KNOWN FAR AND WIDE AS A BEAUTY. MANY KNIGHTS TRY TO WIN HER HAND.

ROBIN AND MARIAN MEET WHILE DRESSED IN DISGUISE. THEY BATTLE WHEN THEY CROSS PATHS FOR THE FIRST TIME.

On guard!

IN THE MIDST OF THEIR FIGHT, THEY BOTH STOP SHORT.

My lady?

THE FIRST DAY OF MAY IS MAY DAY, WHEN MANY CELEBRATE SPRING. IT'S THEN THAT THE TWO ARE REMEMBERED . . . WITH SPECIAL SONGS AND DANCING.

To the king and queen of the forest!

IN ONE OF HIS ADVENTURES, ROBIN LEAVES THE FOREST IN DISGUISE. HE WANTS TO TAKE PART IN A CONTEST AND HOPES TO WIN THE PRIZE.

A PRINCE WANTS TO KNOW WHERE THE BEST ARCHERS LIVE. SO, THE BEST FROM TWO FORESTS COMPETE.

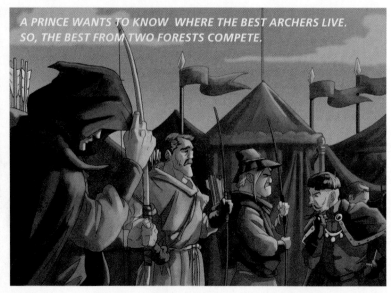

They say the prize is a silver arrow!

THEY SHOOT UNTIL JUST SIX REMAIN STANDING. NOW, CAN YOU GUESS WHO WINS THAT DAY?

THE PRINCE WANTS TO ARREST THE OUTLAW. HIS KNIGHTS CHASE ROBIN, BUT HE AND HIS MEN ESCAPE.

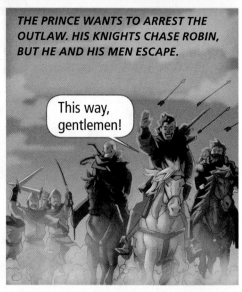

This way, gentlemen!

FOR A WHILE THEY HIDE IN A CASTLE THAT BELONGS TO A MAN ROBIN ONCE HELPED. WHEN THEY MAKE THEIR FINAL ESCAPE, THOUGH, THE PRINCE PUTS THE MAN WHO OWNS THE CASTLE IN JAIL.

ROBIN MUST COME TO THE RESCUE, WHICH HE DOES. ROBIN WILL ALWAYS SHOW UP WHEN HE NEEDS TO HELP ONE OF HIS FRIENDS.

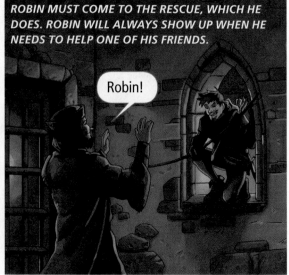

Robin!

THE MERRY MEN LIVE ON IN STORIES. AMONG THEM, A LOYAL SERVANT NAMED WILL . . .

Will Scarlet, at your service . . .

THERE IS MUCH, ALSO CALLED THE MILLER'S SON, AND ALLIN-A-DALE, THE MINSTREL.

This one was first in the fray!

FRIAR TUCK IS A MAN OF THE CHURCH WHO IS ALSO EFFICIENT WITH SWORDS.

You don't say!

Hah!

JOHN LITTLE TAKES THE NICKNAME "LITTLE JOHN." HE HAD BEEN SENT TO HUNT ROBIN, IT'S SAID.

DURING THEIR BATTLE, ROBIN LOSES HIS BALANCE. JOHN GAINS HIS LASTING RESPECT.

HE CALLS THE BIG MAN "LITTLE JOHN," IN THE WAY THAT FRIENDS TEND TO JOKE. HIS MERRY BAND STAYS FRIENDS FOREVER . . . IN THE DEEP FOREST OF DREAMS . . . AND BOOKS.

And so it shall be . . .

⏻ COLLABORATIVE DISCUSSION

Discussing the Purpose How does Robin Hood respond to challenges? Discuss this question with a small group. Cite evidence from the text in your response.

LISTENING TOOLBOX

Class Discussions

You can share your thoughts and exchange ideas with many people at one time in a class discussion. Your classmates can help you understand concepts and can help you think about things in a way you might not have thought about.

- Follow class rules for participating.
- Wait for your turn and don't interrupt.
- Be attentive. Look at speakers when they are talking.
- Ask if you don't understand what's been said.
- Restate in your own words what others have said to make sure you understand.
- Ask questions about the ideas others have shared.
- Build on the ideas shared before yours when you make comments.

Useful Phrases

▷ Would you please repeat that? I'm not sure what you mean.
▷ What I think Lily is saying is ____.
▷ What Stephan said just now makes me think ____.

Speak Out! Have a class discussion to answer the question "What were Robin Hood's goals?" Follow the rules for classroom discussion.

Write On! Which of Robin Hood's adventures from the graphic novel is your favorite? Write a paragraph explaining your opinion.

Vocabulary Strategy: Compound Words

A **compound word** is made up of two words that have been joined together to make a new word with a different meaning. You can figure out a compound word's meaning by identifying the two words that make it up. For example, the word *crosswalk* is made up of the two words, *cross* and *walk*. The word *cross* means "to go from one side to the other," so we can determine that a *crosswalk* is a place where we can *walk* from one side of something to the other.

There are many compound words in "The Legend of Robin Hood." By breaking each compound word into two smaller words, you can identify the definition of the word. Look at the chart below:

Compound Word	Word 1	Word 2	Definition
storyteller	story	teller	a person who tells stories
gentleman	gentle	man	a man with good manners
outlaw	out	law	a person who does not follow the law

Practice and Apply You read that Robin Hood "helps everyday people." Which two words are joined to make the compound word *everyday*? Once you have broken down the word, guess the definition. Then look up the word in a dictionary. Does your guess match the dictionary definition?

Performance Task

Writing Activity: Research Report

You have read about different kinds of revolutions. Your task is to write a report on a real-life figure who took part in the American Revolution.

Planning and Prewriting

Connect to the Theme

There are all sorts of revolutions. There are scientific revolutions, technological revolutions, and cultural revolutions. Some revolutions seem to happen quickly, and some take a long time to begin. Whatever form they take, one thing is for sure—after the revolution, nothing is the same. In this activity you will be writing a research report about a historical figure who took part in the American Revolution. Who will it be?

Choose a Topic

Choosing a person to a write about should be easy—you've come across a few of them in the unit selection. But what if you want to know about others? How do you look up a name without knowing the name you're looking up? Luckily, there are search engines and indexes to guide you. Using the key words "American Revolution" will lead you to some interesting individuals you might never have heard of. Once you've picked a person to write about, make sure your topic is not too big. "George Washington" is too big a topic for a research report. Is there a part of his life you want to focus on? Is there an event you want to research? A better topic might be "General George Washington," or "George Washington's Presidency."

Decide the Basics

Now that you have a topic, you will need to gather your sources, take notes, and make an outline.

Gather Your Sources

Go to the library for information or research your topic online. No matter what sources you use, make sure they're reliable. This is especially true for Internet sources. There's a difference between someone posting an opinion on a website and an online article written by an expert in the field. All sources are not the same!

Check Your Facts

Since you'll be writing a research report about an actual person, you'll be dealing with facts. Facts have to be correct. Using more than one source will help you double-check your facts. It will also help you show multiple points of view. An encyclopedia entry, a news article, and a biography give you different kinds of information. If you're having trouble finding a certain fact in one place you might find it in another.

Take Notes

- Record the date at the top of each note page.
- For each print source, write down the title and the author's name. For each online source, copy the complete URL and the name of the website.
- Write down the important points the author makes. Include the page numbers where you found key information. That way you can easily find it again.
- Paraphrase sections of text instead of copying the author's sentences. When you paraphrase, you give the information in your own words.

Make an Outline

An outline lists all your ideas and puts them in order. It shows which facts are most important and which facts are details. An outline helps you stay on topic, keeps you focused on the points you're trying to make, and sets up a clear message. When you start to write, an outline will help you organize and structure the information you want to present.

Performance Task

Finalize Your Plan

You've got your outline. Now you need to decide how to present the information. Use the diagram in the Writing Toolbox to help you.

WRITING TOOLBOX

Elements of a Research Report

Opening Paragraph	In the **opening paragraph**, present your topic. Introduce the person and why you chose to write about him or her. Hook your readers with an interesting detail or a quotation.
Main Idea and Supporting Details	Each paragraph should include a **main idea** and **supporting details**.
Conclusion	The **conclusion** should sum up how the details support your main idea. You may want to include a final thought about your subject based on the research you did.

Draft Your Research Report

Now start writing! As you write, here are some things to think about:

- **Audience** What effect do you want your report to have on readers? Will it give them a better understanding and appreciation of the person you wrote about?

- **Purpose** Tell why you chose this person early on in your report, so readers can follow the points you're making. Is it clear why you chose this person?

- **Title** The title should identify the individual or refer to him or her in a way that gets the reader's interest.

- **Structure** Use the diagram on the opposite page to help you organize your information. Link your paragraphs together in a way that makes sense. Make sure your sentences flow smoothly.

- **Conclusion** Use a concluding paragraph to tie your ideas together. Restate why you chose to write about this person.

Revise

Self Evaluation

Use the checklist and rubric to guide your analysis.

Peer Review

Exchange your report with a classmate. Use the checklist to comment on your classmate's report.

Edit

Edit your report to correct spelling, grammar, and punctuation errors.

Publish

Finalize your report and choose a way to share it with your audience.

The Power of Storytelling

"Books are the quietest and most constant of friends; they are the most accessible and wisest of counselors, and the most patient of teachers."

— **Charles William Eliot, academic**

Essential Question

Why do people tell stories?

The Language of Storytelling

People have been telling stories since ancient times. Even before we had printing presses, books, and computers, people shared stories. Cave paintings, hieroglyphics (an ancient writing system using symbols), and myths told by the ancient Greeks more than 3,000 years ago are evidence of people's long tradition of storytelling.

Stories are told in many ways. Some of the first stories were likely told or acted out loud. As people discovered ways to write and draw, stories were told with pictures. Today, stories are told in writing. We use dance, drama, song, and pictures to tell stories, too.

Stories open us up to new possibilities. Stories preserve our history. They remind us of things that happened in the past. They also excite our imaginations and open our minds to new ideas for the future. Stories bring us together.

In this unit, you will discover some of the many ways and reasons why people tell stories. You will read a blog entry about *Dia de los Muertos*. Blogs are a way of sharing stories in the digital age. In another selection, you will read slave stories and think about why these stories are important to share. Finally, you will learn how photographs, and even rocks, tell stories.

What are different ways people tell stories?

A Penny for Your Thoughts:
Figurative Language

Stories can be simple and poetic. They can be bold and epic. The words we choose to tell a story paint a picture in the reader's or listener's mind. They set a mood or a feeling. They communicate the plot. **Figurative language** is often used to help make a story memorable. Figurative language compares things in an interesting way or uses words in an unusual way. Here are some examples of figurative language.

Metaphor	A comparison of two or more things	The world is a stage.
Simile	A metaphor using the words *like* or *as* to make a comparison	The girl was as brave as a lion.
Hyperbole	Exaggeration that is not meant to be taken literally	The giant Paul Bunyan was so large that the ground shook for a hundred miles with each step he took.
Personification	Giving animals or things human-like traits, thoughts, or emotions	The sun smiled down on the flowers growing in the field.
Symbolism	Using symbols to signify ideas	The explorers gave the people they met an olive branch to show their intentions. (An olive branch is a symbol of a peace offering.)

↻ Performance Task

Explain why you think people tell stories. Use the information on page 150 and in **Browse** magazine as a guide. Then write a short speech to communicate your ideas about storytelling. Use the supports in your **Activity Book**.

➜ *Browse*
magazine

DOWNLOAD

You have learned how stories can preserve history. Now read a blog about *Dia de los Muertos*, a holiday that preserves the history of people who have passed away.

⏻ SETTING A PURPOSE

As you read, think about the main idea of the blog.

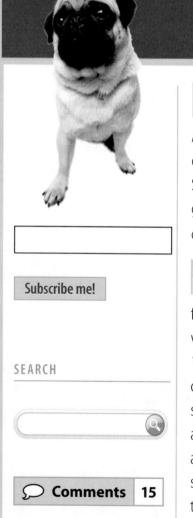

I_LOVE_PUGS

OCT 30
5:00 p.m.
My friend Isabel said she would be spending the weekend preparing for and celebrating *Dia de los Muertos*. In English, this means "Day of the Dead." I told her I didn't know anything about it, but it sounded interesting. She invited me over to learn more about how her family gets ready to enjoy this holiday. I'll share what I learn with all of you!

OCT 31
2:00 p.m.
Isabel's parents explained more about *Dia de los Muertos*. They said the Mexican holiday is a way for families to celebrate the lives of people who are no longer with us. Isabel's mom told me that every year on November 1, they honor dead children. On November 2, they honor dead adults. That sounded kind of sad to me, but her mom said it's not meant to be a sad time. This time is meant to be a celebration. On this holiday, people show that the dead are still a part of their lives and of their community. Isabel says that the holiday is a way for family and friends to keep their memories of the dead alive.

Subscribe me!

SEARCH

🔍

💬 **Comments** 15

OCT 31
2:20 p.m.
I asked Isabel how they celebrate. She said if people live near where their loved ones are buried, they might visit the cemetery to clean and decorate their graves. They might create a little tribute at the grave site. The tribute might include pictures, flowers, or favorite items. For children, visitors might put toys on their graves. Isabel's dad said that they tell stories about the person's life, and hope he or she can hear them. It's a nice way for people to remember the dead and the importance of their family history. Families create tributes with offerings at home, too. Isabel showed me theirs. It included pictures of their family members, candles, pretty orange flowers, sugar skulls, and bread. This bread is called *pan de muerto*, which means "bread of the dead." Isabel's mom said that many communities have parties, parades, and festivals on *Dia de los Muertos*.

OCT 31
3:00 p.m.
Isabel's parents are making tamales. Yum! I looked around Isabel's house and asked her, if it's supposed to be a joyful holiday, how come there are so many skeletons? She said the skeletons aren't supposed to be scary, like I think they are for Halloween. They are meant to be festive. People paint their faces like skeletons, dress up like skeletons, wear skeleton masks, and decorate with skeletons.

OCT 31
5:15 p.m.
I'm home now. Isabel's mom gave me a sugar skull to take home. It's a smiling skull with lots of colorful decorations, including glitter and beads! Her mom reminded me not to actually eat it. It was nice of Isabel's family to take so much time to tell me about the importance of this holiday and the many traditions that go with it. I learned something new about this holiday, and I hope what I learned taught you something, too!

ARCHIVES

October

September

August

July

June

May

April

March

February

UPLOAD

⏻ **COLLABORATIVE DISCUSSION TOPICS**

Discussing the Purpose With a partner, discuss what the main idea of the blog is.

Exploring the Topic With a small group, discuss some of the traditions the blogger learns about *Dia de los Muertos*. Support your opinions with examples.

Staying Safe: It is a good practice not to write about where and when you will be away, especially if your home will be empty for a period of time. Always remember that anyone can see information published on a blog. A blog is public!

Write On! The blogger wrote about the holiday *Dia de los Muertos*. Add a comment to "I_LOVE_PUGS." Tell about a holiday that you enjoy celebrating. Then exchange what you have written with a classmate. Write something in reaction to his or her comment. 💬 Comments | 0

🔄 **Performance Task**

Writing Activity: Scheduling Your Calendar Many bloggers like to write posts ahead of when they want to publish them. For example, if you won't be able to blog during a family vacation, you can set up several blog posts on a calendar to be published while you are away. This way, your blog automatically sends posts and updates your readers.

1 Write three posts that will be published at a later date. Your blog software should have a scheduling feature that allows you to set up your editorial calendar for future publication.

2 Write an entry about a favorite book or movie that you wish to publish at a later date.

3 Send a reminder about an upcoming event, such as a book reading at your local library. Make sure that your blog post gives an accurate date and time. You don't want to invite readers to an event at the wrong location or day!

4 Write a blog post to promote a public event in your area. Set your post up so that the future blog date matches the specific date in mind. Add a special design for fun!

Language Cam video
Watch the video to learn more about the different kinds of stories people tell.

DOWNLOAD

Rocks Tell a Story

You just read about a blogger who learned about the holiday *Dia de los Muertos*. Read ahead to find out what this family learns about the Grand Canyon.

READING TOOLBOX

Interpret Information

Informational texts can present information in different ways. They include facts found from reliable sources. A **source** is something, or someone, that gives information.

Sometimes, an informational text will include information from witnesses or experts. A **witness** is a person who saw an event happen. A witness will tell you what he or she saw first-hand. An **expert** is a person who has a lot of knowledge about a certain topic or subject area. Usually, an expert will be named as an expert in the informational text.

One way to get information from an expert or a witness is by doing an interview. An **interview** is a conversation between two or more people. One person asks another person questions to learn more about a topic.

⏻ SETTING A PURPOSE

As you read, pay attention to the cause-and-effect relationship between the Colorado River and the Grand Canyon.

ROCKS
Tell a Story

By Duncan Teed

Last year, my family visited the Grand Canyon in the northwest corner of Arizona. My parents had been there many times before, but I had not. It was the best trip I have ever taken, because the Grand Canyon is the most incredible place I have ever seen in my life! What the guide said was so fascinating that I asked her if I could record it on my phone. This is what she told us.

GUIDE: Welcome to one of the most remarkable places on earth. We are standing on the South **Rim**. You are
10 looking across at the North Rim. Here at Grand Canyon Village it's 10 miles from rim to rim, but in some places the canyon is 18 miles wide.

> **rim:** outer edge or border

157

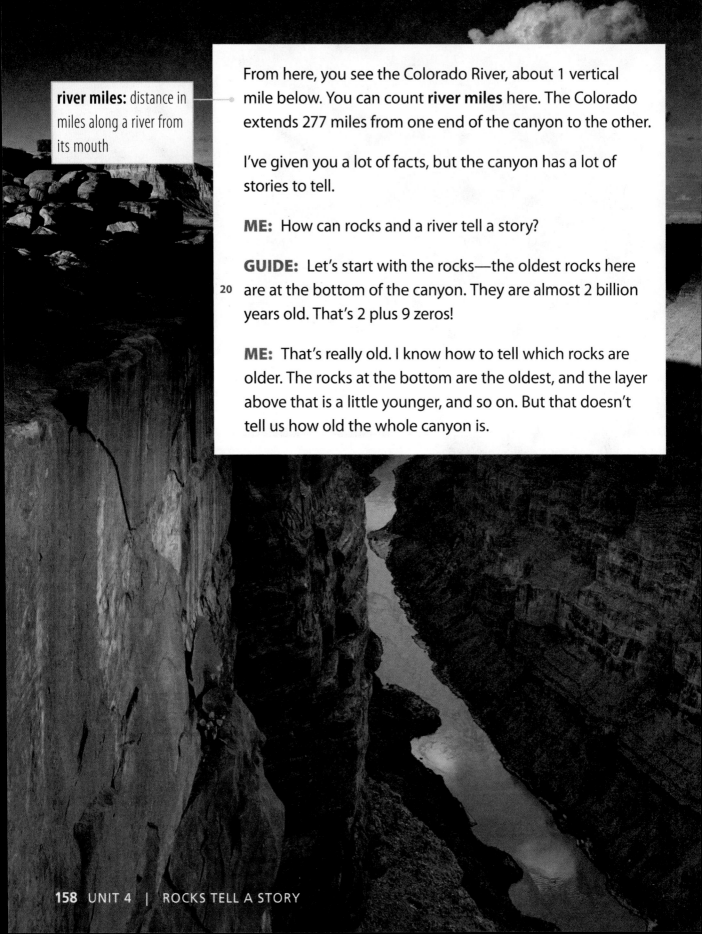

river miles: distance in miles along a river from its mouth

From here, you see the Colorado River, about 1 vertical mile below. You can count **river miles** here. The Colorado extends 277 miles from one end of the canyon to the other.

I've given you a lot of facts, but the canyon has a lot of stories to tell.

ME: How can rocks and a river tell a story?

GUIDE: Let's start with the rocks—the oldest rocks here
20 are at the bottom of the canyon. They are almost 2 billion years old. That's 2 plus 9 zeros!

ME: That's really old. I know how to tell which rocks are older. The rocks at the bottom are the oldest, and the layer above that is a little younger, and so on. But that doesn't tell us how old the whole canyon is.

◀ Temple Butte limestone found in the Grand Canyon, containing fossils of marine creatures such as this bryozoan

◀ Trilobite fossil as found in the Grand Canyon's Bright Angel Shale layer, located in Arizona

GUIDE: Geologists—scientists who study the physical history of the earth—have several ways to calculate the age of rocks. They can determine the absolute age of rocks with **radiometric dating**. As you said, they can determine the
30 relative age by rock layers. If you could climb up the sides of the canyon, you would find nearly 40 layers of rocks.

Radiometric dating is a method scientists use to determine the age of rocks. Read the next paragraph to learn more about it.

ME: I've heard of radiometric dating. That's when you measure how radioactive an old rock is. When some rocks form they have radioactive matter in them, which gets less radioactive over time.

GUIDE: That's right. Scientists call that radioactive decay, and it's a steady process.

Back to the story of how the rocks built up. The earth changed over those billions of years. Volcanoes deposited
40 lava. Mountains formed and shifted. At one time this entire area was under the ocean. We know because geologists have found fossilized sea creatures in the canyon's rocks. **Fossils** also tell geologists what was happening here when dinosaurs roamed the Earth.

Look at the photographs and captions on top of this page for clues about **fossils**.

Layers of the Grand Canyon

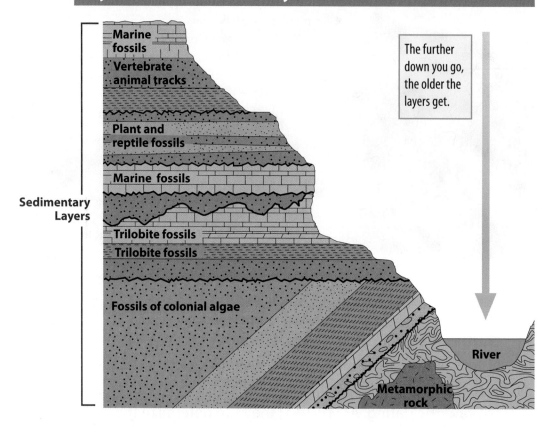

Marine fossils

Vertebrate animal tracks

Plant and reptile fossils

Marine fossils

Trilobite fossils

Trilobite fossils

Fossils of colonial algae

Sedimentary Layers

The further down you go, the older the layers get.

River

Metamorphic rock

ME: So there wasn't a canyon back then, if the rocks were still building up, or the layers wouldn't match up on either side of the canyon. Did the canyon form because of an earthquake or a volcano? Water can wear down rock, but even with two billion years, I can't imagine that little river
50 cutting out this huge canyon.

Which words in the sentence help you understand the meaning of **erode**?

GUIDE: Well, that's a newer story—only about 5 or 6 million years old, but it's still enough time for a "little" river to wear down, or **erode**, the rock. It's still going on today. In another million years or so the canyon will be even deeper. The story continues, though too slow for us to learn the ending now.

ME: Wow. The Grand Canyon does tell stories, if you know how to "read" them!

⏻ COLLABORATIVE DISCUSSION

Discussing the Purpose Explain the effect the Colorado River has had on the Grand Canyon to a partner. Cite text evidence in your response.

Analyzing the Text ⬚ Cite Text Evidence

1. **Identifying Sources** Who is the expert in this selection?

2. **Identifying Sources** Who is the witness in this selection?

Vocabulary Strategy: Word Origins

There are many specialized vocabulary terms specific to the study of geology in this selection. Sometimes, you need to determine the meaning of an unfamiliar word by reading all of the information in the passage. Try identifying context clues in the words and sentences around the word to help you figure out its meaning. If you are still unsure about a word's meaning after reading the passage, use a dictionary to look up the word's meaning.

Practice and Apply In the sentence, "We know because geologists have found fossilized sea creatures in the canyon's rocks" (lines 41–42), what does the word *fossilized* mean? Did you use context clues or a dictionary to find the answer?

DOWNLOAD

You have read about how nature can tell a story. Read the following selection to read the stories of former slaves.

⏻ **SETTING A PURPOSE**

As you read, think about why the author wanted to share these slave stories.

Stories of Slavery

by Monica Bernard

---

enslaved: the state of being owned by another person

People of **African heritage** are people whose ancestors, grandparents, or great grandparents came from Africa.

In 1619, a small group of African men and women arrived on an English ship at Jamestown, Virginia. They came against their will, and most historians believe they arrived already **enslaved**. Today we know almost nothing about the more than 20 Africans who came on that first ship. We know that by 1790, there were about 700,000 people of **African heritage** in the U.S. Some information about their lives comes from white owners or observers.

There are bills of sale, letters, and wills that list the
10 slaves someone owned. But these give a far less personal
account than the enslaved Africans themselves
would tell.

It was illegal for slaves to learn to read and write. Against
all odds, some Africans learned anyway. Some told their
stories in what historians call "slave narratives." Here are
some of their stories.

Venture Smith was born in Guinea around 1729.

The oldest son of a chief, he was raised to become a
chief himself. But when he was about 6 years old, he
20 was captured and sold into slavery. On the slave ship
crossing the Atlantic, an officer bought the boy. The
man took Venture to Rhode Island. Venture grew up
there, as a household slave. As an adult, Venture tried to
escape slavery, but he changed his mind and went back
to his owner. Eventually, Venture Smith was able to buy
freedom for himself and his family. When he was almost
70, he **dictated** his story to a schoolteacher. He said, "My
freedom is a privilege which nothing else can equal."

dictated: said or read aloud and recorded by another

Olaudah Equiano was born in 1745 in what is
30 now Nigeria. Slave traders captured him when he was
about 11. First he was a slave to an African chief. Then
he was taken across the Atlantic on a slave ship and sold
to a Virginia planter. Then a British naval officer bought
him for friends in England. Equiano spent most of the
rest of his life on ships. Eventually one owner allowed
him to work for pay, and Equiano bought his freedom.
As a free man, Equiano **protested** slavery however he
could. In a petition to the Queen of England, he asked for
"your Majesty's compassion for millions of my African
40 countrymen . . ."

> **protested:** showed or expressed strong disagreement

James Roberts was born into slavery in Maryland
in 1753. As a young man, he fought in the Revolutionary
War with his owner. He hoped he and his family would
gain their freedom as a result. Instead, the owner
separated Roberts from his family and sent him to New
Orleans. Roberts fought under Andrew Jackson in the
Battle of New Orleans. But once again, he was sent back
into slavery after fighting for the nation. Eventually,
however, James Roberts gained his freedom.

50 James Roberts wrote his **memoir** as an older man. Like
other former slaves, he wanted future generations to
know what his life in slavery had been like. In sharing
their experiences, later generations could know their
stories of struggle and triumph.

> **memoir:** a written record of personal events, experiences, and thoughts

⏻ COLLABORATIVE DISCUSSION

Discussing the Purpose Why does the author include the stories of former slaves, instead of writing this selection as a list of facts? Discuss this question with a partner. Use the toolbox below to help you.

READING TOOLBOX

Author's Purpose

An author can have one or more reasons, or purposes, for writing a piece. You can read the facts and details in informational texts to help you figure out the *author's purpose*. The purpose of an informational text is to inform or explain. Now that you've read the text, think about the facts and details that help you determine the author's purpose.

↻ Performance Task

Writing Activity: Small Group Research With a small group, conduct research to find out more about Venture Smith, Olaudah Equiano, or James Roberts.

- Take notes and record the sources of your information.

- Work together to compile a list of the notes each group member wrote down. If you find that two of you collected the same piece of information, make sure that you don't repeat the information twice in your list.

- Organize the information into an outline.

- Share what you found with the class.

Podcast: Art of Storytelling Alive and Well in Audio Books

In the last selection, you read about slave narratives from the 1700s. The podcast you'll listen to next discusses a more recent kind of storytelling.

Background on Storytelling

For most of human history, storytelling was the only way to pass on stories. That is, until the invention of writing over 5,000 years ago. Eventually, novels and other kinds of written stories became an important way of sharing culture. In 1932, the American Association for the Blind began to produce audio recordings of books for people unable to read them. Since then, these audio books have become widely available to a variety of listeners, and feature all kinds of written work.

 **SETTING A PURPOSE**

While listening to this podcast, consider the skills a narrator of audio books needs to have. How are these skills similar to those a writer needs to have? How are they different?

Art of Storytelling Alive and Well in Audio Books

Oral and Written Traditions

Oral Tradition	Written Tradition	Audio Books
• stories told aloud • storyteller's voice makes the telling unique • pulls listeners in with a live telling • can be heard by only a few • happens in real time • oldest art form among the three traditions	• stories written down • author's choice of words creates a unique tone • pulls readers in by choice of words • can be read over and over • happens when the listener has access to a book • older than audio books, but newer than the oral tradition	• written stories interpreted aloud • narrator is an actor who brings the words alive • pulls listeners in by creating and sustaining the characters' voices • can be heard over and over • happens when the listener has access to a listening device • newest art form among the three traditions

⏻ **COLLABORATIVE DISCUSSION**

Discussing the Purpose With a partner, discuss whether audio books are more like oral storytelling or more like written works. Give two examples to support your opinion.

DOWNLOAD

Ode to Family Photographs

Telling stories out loud is one way people share experiences. People can also share their stories through poetry.

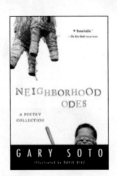

READING TOOLBOX

Analyze Poetic Form

Poetry is a form of literature. The words in a poem are carefully chosen. The words are also written in a certain order. In poetry, **form** is the way words are arranged on the page. The two basic elements of form are line and rhythm. **Line** is the main unit of all poems. Poets use line length and word presentation to point out meaning and create rhythm. **Rhythm** is a pattern of stressed and unstressed syllables in a line of poetry, like rhythmic beats in music.

Creating the form of a poem involves careful choices of words and sounds. To understand how form can help create an effect in poetry ask yourself:

▶ How long are the lines?
▶ Do the sentences always end at the end of the line?
▶ What is the order of the words in each line?
▶ Is there anything special about the font?

⏻ SETTING A PURPOSE

As you read, pay attention to the specific words used in the poem. Also, how does the form of the poem help you understand what the poet is describing?

Ode to Family Photographs

BY GARY SOTO

An **ode** is a poem that expresses praise or enthusiastic emotion.

This is the pond, and these are my feet.
This is the rooster, and this is more of my feet.

Mamá was never good at pictures.

This is a statue of a famous general who lost an arm,
5 And this is me with my head cut off.

This is a trash can chained to a gate,
This is my father with his eyes half-closed.

This is a photograph of my sister
And a giraffe looking over her shoulder.

10 This is our car's front bumper.
This is a bird with a pretzel in its beak.
This is my brother Pedro standing on one leg on a rock,
With a smear of chocolate on his face.

Mamá sneezed when she looked
15 *Behind the camera: the snapshots are blurry,*
The angles dizzy as a spin on a merry-go-round.

But we had fun when Mamá picked up the camera.
How can I tell?
Each of us laughing hard.
20 Can you see? I have candy in my mouth.

This sentence **compares** the angles in the photographs to a ride on a merry-go-round. Can you guess why? What word helps you understand it?

⏻ COLLABORATIVE DISCUSSION

Discussing the Purpose With a partner, discuss the language and form of the poem.

- Reread the title of the poem. What word helps you figure out how the poet feels about his family?

- Look at the parts of the poem that are in *italics*. What do the sentences in italics show?

Write On! Write a paragraph about the memory from the poem that you like best. Include reasons for why you like it.

LISTENING TOOLBOX

Active Listening
Always be respectful of others when they are speaking.

▶ **Give your full attention to the speaker.** You may think you know what the person is going to say next, but you may be wrong!

▶ **Let the speaker finish before you begin to talk.** You can't really listen if you are busy thinking about what you want to say next.

▶ **Ask questions.** If you are not sure you understand what the speaker has said, just ask. Remain calm and collected as you ask your question.

Speak Out! What is your favorite poem? Tell a small group about the poem, and why it is your favorite. If you can, recite a section from the poem.

DOWNLOAD

The Land of Stories: The Wishing Spell

In "Ode to Family Photographs," you read about a poet's memories of his family. In this selection, you will read about a father who tells his son a story.

Background on Parables

A **parable** is a type of story that teaches a lesson. This lesson might also be called the *moral* or the *meaning* of the parable. The events and characters in parables stand for something else. Understanding the lesson is dependent upon your understanding what the events and characters stand for. Parables come from stories that were told out loud long ago. As you read, think about the lesson of Mr. Bailey's story.

⏻ SETTING A PURPOSE

As you read, pay attention to the elements of the selection. What is the theme of the Walking Fish story?

from *The Land of Stories:*

THE WISHING SPELL

by Chris Colfer

Mr. Bailey always knew when his son needed to talk to him. It didn't have anything to do with observation or intuition, but with location. Occasionally, Mr. Bailey would get home from work and find his son sitting up in the oak tree in the front yard with a **contemplative** look on his face.

> **contemplative:** thoughtful, thinking deeply

"Conner?" Mr. Bailey would ask, approaching the tree. "Is everything okay, bud?"

"Uh-huh," Conner would mumble.

10   "Are you sure?" Mr. Bailey would ask.

> The **interjection** *uh-huh* is used informally to mean "yes." Do you know examples of other interjections?

Yup: informal word
for *yes*

"**Yup,**" Conner would say unconvincingly. He wasn't as vocal about his troubles as his sister was, but you could see it in his face. Mr. Bailey would climb up the tree and have a seat on the branch next to his son and coax out what was troubling him.

"Are you sure you don't want to talk about it?" Mr. Bailey would continue. "Did something happen at school today?"

Conner would nod his head.

20 "I got a bad grade on a test," he admitted on one occasion.

"Did you study for it?" his father asked.

"Yes," Conner said. "I studied really hard, Dad. But it's just no use. I'll never be as smart as Alex." His cheeks turned bright red with embarrassment.

"Conner, let me fill you in on something that took me a long time to learn," Mr. Bailey said. "The women in your life are always going to seem smarter; it's just the way it is. I've been married to your mother for thirteen 30 years, and I still have trouble keeping up with her. You can't compare yourself to others."

"But I'm stupid, Dad," Conner said, his eyes filling with tears.

"I find that hard to believe," Mr. Bailey said. "It takes intelligence to be funny and tell a good joke, and you're the funniest kid I know!"

"Humor doesn't help with history or math," Conner said. "It doesn't matter how hard I try in school. I'm always going to be the dumb kid in class. . . ."

The **suffix -*less*** means "without." Can you guess the meaning of the word *expressionless*?

40 Conner's face went white and **expressionless**; he stared off into nothing, so ashamed of himself that it hurt. Luckily for him, Mr. Bailey had an encouraging story for every situation.

"Conner, have I ever told you the legend about the Walking Fish?" Mr. Bailey asked him.

He looked up at his father. "The Walking Fish?" Conner asked. "Dad, no offense, but I don't think one of your stories is going to make me feel better this time."

"All right, **suit yourself**," Mr. Bailey said.

50   A few moments passed, and Conner's curiosity got the best of him.

> The idiom **suit yourself** means "do as you like."

"Okay, you can tell me about the Walking Fish," Conner said.

Mr. Bailey's eyes lit up as they always did just before he was about to tell a story. Conner could tell this was going to be a good one.

"Once upon a time, there was a large fish who lived in a lake by himself," Mr. Bailey told him. "Every day, the fish would watch **longingly** as a boy from the village

60 nearby would play with all the horses and dogs and squirrels on land—"

> **longingly:** with desire or need

"Is a dog going to die in this story, Dad?" Conner interrupted. "You know I hate stories when dogs die—"

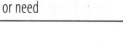

"Let me finish," Mr. Bailey went on. "One day, a fairy came to the lake and granted the fish a wish—"

"That's random," Conner said. "Why do fairies always just show up and do nice things for people they don't know?"

70   "Employment obligation?" Mr. Bailey shrugged. "But **for argument's sake,** let's say she dropped her wand in the lake and the fish retrieved it, so she offered him a wish as a thank-you. Happy?"

"That's better," Conner said. "Go on."

"The fish, predictably, wished for legs, so he could play with the boy from the village," Mr. Bailey said. "So the fairy turned his **fins** into legs and he became the Walking Fish."

"That's weird," Conner said. "Let me guess, the 80 fish was so freaky-looking, the boy never wanted to play with him?"

"Nope, they became great friends and played together with the other land animals," Mr. Bailey told him. "But, one day, the boy fell into the lake and couldn't swim! The Walking Fish tried to save him, but it was no use; he didn't have fins anymore! Sadly, the boy drowned."

Conner's mouth hung open like a broken glove compartment.

for argument's sake: in order to consider the possibility

fins

90   "You see, if the fish had just stayed in the lake and not wished to be something else, he could have saved the boy's life," Mr. Bailey finished.

"Dad, that's a horrible story," he said. "How does a boy live by a lake and not know how to swim? Dogs can swim! Couldn't one of them have saved him? Where was that fairy when the boy was drowning?"

"I think you're missing the point of the story," Mr. Bailey said. "Sometimes we forget about our own advantages because we focus on what we don't have. Just

100   because you have to work a little harder at something that seems easier to others doesn't mean you're without your own talents."

Conner thought about this for a moment. "I think I get it, Dad," he said.

Mr. Bailey smiled at him. "Now, why don't we get down from this tree, and I'll help you study for your next test?"

"'I told you, studying doesn't help," Conner said. "I've tried and tried and tried. It never helps."

110   "Then we'll come up with our own way of studying," Mr. Bailey told him. "We'll look at pictures of people in your history book and make up jokes about them so you'll remember their names. And we'll create funny **scenarios** to help you with all of those math formulas."

scenarios: possible situations

Conner slowly but surely nodded and agreed to it.

"'Fine," he said with a half smile. "But for future reference, I liked your story about the Curvy Tree much better."

UPLOAD

⏻ COLLABORATIVE DISCUSSION

Discussing the Purpose Talk with a partner about the elements of the selection. What is the theme of this selection? Who are the characters? Use the toolbox below to help you.

READING TOOLBOX

Identifying Story Elements

The elements or parts of a story are:

▶ The message or big idea of the story is the **theme**. The theme is implied, rather than stated directly. The reader has to infer what the theme is from the text.

▶ The **plot** is what happens in the story. It is what the story is mainly about.

▶ The **characters** are the people in the story.

▶ The **setting** is where and when the story takes place. The setting also helps set the mood for the story.

Vocabulary Strategy: Idioms

There are many idioms in this selection. An **idiom** is a common expression whose meaning is different from the dictionary definition of its individual words. Context clues can help you understand the meaning of idioms.

Look at the idiom "suit yourself" (line 49). This idiom means "do as you like." What clues in the text help you better understand the meaning of this idiom?

SPEAKING TOOLBOX

Using Academic Language

During a class discussion, be mindful of the differences between the expressions and exclamations that you use with your friends, and the academic language appropriate for the classroom. Here are some examples of expressions that you can use when contributing your opinions or when asking someone for more information.

Everyday Language	Academic Language
Huh?	Will you please repeat that?
What?	Will you please restate your idea?
What do you mean?	Can you explain what you mean by ____?
I don't get it.	I don't quite understand your (response/suggestion/example).
That's not true.	I don't agree.
Think about . . .	Consider . . .
I think . . .	I believe . . . /In my opinion . . . / From my perspective . . .

Speak Out! What is the lesson in the Walking Fish parable? Do you think this story is helpful to Conner? Share your opinion with a partner.

A Tale from The Arabian Nights

In "The Land of Stories: The Wishing Spell," Mr. Bailey tells Conner a story. In "A Tale from The Arabian Nights," Scheherazade tells her husband a story about Sinbad the sailor.

Know Before You Go

ARABIC FOLKLORE *The Arabian Nights* is a collection of stories written in Arabic during the Islamic Golden Age (eighth century–thirteenth century) and rooted in Arabic, Persian, Indian, Egyptian, and Mesopotamian folklore.

A NEVER-ENDING STORY Although each story in *The Arabian Nights* can stand on its own, they are also connected to a larger story—about a queen named Scheherazade who entertains her husband, the Sultan, by telling him a different story each night for 1,001 nights. To keep him interested, she ends each story with a cliffhanger.

1,001 VERSIONS The stories in *The Arabian Nights* were gathered over hundreds of years by many authors, translators, and scholars. As a result, there are different kinds of tales, including adventure stories, love stories, poems, and farces.

⏻ SETTING A PURPOSE

Think about how you would tell the story to make it exciting for the listener.

The Characters

Scheherazade

The Sultan

Sinbad

A Tale from The Arabian Nights

retold by Dina McClellan

ONCE THERE WAS A SULTAN WHO MARRIED ONE WOMAN AFTER ANOTHER. WHEN HE WAS BORED WITH ONE, HE MARRIED SOMEONE ELSE.

WHEN IT WAS ANNOUNCED THAT HIS NEW BRIDE WAS SCHEHERAZADE, PEOPLE THOUGHT THAT THINGS MIGHT WORK OUT THIS TIME.

I hear she's very clever.

I hope so. The Sultan is easily bored.

BUT SHEHERAZADE WORRIED THAT THE SULTAN WAS ALREADY BORED WITH HER. HE HARDLY LOOKED AT HER, OR LISTENED TO ANYTHING SHE SAID. ONE EVENING, AS HE HEADED OFF TO BED . . .

Would you like me to tell you a bedtime story?

If you must. But make it short— I'm tired.

AND SCHEHERAZADE BEGAN TO TELL HIM THE STORY OF SINBAD THE SAILOR . . .

SINBAD WAS A GREAT ADVENTURER WHO GAVE UP A LIFE OF COMFORT IN ORDER TO SAIL AROUND THE WORLD.

ON ONE VOYAGE SINBAD AND HIS CREW LANDED ON AN ISLAND COVERED WITH WILDFLOWERS AND FRUIT TREES.

WHILE HIS CREW WENT EXPLORING, SINBAD STRETCHED OUT IN THE SUN AND, LULLED BY THE MURMUR OF A NEARBY BROOK, FELL INTO A DEEP SLEEP.

HE STARTLED AWAKE SOME HOURS LATER, ONLY TO REALIZE THAT HIS SHIP HAD SAILED OFF WITHOUT HIM. FROM THE SHORE, HE COULD SEE IT DISAPPEARING BEHIND THE HORIZON.

SINBAD WAS GRIPPED BY FEAR. HE WAS ALL ALONE, NO HUMANS IN SIGHT. HE'D NEVER SURVIVE. WHAT MADNESS HAD DRIVEN HIM TO GIVE UP HIS COMFORTABLE LIFE?

SINBAD LOOKED AROUND FRANTICALLY FOR A MEANS OF ESCAPE BUT SAW ONLY A HUGE DAZZLING OBJECT SOME DISTANCE AWAY.

AS HE NEARED THE OBJECT, HE SAW THAT IT WAS SMOOTH, ABOUT FIFTY PACES AROUND, AND THAT THERE WAS NO OPENING WHATSOEVER.

HE DIDN'T HAVE TO WAIT TOO LONG TO FIND OUT WHAT IT WAS. FOR SUDDENLY HE WAS ENGULFED IN SHADOW, AND SINBAD SAW DIRECTLY ABOVE HIM A BIRD OF EXTRAORDINARY SIZE.

HE REALIZED THAT THE BIRD WAS THE GIANT MYTHICAL CREATURE CALLED A ROC—AND THAT THE SMOOTH OBJECT WAS THE ROC'S EGG!

AND SURELY ENOUGH, THE ROC SETTLED ITSELF DOWN ON THE EGG AS IF TO KEEP IT WARM.

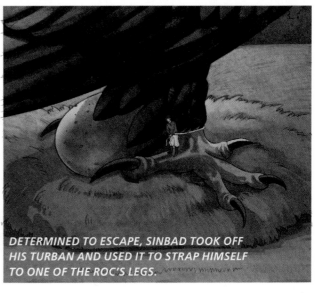

DETERMINED TO ESCAPE, SINBAD TOOK OFF HIS TURBAN AND USED IT TO STRAP HIMSELF TO ONE OF THE ROC'S LEGS.

WHEN THE ROC TOOK OFF THE NEXT MORNING, IT TOOK SINBAD ALONG. THE ROC CARRIED SINBAD OVER MANY MILES . . . SO HIGH THAT THE ENTIRE EARTH SEEMED TO DISAPPEAR . . .

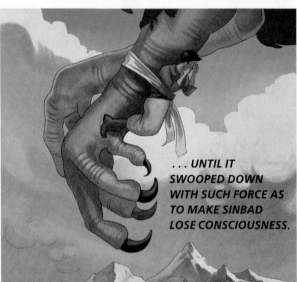

. . . UNTIL IT SWOOPED DOWN WITH SUCH FORCE AS TO MAKE SINBAD LOSE CONSCIOUSNESS.

WHEN THE ROC LANDED, SINBAD QUICKLY UNTIED HIMSELF, AND LAY LOW UNTIL IT HAD FLOWN AWAY.

SINBAD FOUND HIMSELF IN A DEEP AND NARROW VALLEY THAT WAS COMPLETELY SURROUNDED BY MOUNTAINS SO TALL THERE WAS NO WAY TO CLIMB THEM.

IT WAS THEN THAT SINBAD NOTICED THE SNAKES. THE VALLEY WAS SWARMING WITH THEM, AND THEY WERE SO HUGE THEY COULD SWALLOW AN ELEPHANT WHOLE. SINBAD REALIZED THE SNAKES WERE PROBABLY THE ROC'S NATURAL PREY.

SINBAD SAT DOWN TO THINK. HE WAS UNUSED TO GIVING UP. THERE HAD TO BE A WAY OUT. ALSO, HE WAS GETTING HUNGRY.

AND SINBAD NOTICED SOMETHING ELSE, TOO—THE VALLEY FLOOR WAS COVERED WITH DIAMONDS! WITH A SIGH OF REGRET, SINBAD REALIZED THAT, GIVEN HIS PREDICAMENT, DIAMONDS WERE WORTHLESS TO HIM.

SINBAD FIGURED THAT THE SNAKES HIBERNATED DURING THE DAY IN ORDER TO AVOID THE ROC. SO IN ORDER TO AVOID THE SNAKES, SINBAD SPENT THE NIGHT IN A CAVE.

WHEN HE CAME OUT, THE SNAKES WERE GONE. SINBAD SAT ON A ROCK TO THINK THINGS THROUGH.

THE THINKING DIDN'T LAST LONG, HOWEVER, AS A HUGE CHUNK OF FRESH MEAT FELL FROM THE SKY AND LANDED ON THE GROUND WITH A THUD.

SINBAD STARED IN DISBELIEF AS MORE CHUNKS OF MEAT RAINED DOWN UPON HIM.

THEN HE REMEMBERED:

MERCHANTS CAME TO THIS VALLEY WHEN EAGLES WERE HATCHING THEIR YOUNG. THE MERCHANTS WOULD THROW DOWN MEAT IN THE HOPE IT WOULD STICK TO THE DIAMONDS.

THEN, WHEN THE EAGLES CARRIED THE MEAT BACK TO THEIR NESTS, THEY'D CARRY THE DIAMONDS BACK TO THEIR YOUNG . . .

. . . LEAVING THE MERCHANTS IN A POSITION TO RAID THE NESTS AND COLLECT THE DIAMONDS.

SINBAD HAD AN IDEA: HE'D STASH AWAY A FEW DIAMONDS, STRAP HIMSELF TO A CHUNK OF MEAT, AND WAIT FOR AN EAGLE TO SWOOP DOWN, SEIZE THE MEAT, AND CARRY IT BACK TO ITS NEST.

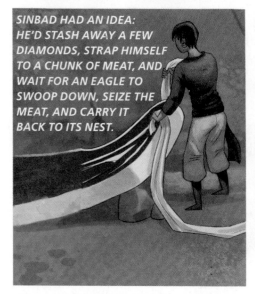

ALL THIS WENT ACCORDING TO PLAN.

WHEN THE MERCHANTS RAN OVER TO THE NEST — INTENDING TO SCARE OFF THE EAGLES AND COLLECT THE DIAMONDS— THEY WERE AMAZED TO FIND A MAN THERE!

AFRAID HE'D BE SEEN AS COMPETITION AND LEFT THERE TO DIE, SINBAD OFFERED THE DIAMONDS TO THE MERCHANTS AS A SIGN OF GOOD FAITH.

THE MERCHANTS WERE THRILLED, AND INVITED SINBAD TO JOIN THEM ON THEIR SHIP BOUND FOR HOME. BUT WHEN THE SHIP REACHED BAGHDAD—

SCHEHERAZADE PAUSED, AND LOOKED AT THE SULTAN, THINKING HIM ASLEEP. BUT HE WAS WIDE AWAKE, COMPLETELY ENTRANCED BY THE STORY AS WELL AS THE STORYTELLER.

THE SULTAN BEGGED HIS WIFE TO GO ON WITH THE STORY, BUT SHE REFUSED.

Enough for tonight. I'll be back tomorrow to finish the story.

AND, TRUE TO HER WORD, SHE CAME BACK. BUT SHE DIDN'T FINISH THE STORY. IN FACT, THE STORY WOULD GO ON FOR DAYS AND DAYS AND DAYS . . .

COLLABORATIVE DISCUSSION

Discussing the Purpose With a small group, discuss the theme of the story. How do Scheherazade and Sinbad respond to their challenges?

⟳ Performance Task

Speaking Activity: Character Traits Character traits are the qualities shown by a character. These qualities can include physical traits, such as strength and speed. Character traits can also be expressions of personality. For example, maybe the character is courageous.

- Reread the selection. Pay attention to the way the characters act and what they say.

- Discuss the following questions with a partner. Remember to cite text evidence in your responses.

- Discuss the character traits of Scheherazade. What physical traits does she exhibit? What are her expressions of personality?

- Discuss the character traits of Sinbad. What physical traits does he exhibit? What are his expressions of personality?

READING TOOLBOX

Point of View

An author's style involves choices about *how* something is said instead of *what* is said. **Point of view** is a style element. In a first-person point of view story, the **narrator**, or the voice that tells the story, is a character in the story and uses first-person pronouns such as *I*, *me*, and *we*. In a third-person point of view story, the story is told by someone who is not in the story. The pronouns *he*, *she*, *it*, and *they* are examples of third-person pronouns.

↻ Performance Task

Writing Activity: Short Narrative Write a short narrative about another adventure Sinbad could have.

- Pick a point of view. Will you tell the story from Sinbad's point of view? Or will you use a third-person narrator?

- Think about what the adventure will be. What is the setting of the story?

- Remember to include Sinbad's character traits in your story. This will help you develop your narrative.

Performance Task

Writing Activity: Narrative

You have been reading stories and informational texts about storytelling. Now, it's your turn to write a narrative that shows the power of storytelling.

Planning and Prewriting

Connect to the Theme

Your narrative could be based on a personal experience, or it could be completely fictional. If you choose fiction, your narrative can be real or it can be imaginary! What things on this list are you interested in writing about?

Realistic	**Imaginary**
• Flying a plane	• Flying an alien spaceship
• Going to a new school	• Having a superpower
• Taking care of a pet	• Taking care of an imaginary animal
• Visiting a museum	• Visiting the future
• Finding a snake in a park	• Falling into a ravine filled with snakes

If you are writing about a person or event, you could write about:

Realistic	**Imaginary**
• A person you know or a celebrity	• A fictional character
• A historical event	• An imaginary event

Write Down Three Narrative Ideas

Write three possible ideas based on one of the situations on the list that you think can be the start of a narrative.

Read your ideas. How excited are you about each one? Rate them, from 0 (not excited) to 5 (really excited). Which one has the highest rating? That's your narrative!

Decide the Basics

Now that you have your idea, it's time to plan the structure of your narrative. Think about your main conflict or problem, your characters, your setting, and your point of view.

Conflict or Problem

A **conflict** is a struggle between opposing forces that is the focus of the narrative. Think about:

- What is the conflict in your narrative?
- Who faces this conflict?
- Is your conflict exciting enough? If not, go back and think of a problem that would be more interesting or exciting.

Characters

Characters are the people, animals, or imaginary creatures who take part in the action. Think about:

- Who is the main character?
- Are there other characters?
- How do you describe your characters?
- Do you feel strongly about your characters? Do you love them or dislike them? If you don't feel strongly about your characters, neither will your reader.

Setting

The **setting** is the **time** and **place** of the action. Think about:

- **Time:** When is your narrative set?
- **Place:** Where is your narrative set?
- Is the setting going to play an important role in your narrative?

Point of View

The **point of view** refers to how a writer narrates (or tells) a narrative. When a story is told from the **first-person** point of view, the narrator is a character in the narrative. In a narrative told from the **third-person** point of view, the narrator is not in the story. The narrator affects the information readers receive.

Performance Task

Finalize Your Plan

You know the basics of your narrative: the conflict, the characters, the setting, and the point of view. Now it's time to plan your plot structure. Follow the structure of the diagram in the Writing Toolbox.

WRITING TOOLBOX

Elements of a Narrative

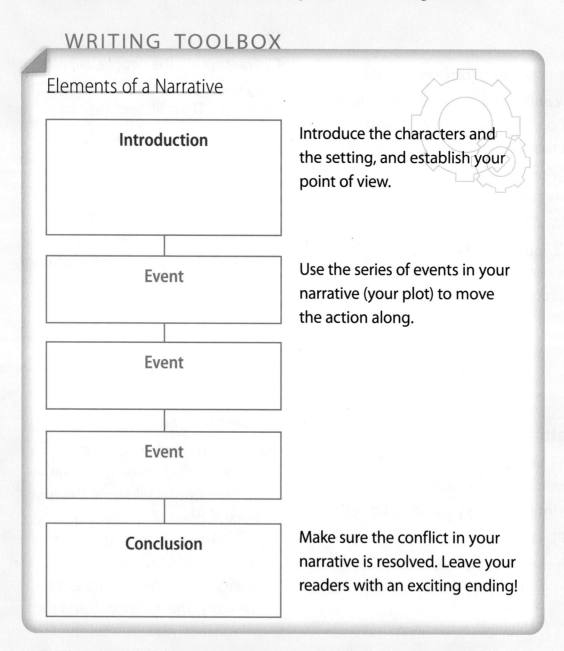

| Introduction | Introduce the characters and the setting, and establish your point of view. |

| Event | Use the series of events in your narrative (your plot) to move the action along. |

| Event |

| Event |

| Conclusion | Make sure the conflict in your narrative is resolved. Leave your readers with an exciting ending! |

Draft Your Narrative

You have the basics of your narrative. Start writing! As you write, think about:

- **Purpose and Audience** What effect do you want the narrative to have on readers? Who will read or listen to your narrative?

- **Main Character, Setting, and Conflict** Introduce the main character, setting, and conflict.

- **Point of View** Establish your point of view quickly.

- **Transitions** Use transitional words and phrases to help your reader follow the sequence of events.

- **Descriptive Language** Use descriptive words and sensory language to create a detailed picture.

- **Ending** Make sure the story has an exciting ending.

- **Conflict Resolution** Tell how the conflict is resolved.

Revise

Self Evaluation Use the checklist and rubric to guide your analysis.

Peer Review Exchange your narrative with a classmate. Use the checklist to comment on your classmate's narrative.

Edit

Edit your narrative to correct spelling, grammar, and punctuation errors.

Publish

Finalize your narrative and choose a way to share it with your audience.

Under Western Skies

Go west, young man, and grow up with the country.

— **Horace Greeley, newspaper editor**

Essential Question

What does it mean to live "under western skies"?

The Language of Exploration

Explorers want to discover and find out about unknown lands. Explorers are adventurous people who enjoy learning about new places and new things. Some of the early European explorers who came to North and South America include Christopher Columbus, Amerigo Vespucci, Ponce de León, and Francisco Vásquez de Coronado.

Pioneers began exploring "the Western Frontier" in the early 1800s. Although European settlers established towns and cities along the eastern coast of what is now the United States beginning in the 1500s, it wasn't until after the Louisiana Purchase in 1803 that pioneers began settling the west. Pioneers moved to the west in search of new land and opportunities. They wanted a chance to start a new life for themselves.

Today, space is considered a new frontier with astronauts and space probes as explorers. Space exploration and the search for other life forms on distant planets is now underway. Although extraterrestrial life is still considered science fiction, explorers can't help but wonder what else might be out there.

In this unit, you will discover ways in which people explore and develop new lands. You will find out about life on a ranch in the *Bar None Canyon Ranch* blog. You will read about the hope and difficulties of pioneers moving west. You will also learn about the work of the SETI Institute and their quest to find other forms of life in the universe.

Why do people explore new lands?

Mind Your 'Tude: Directional Words

When people began traveling long distances over land and sea, they needed a way to help them tell direction and describe exactly where they were at any moment. After centuries of experimentation and debate, people came up with the modern system of latitude and longitude that we use today. Adding a third dimension, we use altitude to describe how far above or below we are from sea level. Together, latitude, longitude, and altitude give explorers a way to describe their travels and discoveries.

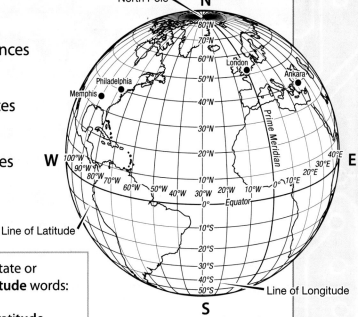

Longitude describes distances east and west on Earth.

Latitude describes distances north and south on Earth.

Altitude describes distances above sea level.

-**tude** is a suffix that means in the state or condition of. Here are some other -**tude** words:

atti**tude**   multi**tude**   grati**tude**

⟳ Performance Task

Talk with a partner about exploration. What traits must explorers have? How might they feel during their journeys? Why do you think they travel to new lands? Use the information on page 196 and in **Browse** magazine as you gather your thoughts. Then look in the **Activity Book** for additional support. When you are ready, discuss why explorers explore.

➜ **Browse**
magazine

DOWNLOAD

Ranch life can be exciting. There is a lot to do! Read the blog to find out about some of the activities that happen on a ranch.

⏻ SETTING A PURPOSE

As you read, pay attention to the specific words used to describe life on the ranch.

Bar None Prairie Ranch Blog

**June 6
9:15 a.m.** It's another great day at the Bar None Prairie Ranch! We have a great day planned for guests and visitors. Our morning horseback riding lessons are just getting started. You can catch a class every day between 10 a.m. and 2 p.m. Classes involve an orientation to riding, getting matched with your horse, and plenty of instruction. Don't be nervous if it's your first time on a horse. Safety and fun are our top priorities! Check the daily schedule to see which guided ride is the best fit for you. Feeling adventurous? Sign up for our half- or whole-day rides. While you're busy enjoying your day's activities, remember to appreciate the breathtaking views of the mountains, meadows, forests, and rivers.

**June 7
5:30 a.m.** It's perfect weather tonight for our campfire! We hope you'll join us for our sing-alongs. Need another option for the evening? Don't forget the moonlight ride! And tomorrow night we're having a country dance with an amazing band you won't want to miss!

Enter your email address:

Subscribe me!

SEARCH

💬 **Comments** 10

June 8
11:45 a.m. Today's post brings you a sneak peek at some "behind the scenes" action here at the ranch. While you're enjoying rides and activities, our staff members are grooming horses, caring for cattle, feeding and cleaning up after chickens and goats, and distributing water and food. We are constantly maintaining our trails, checking fences, and doing upkeep on buildings, cabins, and property. We're taking care of the business side of the ranch at all times, too, with marketing and accounting. Did you enjoy your food here this week? Our kitchen staff prepares meals from scratch with fresh ingredients. It's all hard work, but we take great pride in our ranch.

June 9
8:00 a.m. Today we're doing water events! Depending on what you signed up for, you might be kayaking, white-water rafting, taking a scenic float trip, or fishing. Tired out from all the horseback riding? Consider bird watching, reading by the river, or napping in one of our hammocks. Enjoy the beautiful scenery and fresh air. And don't forget that the equestrian show is happening in just two days! It's at 1:00 p.m. at the main corral.

June 10
8:15 a.m. This afternoon we're offering children's programs down by the corral. Activities include riding miniature horses, taking a nature walk, making crafts, and panning for gold. Tonight is also our kids' hot dog roast and hayride, followed by our campout for ages 12 and under. Our older guests can enjoy a guided hike to one of the tallest peaks in the area.

June 11
8:20 a.m. Today is all about the horses! Our ranch roping demonstration will start after lunch. Other activities today include a cattle roundup, a family rodeo, and an equestrian show. Need something to do before then? Check out the game of horseshoes happening on the front lawn. There's always a lot going on at the ranch!

ARCHIVES

June

May

April

March

February

January

December

November

October

September

August

UPLOAD

⏻ **COLLABORATIVE DISCUSSION**

Discussing the Purpose How does the information in the blog help you understand what ranch life is like? How is this blog different from a personal blog? Discuss your answer with a partner.

What Would You Do? In a small group, talk about the activities that the Bar None Prairie Ranch mentions in their blog. Which activity would you want to do? Tell your group why you would want to take part in that activity.

Write On! The Bar None Prairie Ranch gives readers the opportunity to post a comment about their blog. What other facts do you want to know about life on the ranch? Write a comment to the "Bar None Prairie Ranch Blog," asking about ranch life "behind the scenes." Then exchange comments with a classmate. 💬 Comments 0

↻ **Performance Task**

Writing Activity: Helpful Tips When Writing Blog Posts
When you are writing blog posts, think about the tone of your blog and your audience.

1 Do you want your blog to be informative, educational, or entertaining? Think about your topic. If you are giving your readers tips about the newest technology tool, the tone of your blog should be informative. If you are blogging about moving to a new place, your tone can be more conversational.

2 Think about your audience. Some bloggers consider their readers to be a community. They might think of blogging as an email format and introduce their posts in an informal style. For example, saying "Hi, readers!" is conversational. Other bloggers use a more formal style. Even if your tone is conversational, be sure to proofread your blog posts. Pay attention to your spelling and grammar.

3 Use language that is respectful. Using appropriate language shows that you can share meaningful and thoughtful content. Do not call anyone names, and always maintain a polite tone.

4 If your blog entry is time-sensitive, or needs to be read right away, use software that allows your readers to subscribe to your blog. They will automatically be updated when you publish a new entry. For blogs that provide daily or weekly updates about scheduled events, this is a handy tool.

Language Cam video
Watch the video to learn more about life under western skies.

SETI: LISTENING TO THE WESTERN SKY

In the Bar None Prairie Ranch blog, you read about what life is like on a ranch. But is there life among the stars? Read this selection to find out about SETI and the work they do.

Background on Astronomy

Scientists have been watching the sky with telescopes for hundreds of years. Early telescopes made it easier to see the stars and planets. In the twentieth century, astronomers (scientists who study outer space) began to use radio telescopes. These telescopes detect radio waves and other invisible radiation, rather than visible light. This meant that a new kind of information could be recorded about space objects. This information could include radio transmissions from space—if any exist.

⏻ SETTING A PURPOSE

As you read, pay attention to the facts and details that explain what SETI does, and why they do this work.

SETI:
Listening to the
Western Sky

by Silvia Conovas

Out west in Hat Creek, California, many large **telescopes** stand in otherwise deserted fields. As the earth turns, they slowly turn as well, following the stars. They listen to the universe. They are part of **SETI**, The Search for Extra-Terrestrial Intelligence. They are listening for aliens. While this may seem like science fiction, the Center for SETI Research is very serious. Based in California, SETI has been around since 1984. The Center argues that there are probably alien civilizations somewhere out there.

10   There are billions and billions of stars in our galaxy. Our sun is a star like those stars. While many of those stars are much brighter or **dimmer** than our sun, many are very similar to ours. The reason the sun appears so much larger and brighter than other stars is because the sun is much closer. The stars are incredibly far away. But around those stars we have started to see exoplanets, which are planets that orbit other stars besides the sun. Some of these planets are similar to the earth.

The word *telescopes* has a **prefix** that means "at a distance." Can you identify it?

SETI is an **acronym**— a word formed from the first letters of a series of words.

What words help you understand the meaning of **dimmer**?

▲ *Hat Creek Allen Telescope Array. These radio-telescope antennas are used for radio-astronomy and Search for Extraterrestrial Intelligence (SETI).*

Life could evolve on such planets, as it did on the earth.
20 It's even possible that somewhere a planet's residents have built technology and use radios, as we do. SETI is listening for the radio signals they could be sending. Even though we cannot be certain we will hear anything, SETI thinks it is **worth** listening. If there is even a small chance of finding intelligent life, that incredible discovery would be worth the effort.

worth: important or good enough to defend

Of course, listening to the sky is easier said than done. For one thing, the earth is constantly spinning as it orbits the sun. This means the telescopes have to move constantly
30 to keep focused on one part of the sky. They also need to be upgraded to extend their range. And more telescopes must be built as SETI expands the region it listens to.

There are some people who disagree with SETI. They think that SETI is a waste of money. Some are worried that aliens might be hostile. But the scientists at SETI consider the chance worth the cost. They also point out that any alien civilization would be much too far away to be a danger.

SETI has been monitoring the sky for a long time and hopes to listen to a million stars and more. So far all we
40 have heard is silence. But, possibly, someday we will know for sure whether or not we are alone in the universe.

How Likely Is It?

Scientists aren't sure what conditions are required for life to emerge. We don't know how common life is in our universe. That's something that scientists at the Carl Sagan Center at SETI want **to figure out**. They hope to discover how the evolution of life on the earth began. Once we know that, we'll have a better idea of how likely it is we'll ever hear from other planets.

The phrasal verb **to figure out** means "to understand or solve."

COLLABORATIVE DISCUSSION

Discussing the Purpose With a partner, discuss what SETI does. Why does SETI study the stars? Cite evidence from the text in your response.

SPEAKING TOOLBOX

Presentation

When you give a presentation, let your listeners know that you are speaking to *them*, not *yourself*.

▶ **Don't mumble!** Speak loudly enough to be heard. Remember to speak at a normal speed.

▶ **Use a friendly, confident tone.** Tone lets the listener know your mood. It can also change the meaning of a sentence.

▶ **Use physical clues.** Your posture, hand gestures, and facial expressions can help listeners understand your points.

⟳ Performance Task

Speaking Activity: State Your Opinion Do you think the work SETI does is important? Why, or why not? Give a presentation to a small group that answers that question.

- First, take some time to form your opinion. What information in the selection made you decide on this opinion? Citing text evidence when you are speaking makes your opinion stronger.

- Next, consider what you want to say. Write down examples from the text to support your opinion.

- Remember to speak at a normal rate. Pause after punctuation. Don't forget to make eye contact with your listeners.

Vocabulary Strategy: Greek Affixes

An **affix** can be added to a base word to create a new word. You know that an affix that can be added to the beginning of a word is a **prefix**, while an affix added to the end of a word is a **suffix**. Many affixes come from ancient Greek words. Knowing the meaning of Greek affixes can help you identify and define words that share the same affix and have similar meanings.

The Greek prefix *tele-* means "far off" or "distant." A *telescope* is a device that we use to see stars and other distant objects in the sky. Other words that contain the Greek prefix *tele-* include *television*, *teleport*, and *telephone*. How does the prefix *tele-* give you a clue about the meaning of the word *telephone*?

Greek Affix	Meaning	Example	Other Words
bio-	life	biography	
hydr-	water	hydrate	
-phon	sound	microphone	
-meter	measure	thermometer	

Practice and Apply Use a chart like the one above to explore the meaning of words with Greek affixes. Be sure to use a dictionary to gain a better understanding of how an affix gives a clue about a word's meaning.

DOWNLOAD

Who Was the Real Daniel Boone?

SETI uses telescopes to explore the sky. Read this selection to learn about Daniel Boone, an early explorer of the western frontier.

Background on Daniel Boone

Daniel Boone is a famous frontiersman from American history. Born in Pennsylvania in 1734, he loved spending time in the woods, and learned to hunt to feed his family.

Boone participated in the French and Indian War in 1755. After finishing his service, he began leading expeditions into Kentucky.

One of his first expeditions ended in disaster. But Boone returned, built a fort, and helped establish a successful settlement. He spent much of the rest of his life exploring, and tales about his accomplishments circulated far and wide.

⏻ SETTING A PURPOSE

As you read, think about the main idea of the selection. Look for details that support the main idea.

Who Was the Real
Daniel Boone?

by Shane Dixon

Daniel Boone is a popular figure in history. But much of what comes to mind when people think of Daniel Boone is incorrect. Who was Daniel Boone, really?

Daniel Boone was a frontiersman who wore a **coonskin** *cap.*

FALSE: Daniel Boone never wore a coonskin cap. In fact, he **despised** them. It would have been hard to hunt with the sun in his eyes, so his choice of headgear was a beaver hat with a wide brim to block the sun. The coonskin cap image began when an actor played the role of Daniel Boone on television in the 1960s.
10 He wore a coonskin cap, and the image stuck.

coonskin: the skin of a raccoon

despised: strongly disliked

Daniel Boone was a tall, tough fighter.

FALSE: Daniel Boone, about 5' 8" tall, was a gentle man. Over time, he became a legendary figure, a giant who conquered the frontier. In the famous television program in the 1960s, Boone was portrayed as "the **rippin'est**, roarin'est, fightin'est man the frontier ever knew." The program's theme song proclaimed, "As tall as a mountain was he."

> The word **rippin'est** comes from the adjective *ripping*, which means "splendid or excellent."

Daniel Boone disliked Native Americans.

FALSE: In his life on the frontier, Daniel Boone had many encounters with Native Americans. Two of his sons were killed in battles with them. But Boone said he fought with Indians only when he had to. He greatly regretted the deaths of three Native Americans in battle. Overall, he thought they had been quite kind to him.

Why are there so many false stories about Daniel Boone? Boone became an American hero in his own lifetime. He was leading pioneers west just when the 13 colonies broke away from England in the fight for independence. Soon thereafter, in 1784, a writer named John Filson wrote what he called an autobiography of Boone. (Of course, it was not a true autobiography, since Boone did not write it himself.) The book turned Daniel Boone into one of the United

40 States' first celebrities. His pioneer spirit matched that of the new nation. Almost 200 years later, the popular television series *Daniel Boone* continued the legend of Daniel Boone. Actor Fess Parker represented him as an action hero.

In real life, Daniel Boone was a natural woodsman. He had been hunting since he was 12 years old. And he was a **trailblazer**—literally. He was curious about the world. He had what people

50 call **wanderlust**.

trailblazer: a person who makes a trail, or path, for others to follow

wanderlust: the desire to travel

Boone's life was not all about being the brave pioneer, however. After settling in Kentucky, Boone went into debt and struggled over conflicting land claims. Kentucky historian James Klotter wrote, "He's an everyday man often **thrust into** difficult circumstances and responding in mostly honorable ways. He's kind of what we want our heroes to be."

thrust into: pushed or forced into something

60 Boone may not have been the person we imagine him to be, but he remains an important American icon. He became famous for his adventures, and even if his story has been made larger than life through the years, his legacy endures.

⏻ COLLABORATIVE DISCUSSION

Discussing the Purpose What is the main idea of this selection? Discuss this question with a small group. Find at least three supporting details to support your answer.

READING TOOLBOX

Main Idea and Details

If you're looking for the main idea of an informative article, look at the first paragraph, called the **introduction**. If you're looking for the main idea of one paragraph, you'll probably find it in the first sentence.

Supporting details of an article are found in the paragraphs after the introduction. These paragraphs are called the **body**. The supporting details of a paragraph are found in the sentences that follow the first sentence.

The last paragraph of an article, the **conclusion**, brings together the most important details given in the body and restates the main idea.

Write On! Write a short essay to answer the question: Why do you think that Daniel Boone has remained such an important figure in American history? Include an introduction, body, and conclusion in your essay. Support your opinion with reasons from the text.

Podcast: No Boss but the Land and Cattle: A Rancher's Coming of Age

You have just read about Daniel Boone, a real person who became a legend of the American West. In this podcast, you'll hear from some real modern-day cowboys.

Background on Ranching

People have been raising cattle in North America for hundreds of years. Cattle ranching involves not only taking care of cows, but also taking care of the farm and the horses ranchers ride when they work.

The image of a cowboy herding cattle on horseback is often considered a symbol of America. Not all ranchers are "cowboys"—many women do this kind of work, too. Much of the romantic image of ranching comes from popular entertainment such as western movies.

⏻ **SETTING A PURPOSE**

In this podcast, the Howells explain many different parts of life on the ranch. Which parts seem interesting or exciting? Which seem difficult?

No Boss but the Land and Cattle: A Rancher's Coming of Age

Main Idea and Details in the Podcast

Main Idea	A father and son share their viewpoints about life on a ranch.
Detail	Growing up, Rodney spent a lot of time learning about the land and playing outdoors.
Detail	Rodney was able to spend time with his sons while they were growing up.
Detail	Brett and Brady helped their father on the ranch from the time they were young, including weekends.
Detail	Brady is now a lawyer, but he thinks there is a possibility that he will take over the farm from his father one day.

⏻ **COLLABORATIVE DISCUSSION**

Discussing the Purpose In a group, discuss what it would be like to work as a rancher. Does ranching sound like the kind of job you'd like to do?

The Pioneers

You have listened to a podcast about life on a ranch in the west. This poem tells about the pioneers who set out to settle in the West.

Background on the Oregon Trail

In 1803, the United States bought a piece of land from France that stretched from present-day Louisiana to Montana. The path that early pioneers used to travel from the East to the West was known as the Oregon Trail. Between the mid-1840s and the late 1860s, more than 400,000 people made the 2,000-mile trip over the Oregon Trail. The new land out West was a land of opportunity for these pioneers. Many people traveled to this new land, including missionaries, fur traders, farmers, and gold miners hoping to make their fortune in California.

⏻ SETTING A PURPOSE

As you read, think about the specific words and punctuation used in the poem.

The Pioneers

by Charles Mackay

rouse: come alive, wake up

ply: to work hard with a tool

hatchet

spade

Rouse! brothers, rouse! we've far to travel,
   Free as the winds we love to roam,
Far through the prairie, far through the forest,
   Over the mountains we'll find a home.
5 We cannot breathe in crowded cities,
   We're strangers to the ways of trade;
We long to feel the grass beneath us,
   And ply the hatchet and the spade.

Meadows and hills and ancient woodlands
10   Offer us pasture, fruit, and corn;
Needing our presence, courting our labour;—
    Why should we linger like men forlorn?
We love to hear the ringing rifle,
    The smiting axe, the falling tree;—
15 And though our life be rough and lonely,
    If it be honest, what care we?

Fair elbow-room for men to thrive in!
    Wide elbow-room for work or play!
If cities follow, tracing our footsteps,
20   Ever to westward shall point our way!
Rude though our life, it suits our spirit,
    And new-born States in future years
Shall own us founders of a nation—
    And bless the hardy Pioneers.

> **forlorn:** sad, with no hope

⏻ COLLABORATIVE DISCUSSION

Discussing the Purpose With a small group, discuss the language and punctuation used in the poem. What message does the poet have for the pioneers?

READING TOOLBOX

Make an Outline

When you are preparing to give an oral opinion, it can be helpful to make an outline of important points before you speak. An outline can help you keep your points organized. You can quickly look at your outline while you are speaking to make sure you are on track.

▶ Ask yourself, "What are the most important things for my listeners to know?"

▶ Ask yourself, "What is the best order for telling the information? What will paint a clear picture for listeners?"

▶ Make sure that your ideas are clear and state your key points, or main ideas.

Write On! Make an outline of the events in the poem.

Speak Out! Tell a partner about the events that happened in the poem. Look at your outline to help you.

DOWNLOAD

Rachel's Journal

You read a poem about pioneers getting ready to travel west. In this selection, you will read about Rachel, a girl who is traveling west on the Oregon Trail.

READING TOOLBOX

Determining the Theme

A **theme** is a message, or big idea, about life or human nature that the writer shares with the reader. The theme is stated indirectly, and a reader must **infer** what it is from evidence in the text.

To help you determine the theme of a story, think about:

▶ **Title** Does it contain an important idea?

▶ **Characters' and narrator's words and actions**
What do they do and say? Do they change? If so, how?

▶ **Setting** Does the location of the story have any special meaning?

▶ **Descriptive words, phrases, and details**
Do the particular words the author chose bring up certain feelings or thoughts?

Keep in mind that a theme is different from a topic. The topic is what the story is about, while the theme is the bigger message the story tells.

⏻ SETTING A PURPOSE

As you read, think about the theme of the selection.

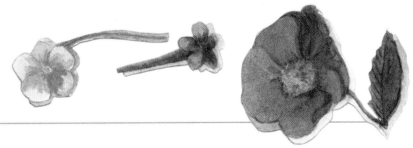

from

Rachel's Journal

by Marissa Moss

April 28, 1850

The wide expanse of the Great Plains is now before us. As far as we can see, there is tall grass all around, dotted with beautiful wildflowers. At first the other wagon trains were so thick about us, we saw more of **schooner** "sails" than of the prairie. Now the crowds have thinned out, and when we camped for the night we felt truly alone, like small **specks** in a vast ocean of wilderness. I ached for home for the first time, but Ben played his fiddle while Mother sang, and that cheered us all.

schooner: a sailing ship

specks: small spots

May 3, 1850

10 I am used to bumping around in the wagon (Pa says I have got my sea legs), but I cannot get used to the mosquitoes. One leg is swollen up and I have a horrid bump over my eye. Prudence has it worse, though. She has a bright red bite on her nose.

221

churning: stirring cream to make butter

The jolting ride spares me the chore of **churning** butter, but I still have to collect fuel for the fire each night. Yesterday there was no wood to be found. Mrs. Sunshine suggested
20   that we twist grasses together into coils and burn that. Mr. Elias laughed and said there was plenty of fuel all around us, lying almost at our feet. I could not see at all what he meant, but then he picked up a buffalo chip and lit it. Now I gather "meadow muffins." It takes quite a pile of them for a lasting fire, but at least they are light and easy to find.

Prudence declares it is one thing to gather them (which she grudgingly does), but another to eat anything cooked with
30   them—the thought of supper smoked in buffalo droppings curdles her milk. I think they make a fine fuel, and they do not smell at all (so long as they are good and dry. I surely would not pick up a wet one!) So I was content to feast on beans and rice. I smacked my lips loudly, praising the delicious meal, but Prudence turned away and went to bed, too fine for such coarse fare.

June 25, 1850

We are all used to traveling together now, and for the most part we get along fine (even Prudence and me). The two Sunshine brothers constantly argue, but only with each other, so we pay them no mind. Pa still finds Mr. Bridger's laziness **galling**, but he is very fond of Mr. Elias. Mrs. Elias, Mrs. Arabella Sunshine, and Mother gossip together and exchange recipes, dreaming of the days when they can really cook again. Will and Ben are fast friends with Samuel and Almanzo, and the four often play cards (when they tire of tossing buffalo chips.) As for me, I like to ride with Emma. Quilting and embroidery are more bearable if you have company. (Though it does not improve my work, it improves my mood.)

galling: irritating

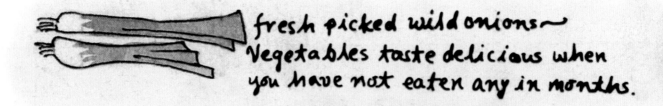
fresh picked wild onions~
Vegetables taste delicious when
you have not eaten any in months.

July 4, 1850

50 We finally came to the first landmark on the broadsheet—
Courthouse Rock. It looked so close, Mother allowed us
to ride out so that we could add our names to it, as many
others come before us have. Even Prudence wanted to go.
But instead of a couple of hours, it took the rest of the day
to reach it—the prairie gives the **illusion** of small distances
as there is nothing to provide a sense of scale. Having come
so far, however, we were determined not to return until we
had climbed that rock. My britches proved an advantage,
and I was the only girl to make it to the top. Ben, Will,
60 Samuel, Almanzo, and I viewed the sunset from on high. It
was glorious! We galloped back in the dark, but the moon
was full and the campfire was clear before us. Racing across
that broad expanse, tasting the crisp night air, with so
many stars twinkling above us and the moon's silvery light
casting purple shadows before us, I felt like I was a hawk
soaring. I did not want to stop, ever.

> **illusion:** something that gives a false impression of what it is

ham

fruit pies (canned, not dried)

fruitcake Mother baked in Illinois and saved for today

biscuits

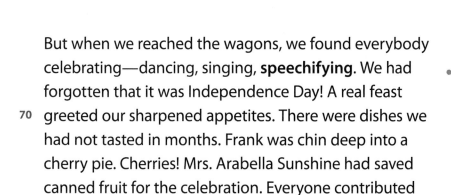

I cannot recall how it feels to be inside a house anymore.

We passed a schoolhouse ~ oh, dear, we are back in civilization.

But when we reached the wagons, we found everybody celebrating—dancing, singing, **speechifying**. We had forgotten that it was Independence Day! A real feast

70 greeted our sharpened appetites. There were dishes we had not tasted in months. Frank was chin deep into a cherry pie. Cherries! Mrs. Arabella Sunshine had saved canned fruit for the celebration. Everyone contributed something.

I was too excited to sleep, so I just looked up at the stars thinking how odd it was to celebrate America's birthday when we were leaving the United States. If we love our country so much, why are we going so far away?

> The word **speechifying** comes from the verb *speech*. Can you guess what it means?

pickles

sausages

cheese

Praise Lily, the milch cow!
butter

bread (without mice spice)

I saved some seeds so we can plant watermelon in our new California garden. But first I will give some to Prudence.

October 23, 1850

This morning we woke up early. The guidebook showed
80 that there were only a dozen or so miles ahead, and no
one wanted to sleep. We descended the last stretch of
8 miles. The road is smooth and level, dotted with farms
and **homesteads**. We are finally, safely here!

homesteads: pieces of land claimed by a settler

The other families we meet are all so friendly. One fruit
seller welcomed us with a watermelon and astonishing
news—California has just been admitted to the Union. We
are not only back in civilization, we are back in the United
States of America!

Pa grinned at Mother and handed her the first slice of
90 melon. Tomorrow we would find our homestead. Today,
I looked back at the wagon, at our family, bigger by one.
We were not at the edge of the world after all. Not in a
strange place. Not in between anymore. We finally were
somewhere. We were home.

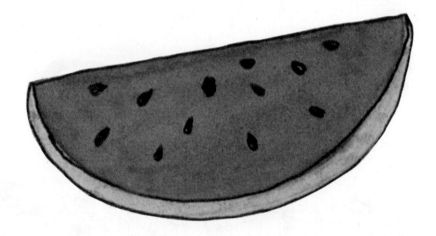

COLLABORATIVE DISCUSSION

Discussing the Purpose Discuss the theme of the selection with a small group.

Analyzing the Text [Cite Text Evidence]

Compare and Contrast How are the pioneers in the poem "The Pioneers" similar to the characters in "Rachel's Journal"?

◌ Performance Task

Speaking Activity: Practice for an Oral Opinion Work with a partner to practice delivering an oral opinion that answers the question "Would you have liked to be a pioneer on the Oregon Trail?"

- Using your discussion as a guide, write notes. List key points, or main ideas. These will be your talking points, which are the most important ideas that you want your listeners to know.

- Review your information. This will help you feel more confident about delivering your oral opinion.

- Practice delivering your opinion several times with your partner.

- Timing yourself is important. Keep track of how fast or slowly you speak, and the total time it takes for you to deliver your oral opinion.

- Ask your partner for feedback: Did you speak clearly? Did you express your ideas with feeling? Did you speak at the proper speed? Did you make eye contact?

The Quillworker Girl

Rachel and her family faced challenges while traveling west. The Quillmaker Girl and her family face challenges of a different kind.

GENRE Native American myths use animals, seasons, and other facts of nature as signs for something else. The stories show lessons about life and express awe.

BACKGROUND Many people see pictures in the stars. They identify *constellations*. Those are star groupings named for familiar objects. To picture constellations, imagine lines from star to star. For example, many ancient peoples saw a bear in one star grouping. Different peoples identified different constellations over time.

The Big Dipper is made of seven stars that appear in different positions each season.

The Big Dipper is not big enough to be a constellation. But its seven stars are part of Ursa Major, or Big Bear.

⏻ SETTING A PURPOSE

As you read, pay attention to how the characters respond to challenges.

The Quillworker Girl

A Native American Myth retold by Eden Foster

MANY YEARS AGO THERE LIVED A CHEYENNE GIRL WHO MADE THE MOST BEAUTIFUL QUILL-WORK ANYONE HAD EVER SEEN.

This teepee will be beautiful!

SHE USED PORCUPINE QUILLS TO DECORATE ALL KINDS OF THINGS. HER DESIGNS WERE WELL KNOWN FOR BEING THE BEST ANYWHERE.

ONE DAY SHE SET TO WORK ON A HANDSOME SET OF MEN'S BATTLE CLOTHES. HER MOTHER HAD NO IDEA WHO THEY WERE FOR.

Who might that be for?

SHE MADE SEVEN SETS OF CLOTHES, EACH WITH UNIQUE COLORS AND PATTERNS. ONE WAS SMALLER THAN THE REST.

And now, I'll finish the small one…

THE MOTHER WAITED PATIENTLY UNTIL ON THE LAST DAY OF HER WORK, THE GIRL EXPLAINED.

I know, that very far away, live seven brothers who have no sister. They are very special and the whole world will look up to them one day.

I will be their sister. I will find them and give them these clothes as a gift.

I must go with you. How do you know where they are?

I don't know how, but I know. I fear it is too far for you to travel. I will go on my own.

I see that you know what you must do. I will help you prepare.

Thank you!

THE GIRL SAID GOODBYE TO HER MOTHER AND SET OFF ON HER JOURNEY.

Be brave. Be careful. And be strong!

SHE WALKED FOR MANY MILES. SOMEHOW, SHE KNEW WHERE TO TURN AND WHEN TO REST.

SHE KNEW WHEN SHE WAS GETTING CLOSE.

SHE SAW THE BRANCHES OF A TALL TREE BEYOND A WIDE STREAM. THEN THE TOP OF A LARGE TEEPEE APPEARED. SHE HAD ARRIVED.

BEFORE SHE COULD FINISH HER SENTENCE, A YOUNG BOY HAD ALREADY COME OUT TO GREET HER.

It is I! The-Young-Girl-Looking-For-Brothers.

I am the youngest brother. The other six will be surprised to see you. But I knew you were coming.

How?

I have gifts. One is the gift of no touch. You'll know what that is some day.

THE GIRL SUSPECTED THAT SHE ALREADY KNEW.

You have no sister and I have no brothers. I will take you as my brothers if you will have me. My parents have each other and they don't need me as much as you do.

WHEN THE REST OF THE BROTHERS RETURNED FROM THEIR HUNT THEY WERE INDEED SURPRISED.

THEY MARVELED AT THE BEAUTIFUL CLOTHES AND THEIR NEW SISTER.

THE FAMILY LIVED HAPPILY UNTIL ONE DAY, A BABY BUFFALO APPROACHED THE TEPEE.

What is it, little buffalo?

My nation has heard of your talented sister. I want to bring her back with me.

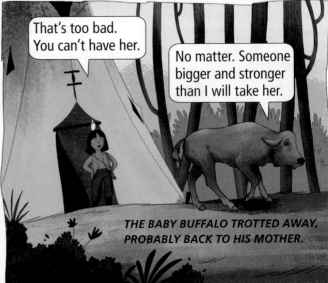
That's too bad. You can't have her.

No matter. Someone bigger and stronger than I will take her.

THE BABY BUFFALO TROTTED AWAY, PROBABLY BACK TO HIS MOTHER.

THE GIRL SUSPECTED THAT SHE ALREADY KNEW. THE BABY BUFFALO WAS TELLING THE TRUTH. EACH DAY, A LARGER BUFFALO CAME AND TRIED TO TAKE THE GIRL AWAY.

I don't know how big the next buffalo will be. I know he will kill you if you don't give him what he wants.

THE BUFFALO WHO CAME WAS THE LARGEST IN EXISTENCE. HE SNARLED AND BEAT HIS HOOVES. THE EARTH BENEATH HIM SHOOK.

What do you want, giant buffalo?

You will all die unless you give me your sister!

Never!

Then I must kill you now!

Sister! Brothers! He is coming for you!

You have to use your medicine gift! Now!

I know! I am!

THE TREE FELL AND THEY LOST HOLD OF THE BRANCHES. THEY WERE CAUGHT IN THE CLOUDS. THE GIRL WEPT.

How will we get down again?

I know what to do. Don't be sad. I will make us into stars!

Take my hand!

A GREAT BRIGHT LIGHT SHONE ON THEM. IT WAS COMFORTING AND FULL OF WARMTH.

THEY TRANSFORMED INTO THE CONSTELLATION THAT SOME CALL THE BIG DIPPER.

THE GIRL WAS RIGHT! THE WORLD DOES LOOK UP TO HER BROTHERS. WHEN WE LOOK INTO THE NIGHT SKY, WE SEE THEM!

WE SEE HER MOST CLEARLY. SHE IS THE BRIGHTEST STAR IN THE BIG DIPPER, SPREADING HER LIGHT ACROSS THE SKY.

UPLOAD

⏻ **COLLABORATIVE DISCUSSION**

Discussing the Purpose How do the Quillworker Girl and her brothers respond to challenges? Discuss this question with a partner. Cite evidence from the text in your response.

LISTENING TOOLBOX

Listening to an Oral Opinion

▶ **Listen for evidence.** Identify the speaker's position and follow his or her opinion.

▶ **Listen for persuasive tricks.** Don't let yourself be convinced by the speaker without thinking carefully about what he or she is saying. Don't fall for faulty logic.

▶ **Respond to the speaker.** Challenge facts and ask for explanations at suitable times in the opinion.

Useful Phrases

▷ That's a good point, but ____.

▷ Could you explain what you mean by ____?

▷ I don't agree that ____.

Speak Out! Work with a small group to compare and contrast the characters in "The Quillworker Girl." Then, pick one character. Give an oral opinion on which character handled a problem best. Provide reasons and evidence to support why you think that character best responded to a problem.

Vocabulary Strategy: Word Connotation

Some words can make us feel a certain way. The associations that word brings to mind are called its **connotations**. Read the two sentences below:

Joseph removed the piece of chalk from Julie's hand.

Joseph snatched the piece of chalk from Julie's hand.

Even though *removed* and *snatched* both mean "to take," the word *snatched* has a negative connotation because it suggests that the chalk was taken with the use of force. A **negative connotation** suggests something bad. A **positive connotation** suggests something good. Good writers understand that the way the reader feels about a character or an event depends on the context clues that connotations provide. Read this sentence from "The Quillworker Girl:"

The buffalo who came was the largest in existence. He snarled and beat his hooves. The earth beneath him shook. (p.233)

The word *snarled* has a negative connotation. It suggests that the buffalo is angrier than the buffalo that have come before him. While the word *growled* has a similar meaning to the word *snarled*, it's important to use the word that has the correct connotation. This buffalo is forced to come because none of the smaller buffalo could take the girl away. The world *growled* would suggest that the buffalo was only warning the brothers and the girl that he may attack. The word *snarled* is a better choice because *snarled* suggests how angry he is.

Practice and Apply   What is another word in the sentence above that shows that *snarled* has a negative connotation? How do you know?

Performance Task

Speaking Activity: Oral Opinion

In this unit, you have read about exploration from different points of view. Your task is to present an oral opinion on this theme, using evidence from the selections to support your ideas.

Planning and Taking Notes

Connect to the Theme

The dictionary tells us that *to explore* means "to travel through an unfamiliar area," but also "to discuss something in depth." The two meanings are not all that different. Whether we're exploring the Arctic or exploring a new idea, we're crossing into unfamiliar territory. We're taking a risk. We don't know exactly how things will turn out.

When the fifteenth-century explorers took off for parts unknown, they had no idea what would happen to them. When people set out to explore an issue they never know how it will affect their thinking. Your task is to present an oral opinion based on the theme of "exploration." But first you need an issue. What will it be?

Write Down Possible Topics

In this activity, you will give an opinion on the theme of exploration and support it with evidence from the text. Think about the selections you read. What is an opinion you could give based on the selections? Write it in the form of a sentence. Here are some examples:

- The early explorers did not learn anything important.
- We do not need to explore space.
- The pioneers who traveled west were brave.

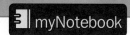

Decide the Basics

Now that you have decided on an issue and made an opinion, you'll have to back up your opinion with reasons from the text. You'll need to organize your thoughts and decide how to express yourself.

State Your Opinion

- Write your opinion in the form of a statement.
- Make sure your opinion is clearly stated at the beginning of your oral opinion. Try to grab the listener's attention in your opening statement.
- Begin your oral opinion with a fact or a question that will make listeners curious.

Find Reasons

Reasons are examples from the text that back up your opinion.

- Use only those examples that support your opinion.
- Make sure your reasons are presented in logical order.

Vocabulary

- Remember that this is an oral presentation—listeners get one chance to hear it. Use time-order words (*first*; *then*; *finally*) to help them out.
- Include connecting words and phrases such as *at the beginning, for example*, and *however* to make your opinion easier to follow.

Prepare for Speaking Out Loud

- Speak loudly enough to be heard, at a normal speed. Speak clearly.
- Pay attention to tone and word choice.
- Use language that sounds natural.
- Use physical cues. Hand gestures, facial expressions, and eye contact can help listeners understand your points.

239

Performance Task

Presenting the Information

You've got the basics down. You have made an opinion based on the selections and the evidence to support it. All you need is a way to present the information—in other words, a structure. Having a clear, logical structure is important when it comes to presenting information orally.

Use the diagram in the Writing Toolbox to help you collect your ideas in an outline.

WRITING TOOLBOX

Elements of An Oral Opinion

Introduction	**The introduction should state your opinion.** Try to grab the listener's attention in the first statement.
Reasons	**Provide reasons that support your opinion.** You may want to use this section to respond to opposing viewpoints, or opinions you don't agree with. Back up your ideas with evidence from the text.
Conclusion	**The conclusion sums up your ideas.** Restate your opinion and summarize the reasons you used to support it. You can also use this section to ask a question for your listeners to think about.

Speaking in Front of an Audience

You've got it all planned out. You've stated your opinion and you have all the evidence you need to support it. You have a way to organize your ideas. It's time to prepare your oral opinion. Here are some things to think about:

- **Practice** Rehearse your presentation as much as possible—in front of a mirror, to a family member, or even to a pet. The more you practice, the more comfortable you will be when you speak.

- **Audience** Know your audience. You will be speaking to your teacher and classmates.

- **Purpose** Show your audience that you believe in your opinion.

- **Clarity** Present your information in a clear and straightforward way.

- **Support** Make sure your reasons support your opinion.

- **Style** Use a formal but relaxed tone.

- **Conclusion** Tie your ideas together at the end. You may want to restate or sum up your main points. You may want to offer insights of your own about the topic.

- **Listening** When you are listening to another classmate give his or her oral opinion, be respectful. If you have a questions or comments, wait until the presentation is over before you speak.

Revise

Self Evaluation

Use the checklist and rubric to guide your oral presentation.

Peer Review

Use the checklist to comment on your classmate's presentation.

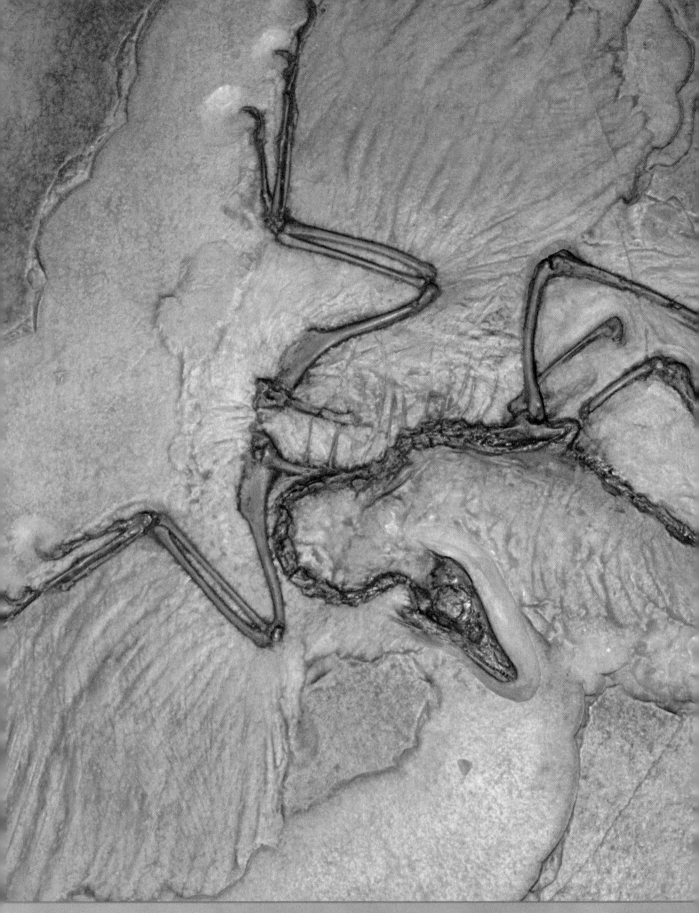

Journey to Discovery

The world is full of obvious things which nobody by any chance ever observes.

— Arthur Conan Doyle, writer

Essential Question

Why do people want to make discoveries?

The Language of Discovery

Earth holds many hidden treasures that have yet to be discovered. If you look closely enough, you will find fascinating creatures, rocks, elements, or artifacts on almost every part of Earth. With careful study, each of these can tell a story about Earth and its history.

There are many paths on the journey to discovery. Discovery is about finding out something new. People make discoveries about all kinds of things. We discover materials with interesting properties. We discover new living things or find out more about ancient civilizations. We explore caves, mountaintops, deep sea vents and many other distant or hard-to-reach places to learn about them.

A discovery can be intentional or accidental. Sometimes a discovery is made when someone wants to solve a particular question. Often, discoveries are made when someone finds something without looking for it.

Discovery begins with exploration, observation, and a willingness to examine ordinary objects more closely. Discovery begins with curiosity and fascination about the world. It requires a little bit of daring and an open mind. Discovery leads to new understandings of our world and can lead to new inventions and progress.

In this unit, you will discover many paths on the journey to discovery. You will learn about Sacajawea, John James Audubon, and others who, either intentionally or accidentally, discovered something new.

> **Why are discoveries important?**

The Cover Up: Word Groupings

Cover is a root word for many other words we commonly use or see in text. A **root** is the part of a word that gives the basic meaning. To *cover* means to hide or put a protective layer over something, so words with the root word *cover* have something to do with hiding or protecting. Knowing the meaning of root words and common prefixes and suffixes can help you learn new words.

Here are some words related to *cover*:

Discover *Cover*

Discover	verb	To find out or reveal
Uncover	verb	To take off a protective layer
Covering	noun	Something that can be used as a protective or outer layer
Undercover	adjective	Work done in secret
Coverless	adjective	Not having a protective or outer layer
Covert	adjective	Secretive or hidden

↻ Performance Task

Writing Activity: Write a Short Report About a Discovery. Describe a discovery that you or someone else has made. Explain how the discovery happened. Tell why the discovery was interesting or important. Flip through **Browse** magazine if you need help with brainstorming topics. Use the supports in the **Activity Book** as you prepare your report.

→ *Browse* *magazine*

DOWNLOAD

You have read about different kinds of discoveries. Now read about a blogger who makes some discoveries at camp.

⏻ **SETTING A PURPOSE**

As you read, pay attention to the specific words that Looking4Dinosaurs uses to talk about archaeology camp.

Looking4Dinosaurs

August 12, 4:45 p.m.

Enter your email address:

Subscribe me!

SEARCH

💬 **Comments** **10**

You're never going to believe where I was this last week. If you guessed archaeology camp, you're right! It would be no surprise to anyone who knows me that I loved it. I want to be an archaeologist when I grow up. My mom can tell you about all the holes I used to dig in our yard, hoping to find some hidden object.

You're probably picturing me spending all week under the hot sun, digging in the dirt, and maybe finding a little piece of something. We did do a lot of digging at excavation sites, and it sure was hot, but there was a lot more to our days. First, they taught us about the history of the site we would be working on. Then, the camp leaders taught us about the many tools we would be using. We had to learn how to dig properly and how to screen the dirt we dug up. Besides digging alongside professional archaeologists, we learned how to identify artifacts and analyze, record, and catalog objects. Speakers came to tell us more about their jobs discovering, preserving, and mapping sites and objects. Some speakers also talked about their finds. These lectures were mainly indoors, so speakers could show slides. Those lectures were a great break from the hot sun!

I found a couple of arrowheads during the week. Other objects that were found included nails, bits of bone, beads, glass, and even what looked like a little bottle. It wasn't always easy to tell exactly what we were looking at. Honestly, it didn't really matter *what* we were finding; we were just happy to find anything at all! We kept saying how cool it was to be finding things that have been buried for so many years. Thinking about the history of an object and trying to figure out the story that went along with it was really challenging and exciting. Learning about other cultures and other time periods was amazing. We made a lot of great discoveries. At the end of camp, we had an exhibit of all of our findings, so we could share what we learned with our families and friends.

Archaeology camp is great if you like history, science, and getting your hands dirty. Being an archaeologist requires good reasoning skills, careful record-keeping, and a lot of patience. I figure if I start working hard on all of those traits now, I'll be ready for the hard but rewarding work of making new discoveries as an archaeologist when I'm older.

I think next year it would be cool to go to a camp where we look for dinosaur bones. I told my mom that, and she said that my camp sounded like so much fun, maybe the whole family will go on a dig next year!

ARCHIVES

August

July

June

May

April

March

February

January

December

👍 Like   👎 Dislike

⏻ COLLABORATIVE DISCUSSION

Discussing the Purpose With a partner, talk about the words Looking4Dinoaurs uses to talk about archaeology camp. What words best show her feelings?

Finding Text Evidence In a small group, discuss one or two reasons why the blogger enjoyed her time at camp. Cite evidence from the text in your response.

Staying Safe What are the possible risks of communication online? How can bloggers stay safe? Work in a group. Make a list of rules that bloggers should follow to help limit risks.

Write On! Looking4Dinosaurs wrote about her time at archaeology camp. Add a comment to Looking4Dinosaurs telling what part of archaeology camp you found most interesting and why. Then exchange what you have written with a classmate. Write something in reaction to his or her comment. ⬚ 💬 Comments | 0 ⬚

↻ Performance Task

Writing Activity: Share and Interact with Other Blogs
Now that you have started your blog, brainstormed ideas, chosen a design, scheduled posts, and are following respectful blogging rules, you are ready to share your blog with others. Interacting with other bloggers is one of the most exciting blogging activities.

1 Leave comments or ask questions on the blogs you follow. By leaving a comment, you have the chance to promote your own blog. Many blogs allow you to include a link to your blog with your comment. If a blogger replies to your comment, you can continue the conversation.

2 Find new blogs that are similar to yours. Start a conversation! Leave comments on these blogs. You might learn something new, or you might be asked to explain something further.

3 Invite your readers to ask a question or leave a comment about one of your blog posts. For example, if you write about a cultural tradition that's important to your family, invite your readers to share their own cultural traditions.

4 Ask your readers to suggest future topics.

Language Cam video

Do you want to learn more about archaeology? Watch the video.

Sacagawea, Explorer

Looking4Dinosaurs learned about the past at archaeology camp. You can learn about an important historical figure, Sacagawea, by reading the following selection.

Background on Early American Exploration

In 1803, the United States bought a huge area of land from France. This event is known as the Louisiana Purchase. The area then known as Louisiana has become most of Kansas, Colorado, Wyoming, Montana, and Minnesota, and also parts of Texas and New Mexico. President Thomas Jefferson wanted to explore and map this territory and find a route through it to the West Coast. An important part of this exploration was making contact with the many different nations of native people who already lived there. Meriwether Lewis and William Clark were the leaders of the expedition.

⏻ **SETTING A PURPOSE**

As you read, think about the relationship between Sacagawea and the Corps of Discovery.

Sacagawea, Explorer

by Olavo Amado

The list of explorers of the Americas is long and storied. One of the most famous women on this list is Sacagawea.

In the winter of 1805 Sacagawea joined the 32 men (and one dog) who made up the Corps of Discovery. Led by Meriwether Lewis and William Clark, the Corps was **commissioned** by President Thomas Jefferson. They were to explore the West from the Mississippi River
10 to the Pacific Ocean. Sacagawea became an important part of the journey.

> **commissioned:** given the order to perform a task

The Corps met Sacajawea in 1805. A year before, the explorers had set out by boat from St. Louis. Traveling along the Missouri River, they reached what is now North Dakota. They spent the winter with the Hidatsa and Mandan Indians. In 1800, Hidatsa warriors had captured Sacagawea from the Shoshone, who lived farther west. Sacagawea was about 12 years old then. By 1805 she was the wife of a French Canadian fur trader,
20 Toussaint Charbonneau. She had just given birth to a baby boy.

Originally Lewis and Clark hired Charbonneau to go west with them. Charbonneau, who spoke Hidatsa and French, could act as a translator when the Americans met Hidatsa people.

As Sacagawea traveled west, she helped the Corps in many ways. For one thing, she knew what plants were **edible** or useful for medicine. And once, when one of the boats **capsized**, Sacagawea saved valuable papers and
30 supplies. Her most important contributions, however, came when the group reached Shoshone country. Sacagawea spoke Shoshone and could translate. It was a complicated process. Sacagawea translated the Shoshone into Hidatsa. Charbonneau translated the Hidatsa into French. One of the members of the Corps translated from French into English so Lewis and Clark could understand.

edible: eatable, fit to be eaten

capsized: turned over, sank

But no one could predict what happened when the Corps met a group of Shoshone warriors. To Sacagawea's amazement, the leader of the group was her long-lost
40 brother! Because of this connection, the Shoshone helped the Corps in **crucial** ways. They sold them much-needed horses, and they let them travel west in peace.

crucial: very important

Sacagawea's very presence continued to help the Corps of Discovery. As they traveled west, they met many new tribes. The Corps was foreign to them, and could easily have been hostile. The presence of Sacagawea, with her child, assured them that the Corps was peaceful, rather than **warlike**.

Break the compound word **warlike** into two smaller words to help you understand it.

When the Corps reached the Pacific Ocean in
50 November 1805, Sacagawea had traveled more than 1,400 miles with them. She had truly been an explorer on a journey of discovery.

Map of the route Lewis and Clark took on their journey

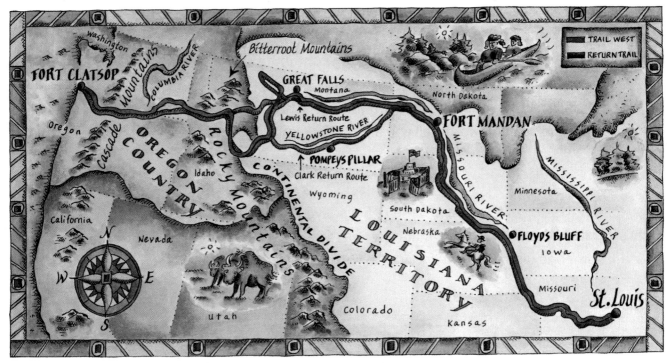

⏻ **COLLABORATIVE DISCUSSION**

Discussing the Purpose What was the relationship between Sacagawea and the Corps of Discovery? Discuss your answer with a small group.

READING TOOLBOX

Character Traits

In a nonfiction selection, the people you read about are not characters, but historical figures. However, they have certain traits. These traits can be physical, such as how they looked. Another kind of trait is how these people acted, or what they said.

▶ When you are reading a nonfiction selection about a historical figure, ask yourself, "What do the actions of this person tell me about him or her?"

▶ Ask yourself, "What did this person contribute to history?"

▶ If there are quotes from the figure, what do the person's words tell you about him or her?

Write On! What were some of Sacagawea's character traits? Write a paragraph that describes Sacagawea to someone who does not know who she is.

Vocabulary Strategy: Location Words

When reading a selection that includes travel, you will sometimes come across words that show location. These are **location words**. Some examples of location words are *north*, *south*, *east*, and *west*. Often, there will be a map that can help you see the journey a person made. By using location words, context clues, and maps, you can tell where people were when specific events happened.

For example, read this sentence from "Sacagawea, Explorer:"

"They were to explore the West from the Mississippi River to the Pacific Ocean."

There are many location words that we use in everyday conversation, including: *near/far, above/below, beside/behind*, and *left/right*. You can use these words to tell others where a person, place, or thing is located. Using location words, how can you identify where the board is in your classroom?

Practice and Apply   Use the words in the box below to identify the location of these items in your classroom: backpack, pencil, clock, teacher.

Location Words	
near	far
above	below
beside	behind
left	right

DOWNLOAD

Sacagawea helped early explorers discover the west. Now read this selection about John James Audubon and one of the many discoveries he made about birds.

⏻ **SETTING A PURPOSE**

As you read, think about the main idea of the selection.

The
Bird Seeker

by Kyle Brown

The landscape is cold and quiet. Though it is summer, bare rocks and deep banks of snow surround the few patches of plants that can grow in this harsh climate. A man sneaks through the snow. Every so often he bends low to poke through the tangled branches and moss in front of him. This is Labrador, Canada, and the famous **naturalist** John James Audubon is at work.

naturalist: one who studies nature

Most people wouldn't choose to spend the summer somewhere freezing. But Audubon did. His goal was to

10   draw and document every bird in North America. That

meant exploring everywhere, no matter how cold. In 1833, he spent all summer studying the birds of these icy Canadian shores.

Audubon spent most of July chasing after the **shore lark**. The male shore lark has spiky feathers that look like horns. He quickly figured out that they must breed in Labrador. They are excellent at hiding their nests, but Audubon wouldn't go home without finding one. After nearly a month of searching and studying less

20 tricky birds, he narrowed down his search. He realized that the shore lark must hide its nests in beds of moss.

shore lark

Two days after he had this realization, he found a nest. The nest was deep in the moss, so the birds sitting in it were hidden under the plants around them. There were few trees to nest on this far north. Audubon realized that the shore lark had adapted, learning to hide its nests rather than to build them high out of a predator's reach.

A few days later, Audubon made the first drawings

30 ever of shore larks and their nests. He later published these drawings in a collection of his studies. This collection was called *Birds of America*, and it documented every species of bird known in the United States at the time.

Birds of America and Audubon's work studying mammals were a great help to biologists. Audubon quickly became famous in England because his books were first published there. He then became famous in the United States, his home country. He inspired many

40 young researchers, including Charles Darwin, another famous naturalist.

Read the following sentence to help you understand what a **conservation group** is.

Audubon's work carries on even today. The Audubon Society, which is named for him, is one of the top **conservation groups** in the United States. The organization works to keep birds and other wildlife and their habitats safe. Audubon's work helped scientists, and his work continues to protect the creatures he spent time studying.

Eastern meadowlarks nesting in yellow false foxglove, from John James Audubon's *Birds of America*

⏻ **COLLABORATIVE DISCUSSION**

Discussing the Purpose What is the main idea of the selection? Discuss the main idea with a small group. Then, find three supporting details from the text.

READING TOOLBOX

Determining Style Elements:
Mood and Tone

Mood is the feeling or atmosphere that the writer creates for readers. Mood is closely related to tone. **Tone** is the writer's attitude toward the subject of the text, or the way the author sounds. Descriptive words and figurative language work together to set the mood and tone of a text. Mood and tone can be described by adjectives such as *angry, intense, serious,* or *humorous.*

Speak Out! Reread the opening paragraph. How does the author set the mood in this selection? Share your ideas with a partner.

DOWNLOAD

Podcast: Living 63 Feet Underwater Helps Cousteau Team Conduct Experiments

Just like John Audubon did in the 1800s, scientists today go to remote places to study animals. In this podcast, you'll hear about someone who lived underwater to study what lives there.

Background on Jacques and Fabien Cousteau

Jacques Cousteau , a famous documentary filmmaker, spent 30 days in 1963 living underwater in the Red Sea. The footage he recorded there became an award-winning documentary. Through his movies, he helped people understand the amazing diversity of life in the ocean and the importance of protecting it.

In 2014, Jacques' grandson Fabien Cousteau went on a similar expedition. Fabien spent 31 days underwater in the Florida Keys. Like his grandfather, Fabien went underwater to learn about the animals and plants that live there. He specifically focused on coral reefs. By staying underwater as long as he did, Fabien was able to gather a lot of information and raise awareness about the importance of researching the ocean.

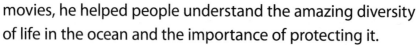 **SETTING A PURPOSE**

As you listen, think about why Fabien Cousteau took his trip underwater. How did it help his work?

Living 63 Feet Underwater Helps Cousteau Team Conduct Experiments

Main Idea and Details in the Podcast

Main Idea	Living in an underwater base for 31 days helped Fabien Cousteau's research on marine life.

Detail	The underwater base had everything Fabien's team needed, such as dive gear and science equipment.

Detail	Fabien and his team could take longer dives in the ocean to study underwater life.

Detail	Fabien's team could see different animals and their behavior up close.

Detail	Fabien's team used new technology to study what was happening to coral reefs.

⏻ COLLABORATIVE DISCUSSION

In a group, discuss what living in the underwater base did for Fabien Cousteau's research. Were there any things that Fabien could do more easily because he lived underwater? Were there any things that would be impossible to do without living underwater?

A Journey to the Center of the Earth

Fabien Cousteau and his team were trying to learn more about the mysteries of the ocean. In "A Journey to the Center of the Earth," Harry and Professor Hardwigg try to solve a mysterious code written on a piece of paper.

READING TOOLBOX

Elements of a Drama

A play, or drama, is a form of literature meant to be performed by actors in front of an audience. Special features of drama include:

▶ **cast of characters** — a list of the characters in the drama. The list appears at the beginning of the play.

▶ **dialogue** — the words that the characters say. The character's name comes before his or her lines of dialogue.

▶ **stage directions** — instructions for how the drama is to be performed in front of an audience. The instructions are often set in parentheses and italic type.

⏻ SETTING A PURPOSE

As you read, think about how Harry and Professor Hardwigg are alike and different.

A Journey to the Center of the Earth

by Jules Verne
adapted by Jessica E. Cohn

Cast of Characters

Narrator

Harry – *young man, nephew to Professor Hardwigg*

Professor Hardwigg – *Harry's uncle, a man with knowledge of many worlds*

Cook – *French woman who cares for the professor and Harry*

Act I
Scene 1

(The story begins in Germany, in the home of Professor Hardwigg. Stage left, there is a dining room. It is small, with an expensive-looking table and four chairs. The professor's study takes up most of the stage. It is filled with books, two armchairs, a desk and chair, and a large table covered with papers.

The curtain rises to show the Narrator facing the audience. He is seated at a chair in the dining room. Harry is standing behind him.)

Break **eventful** into two smaller words to help you understand it.

Look at the picture on the right for a clue about what the author means by **bird prints**.

10 **Narrator:** This story begins, as do so many adventures, on one **eventful** day. It all starts when the professor finds an old yellow book. Inside it is a message written in an ancient alphabet.

Harry: (*to Narrator*) I think the story starts with my hunger. I am hungry now and need to find the cook.

Narrator: Either way, the adventure begins. . . .

(*A door slams. The professor rushes into his study with a book.*)

Professor Hardwigg: Harry—Harry—Harry—*Harry!*

20 **Harry:** (*to Narrator*) My uncle is a man not to be kept waiting. So, I should present myself. Of course, by the time I get there, he will already have forgotten that he called me.

(*Harry goes to the study. His uncle is reading the book and tapping his forehead.*)

Professor Hardwigg: Wonderful! Wonderful—Wonderful!

Narrator: Harry's uncle is admiring a book. A small scrap of paper falls to the floor, and Harry sees that it is covered with primitive letters of some sort. The ancient
30 lettering looks like three sets of **bird prints** set in neat rows and columns, each six or seven characters wide and tall.

Professor Hardwigg: (*picking up the paper, shaking with excitement*) This is old. Very old. It is old Icelandic, I am sure of it.

(*From **offstage**, the Cook calls them.*)

Cook: Supper is ready!

Professor Hardwigg: Forget the dinner!

Harry: Coming!

40 **Narrator:** Only Harry answers the call to food. He slips from the room. His uncle keeps studying the papers.

(*Harry eats in the dining room. He has just finished an apple when he hears his uncle calling.*)

Professor Hardwigg: Harry—Harry—Harry—*Harry!*

Harry: Yes!

Break **offstage** into two smaller words to better understand it.

declare: state, announce

(*Harry returns to the study.*)

Professor Hardwigg: (*excited, hitting table*) I **declare**! I declare to you it is Runic—and contains some wonderful secret, which I must get, at any price.

50 **Harry:** Yes, I . . .

Professor Hardwigg: Sit down! And write what I say!

(*Harry obeys.*)

Professor Hardwigg: I will substitute a letter of our alphabet for that of Runic. We will then see what that will produce. Now, begin and make no mistakes! The first letter is *m!* Now, a period. Now, an *r!*

Narrator: Harry's uncle reads off the letters. Harry copies them. The list grows slowly. The letters don't make sense. Harry is barely done when Professor Hardwigg grabs the
60 papers from him.

Professor Hardwigg: I should like to know what it means. The first row says, "m-*dot*-r-n-l-l-s." The second says, "s-g-t-s-s-m-f."

Harry: I cannot tell what it means at all.

What word in the sentence helps you understand the meaning of **cryptograph**?

Professor Hardwigg: I declare, it is like a **cryptograph**—a puzzle. Unless, indeed, the letters have been written without real meaning. And yet, why take so much trouble?

Harry: Why—

70 Professor Hardwigg: (*confused*) The book and the smaller paper are in different handwriting. The cryptograph is of much later date. To me, it appears that the sentence was written by the owner of the book. But who? (*pause*) Perhaps, by great good luck, it may be written in the volume.

(*With Harry looking on, the professor searches for a name. He finds a blot of ink and looks closely.*)

Professor Hardwigg: (*joyful*) Here, in this faded ink. A name. Arne Saknussemm! Not only was he from Iceland, **80** but he was a celebrated **alchemist**!

Harry: Alchemist?

Professor Hardwigg: The alchemists were the only educated men of the day. They made surprising discoveries. Perhaps this hides the secret to an amazing invention. I believe the cryptograph has profound meaning!

In the Middle Ages, an **alchemist** was a scientist who practiced chemistry and tried to discover how to turn ordinary metals into gold.

Harry: If so, why hide it this way?

Professor Hardwigg: Why—how should I know? But we shall see. Until I discover the meaning of this sentence I
90 will neither eat nor sleep!

Harry: My dear uncle—

Professor Hardwigg: (*forceful*) And neither will you!

Narrator: No food and no sleep does not sound good to Harry. But his uncle is too excited to convince otherwise. The older man keeps talking out loud. He speaks to Harry but mainly to himself. He discovers that the paper has one hundred and thirty-two letters.

Professor Hardwigg: More consonants than vowels. Seventy-nine consonants to fifty-three vowels! This
100 means it is in a southern language. It might be Latin, though it could be Spanish. It might be French, Italian, Greek, or Hebrew. Some of the words are all consonants. Others, all vowels. Very strange, indeed.

Narrator: Meanwhile, Harry writes whatever his uncle tells him to write. And he tries to keep from laughing. The message says nothing. It says . . .

Harry:

mmessunkaSenrA.icefdoK.segnittamurtn

ecertserrette, rotaivsadua, ednecsedsadne

lacartniiiluJsiratrac Sarbmutabeledmek

meretarcsilucoYsleffenSnl.

(The professor listens and then hits the table with his fist . . . and runs out of the room. The Cook enters the study.)

Cook: When will he have his dinner?

Harry: *(sadly)* Never.

Cook: And his supper?

Harry: I don't know. He says he will eat no more, and neither **shall** I. My uncle has determined that neither of us will eat until we decode this horrible message.

Cook: You will both be starved to death.

Harry: I know. Where has my uncle gone?

(The cook shakes her head and exits. Harry picks up the paper and begins to play with the puzzle.)

Narrator: Harry gradually thinks of different ways to group the letters. Nothing makes sense until he realizes something.

110

120

Rarely used today, the word **shall** means "will."

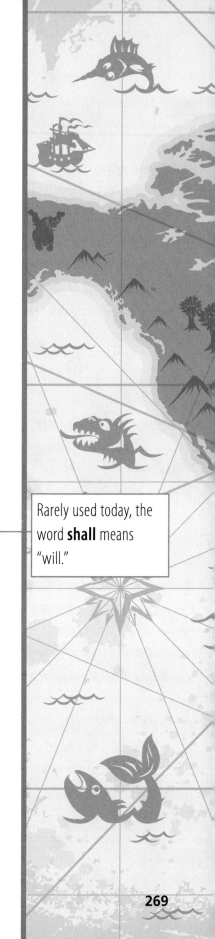

Come apart (break up) and **come together** (make sense) are phrasal verbs.

undertaking: starting a task or a project

Harry: (*talking to himself*) The fourteenth, fifteenth, and sixteenth letters spell *ice*. There is the word *sir* in the eighty-fourth, eighty-fifth, and eighty-sixth letters. Look 130 at this! Here are the Latin words *rota, mutabile, ira, nec,* and *atra.* There is also *luco,* which means "sacred wood."

Narrator: The puzzle begins to **come apart**—and **come together**.

Harry: I see a Hebrew word and some French. It feels as though my brain were on fire!

(*Harry fans himself with the paper. He sees the back and front of it pass back and forth.*)

Harry: And look here! Front to back! Here is the clue! All you have to do to understand this is to read it backward!

140 (*He stretches the paper on the table. He begins to spell backward. Slowly, its meaning becomes clear. The meaning seems to scare him at first. Then, he becomes determined.*)

Harry: Never! Never shall my uncle be made aware of this secret. He would be quite capable of **undertaking** the terrible journey. Nothing stops him! Worse, he would take me with him, and we would be lost forever. This cannot be allowed! My worthy uncle is already mad. *This* would finish him.

(*He picks up the book. Just then, his uncle returns. He* 150 *places the book back on the professor's desk and sits on a chair.*)

Narrator: The professor has decided to use tools of math to read the message. He works late into the night, trying one way and then another. It is as if Harry is not even there. The sounds of the street die away. Harry and Professor Hardwigg miss their supper. The lights go out in the other buildings. Harry holds his secret inside.

Harry: (*to audience*) I know my uncle. His imagination is a perfect volcano. So, I promise never to speak. When the

160 cook offers us breakfast, we do not eat. Noon passes. Two o'clock passes. Still, we do not eat.

(*As he speaks, the cook passes by with a tray of food. Harry shakes his head to say no, even though he is very hungry.*)

Narrator: It occurs to Harry that his uncle may discover the hidden message himself. If so, Harry would have starved for nothing.

Harry: (*clearing throat, sitting upright*) I have made an
169 important discovery, Uncle.

170 **Professor Hardwigg:** You don't mean to say that you
have any idea of the meaning?

(*Harry moves closer and points at the book.*)

Harry: I do. Look at the sentence.

Professor Hardwigg: But it means nothing.

Harry: Nothing if you read from left to right. But look at
it from right to left—

Professor Hardwigg: Backward! Oh, I am such a
blockhead!

Read the following
sentence to help you
understand what **Dog
Latin** means.

Narrator: The message is in **Dog Latin**. This is English in
180 which some aspects have been made to sound like Latin.
If you have heard of Pig Latin, you understand how this
game of words is played.

Harry: It says, "Descend into the crater of Yocul of
Sneffels"

Professor Hardwigg: "which the shade of Scartaris
caresses, before . . ."

audacious: daring

Harry: "the kalends of July, **audacious** traveler, and . . ."

Professor Hardwigg: "you will reach the center of the
earth. I did."

190 **Harry and Professor Hardwigg together:** "Arne
Saknussemm."

Narrator: At last, the professor realizes he is hungry. Happily for Harry, they search the kitchen to see what food is available. After dessert, they return to the study, where the professor makes plans to follow the clues. He sees advantages in their leaving at once.

(*They sit. The professor turns to his nephew.*)

Professor Hardwigg: In the first place, you must keep the whole affair a secret. Many would start the same journey.

200 **Harry:** But I doubt there will be **competitors**.

Professor Hardwigg: A real scientist would be delighted at the chance! If this paper were made public, there would be a stream of them!

Harry: But, my dear sir, is not this paper likely to be a **hoax**?

(*The professor's face becomes gloomy. Then, he smiles.*)

Professor Hardwigg: (*mysterious*) We shall see.

In the next scene, Harry and his uncle begin their adventure. In later scenes, they go to Iceland. Then, as
210 *now, it is an island nation built from volcanoes. They follow a map that leads them inside one of the craters. . . . What will happen in scenes to come? Who will make it home?*

The answers lie in Jules Verne's **A JOURNEY TO THE CENTER OF THE EARTH.**

> Reread the previous sentence to help you understand the meaning of **competitors**.

> **hoax:** something intended to deceive, a trick

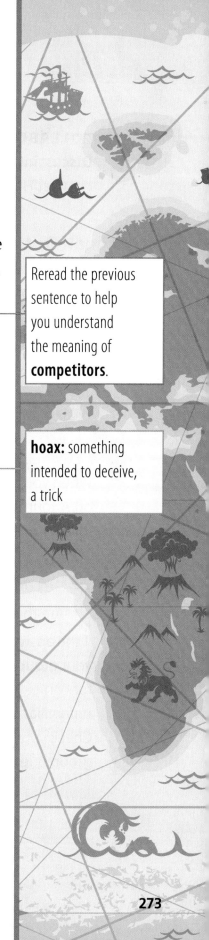

⏻ **COLLABORATIVE DISCUSSION**

Discussing the Purpose With a small group, compare and contrast Harry and Professor Hardwigg.

Speak Out! Take turns rereading pages 268–269 with a small group. Assign one person to read for Harry, one person to read for Professor Hardwigg, one person to read for the Narrator, and one person to read the stage directions.

LISTENING TOOLBOX

Active Listening

When you are rereading and listening to pages 268–269 of "A Journey to the Center of the Earth," ask yourself the following questions:

- Do I know most of the words?
- Do I understand most or all of the dialogue?
- Are the stage directions clear?

If the answer to any of these questions is "no," work with your group to find ways to address the problems. Look for context clues or use a dictionary if the words were unfamiliar. Paraphrase the sentences in your own words. Check your understanding of meaning by asking your group questions.

↻ Performance Task

Writing Activity: Review What is your opinion about the drama and the characters? When you write a review, you are sharing your thoughts about something you read. Write a short review of the drama. Cite appropriate details to support your opinion.

- Before you begin writing, ask yourself, "Would I recommend this selection to a friend? Do I want to keep reading to find out what happens next?"

- Remember that an opinion is your personal view about something.

You can support your opinion with examples from the drama.

- Let readers know your opinion of the selection at the beginning of your review. Then restate your opinion at the end.

Exploring the Deep Ocean

Harry and Professor Hardwigg found a message that would lead them to places beneath the earth. In this selection, you will read about people who travel beneath the ocean's surface.

Background on the *Alvin*

Allyn Vine was a famous oceanographer who did a lot of work to improve vessels used to explore the deep sea.

The deep-sea submarine *Alvin* is named after him. To date, the *Alvin* has made more than 4,400 dives to explore the mysteries of the deep ocean.

There are many creatures found on the ocean floor that people aren't able to see on their own. However, with the help of the *Alvin*, scientists have located over 300 new kinds of animals, including foot-long clams and 10-foot-long tubeworms. The *Alvin* was even used to explore the remains of the famous ship the *Titanic*.

⏻ SETTING A PURPOSE

As you read, think about the relationship between the deep ocean and the creatures that live in it.

Exploring the Deep Ocean

by Susan Escobar

Earth is a watery planet: about three-quarters of it is ocean. We know about the parts of the ocean that we can see—the **intertidal** zone where the water meets the shore, and the thin top layer of the open seas.

But below the **sunlit** surface lies the deep ocean—vast, dark, mysterious, and mostly unexplored. The deep ocean is Earth's largest habitat. It represents about 85% of where life can exist on our planet, but we know little about it. Few people have explored the deep ocean, possibly even fewer
10 than the number of people who have traveled into space.

intertidal: the area of the shore between the low point and the high point of the tide

Break the compound word **sunlit** into two smaller words to understand it better.

What context clues help you understand the meaning of **harsh**?

biodiversity: the wide variety of plants and animals in their natural environment

The prefix *inter-* means "mutually, to each other." Can you guess what **interdependent** means?

Scientists once imagined that the deep ocean's **harsh** conditions—total darkness, freezing temperatures, crushing pressure from the weight of the water—meant few living organisms could survive there. Today we know better. Special submarines and technology have enabled scientists to peek into this dark world. *Alvin*
20 is a specialized submarine that can carry three divers down into the depths of the ocean. It has lights, cameras, and arms to collect specimens. It was built in 1964. In 1977, the *Alvin's* crew was the first to observe the teeming life around hydrothermal vents. We now know that parts of the deep ocean may have as much **biodiversity** as the rainforest.

In most instances, the first link in the deep-ocean food chain is "marine snow"—flakes of dead things and waste matter floating down from the sunlit water above. Like other ecosystems, the deep ocean has a balance of **interdependent** species. All of them have adaptations to
30 deal with the harsh conditions of deep-ocean life.

Take bioluminescence. With no light available, many species make their own. The anglerfish has a spine that acts as a fishing rod dangling above its head. A glowing orb of

light at the end lures prey within range of its huge mouth and teeth. Instead of black ink, the vampire squid squirts out a glowing **bioluminescent** cloud whose light lasts for several minutes.

40   What about camouflage? In the pitch black of the deep ocean, the best way to blend in is to have no color at all. Many deep-ocean animals such as the glass squid are transparent.

Gigantism is another feature of some deep-ocean creatures. The giant squid and the giant isopod are much bigger than similar species that live in shallower waters. This super-size might be related to another deep-ocean phenomenon: long lives. Many deep-ocean creatures live for decades or even centuries.

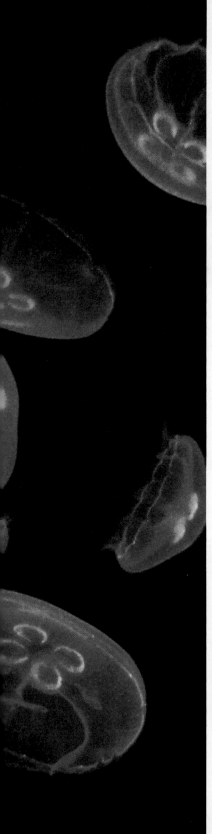

50 Some deep-ocean organisms are adapted to life in and around hydrothermal vents—cracks in the ocean floor through which super-heated mineral-rich water pours out. Giant tubeworms are vent dwellers. They have no internal organs. Instead, they have chambers filled with special bacteria that produce energy from the heat and minerals coming out of the vents.

The range and diversity of life in the deep ocean continues to astonish scientists, just as it continues to expand our understanding of life on Earth. It will continue to open our
60 horizons into the future: scientists estimate that the deep ocean contains 10 million species, most of them still unknown.

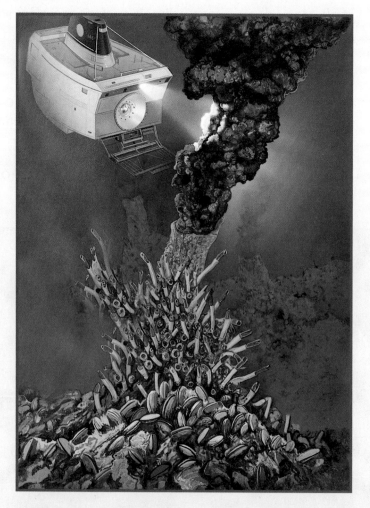

⏻ COLLABORATIVE DISCUSSION

Discussing the Purpose With a partner, talk about what effect living in the deep ocean has on the creatures living in it. Which feature of deep-sea life would you like to learn more about? Why?

SPEAKING TOOLBOX

Partner Discussions

When you have academic conversations with another person, you speak a little less formally than you would if you were talking to a big group. Remember that you still need to be both an active listener and a thoughtful speaker. Here are some tips to help you:

- Paraphrase what you've heard.
- Ask questions if you don't understand.
- Build on your partner's ideas.

Don't interrupt. If you disagree with a point your partner has made, voice objections or alternative opinions politely.

Useful Phrases

▷ Excuse me?

▷ Can you repeat what you just said?

▷ So what you're saying is ___.

▷ That makes me think about ___.

▷ What do you mean when you say ___?

DOWNLOAD

Neil Armstrong

Like the crew of the *Alvin,* Neil Armstrong explored mysteries in unusual places. But while the *Alvin*'s crew explored the deep sea, Neil Armstrong explored space.

Know Before You Go

THE SPACE RACE At the end of World War II, there were two superpowers in the world: the United States of America and the Soviet Union (today's Russia). Both countries wanted to prove that they had the most advanced technology. In 1957, the Soviet Union launched *Sputnik*, the first unmanned satellite, into orbit around the earth. In 1961, Yuri Gagarin became the first person to orbit the planet. That same year, President Kennedy challenged the United States to send a man to the moon and bring him home safely. Eight years later, *Apollo 11* became the first manned spacecraft to land on the moon, and Neil Armstrong became the first man to walk on the moon.

Many of the technologies that are part of our lives today were a part of the space race. Everything from satellites to memory foam was invented to help send human beings into space.

⏻ SETTING A PURPOSE

As you read, think about the relationship between Neil Armstrong and the Gemini program.

Neil Armstrong

by Meredith Mann

NEIL ARMSTRONG KNEW THAT HE WAS MEANT TO FLY. HE WAS BORN IN 1930, BEFORE MOST PEOPLE FLEW IN AIRPLANES, AND TRAVELING IN SPACE WAS ONLY A DREAM.

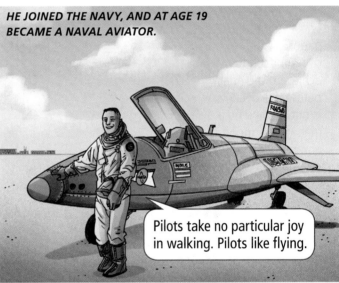

HE JOINED THE NAVY, AND AT AGE 19 BECAME A NAVAL AVIATOR.

Pilots take no particular joy in walking. Pilots like flying.

AFTER LEAVING THE NAVY, HE STUDIED AT PURDUE UNIVERSITY AND LATER EARNED A MASTER'S DEGREE.

NEIL BECAME A TEST PILOT, TESTING AIRCRAFT THAT WENT FASTER THAN ANYTHING EVER HAD BEFORE.

ON MAY 25, 1961, PRESIDENT JOHN F. KENNEDY STOOD BEFORE CONGRESS AND ASKED THE COUNTRY TO MEET A HUGE CHALLENGE.

I believe that this nation should commit itself to achieving the goal, before this decade is out, of landing a man on the moon and returning him safely to the earth.

THE SPACE RACE WAS HEATING UP. WHICH COUNTRY WOULD BE THE FIRST TO THE MOON?

GIANT ROCKETS WERE BEING BUILT TO CARRY PEOPLE INTO SPACE.

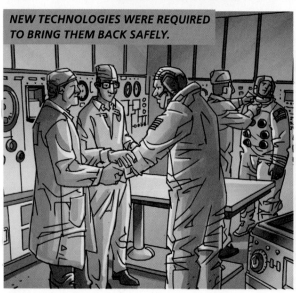

NEW TECHNOLOGIES WERE REQUIRED TO BRING THEM BACK SAFELY.

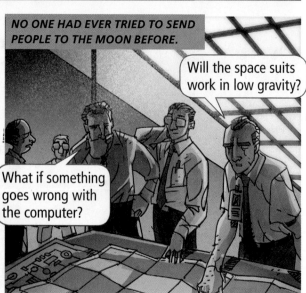

NO ONE HAD EVER TRIED TO SEND PEOPLE TO THE MOON BEFORE.

Will the space suits work in low gravity?

What if something goes wrong with the computer?

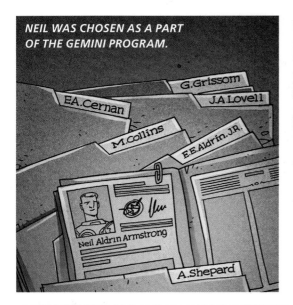

NEIL WAS CHOSEN AS A PART OF THE GEMINI PROGRAM.

E.A.Cernan

G.Grissom

J.A.Lovell

M.Collins

E.E.Aldrin.JR.

Neil Aldrin Armstrong

A.Shepard

AMONG THE ASTRONAUTS, HE WAS KNOWN FOR HIS CALM AND PATIENCE.

NEIL ARMSTRONG AND DAVID R. SCOTT ORBITED EARTH, TESTING HOW TWO MODULES WOULD DOCK IN SPACE.

THEY COMPLETED THE MISSION, BUT A PROBLEM WITH THE GUIDANCE SYSTEM SENT BOTH SHIPS SPINNING OUT OF CONTROL.

NEIL WAS ABLE TO EJECT THE MODULE, AND SUCCESSFULLY LANDED IN THE PACIFIC OCEAN.

AFTER YEARS OF TESTING AND TRAINING, THE TEAM THAT WOULD LAND ON THE MOON WAS CHOSEN.

ON JULY 16, 1969, THEY BEGAN THEIR JOURNEY.

FOR FOUR DAYS, THEY FLEW WEIGHTLESS THROUGH SPACE . . .

. . . UNTIL THEY ACHIEVED LUNAR ORBIT.

ON JULY 20, THEY SEPARATED THE SHIPS. MICHAEL COLLINS STAYED IN THE COMMAND MODULE, WHILE NEIL AND BUZZ TRANSFERRED TO THE LUNAR MODULE.

WITH NEIL AT THE CONTROLS, THE LUNAR MODULE GRADUALLY DESCENDED TOWARD THE MOON'S SURFACE.

BUT THE SHIP HAD MISSED ITS ORIGINAL TARGET, AND HAD TO LAND IN A DIFFERENT SITE.

IF THE ASTRONAUTS RAN OUT OF FUEL, THEY WOULD HAVE TO ABORT LANDING OR CRASH-LAND.

THROUGH EVERYTHING, NEIL STAYED CALM.

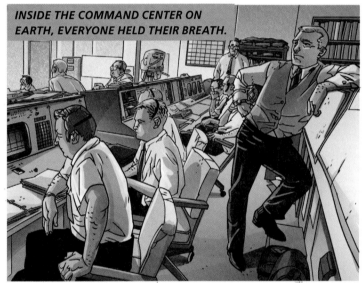

INSIDE THE COMMAND CENTER ON EARTH, EVERYONE HELD THEIR BREATH.

AND WITH ONLY 50 SECONDS OF FUEL AVAILABLE . . .

. . . THE ASTRONAUTS REACHED THEIR DESTINATION.

Houston, Tranquility Base here. The *Eagle* has landed.

AROUND THE WORLD, HALF A BILLION PEOPLE WATCHED AS NEIL EXITED THE LUNAR MODULE.

That's one small step for a man . . .

. . . one giant leap for mankind.

NEIL HAD KEPT THE PROMISE MADE BY PRESIDENT KENNEDY.

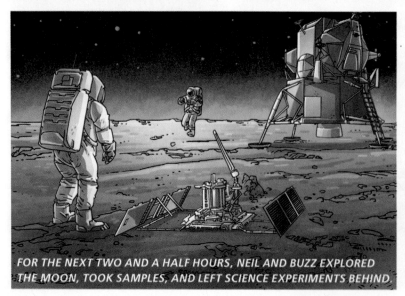

FOR THE NEXT TWO AND A HALF HOURS, NEIL AND BUZZ EXPLORED THE MOON, TOOK SAMPLES, AND LEFT SCIENCE EXPERIMENTS BEHIND.

AND THEN IT WAS TIME FOR THEM TO COME HOME.

AFTER RECONNECTING WITH THE COMMAND MODULE AND SPENDING FOUR MORE DAYS IN SPACE, THEY RETURNED TO EARTH.

CROWDS LINED THE STREETS OF NEW YORK CITY TO CHEER THE HEROES IN A TICKER-TAPE PARADE.

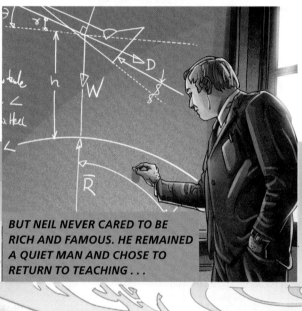

BUT NEIL NEVER CARED TO BE RICH AND FAMOUS. HE REMAINED A QUIET MAN AND CHOSE TO RETURN TO TEACHING . . .

ENCOURAGING PEOPLE TO REACH FARTHER INTO SPACE.

. . . humanity is not forever chained to this planet. Our visions go rather further than that, and our opportunities are unlimited.

UPLOAD

⏻ **COLLABORATIVE DISCUSSION**

Discussing the Purpose With a partner, discuss the relationship between Neil Armstrong and the Gemini program.

↻ **Performance Task**

Writing Activity: Partner Research What does it take to be an astronaut? With a partner, research the training and preparation that astronauts are required to do before they can travel to space.

• Write down all the words and phrases you know about the topic. These are your **search terms**.

• Type your search terms into a search engine.

• Think about your sources. Are they reliable? If the answer is yes, take notes.

• Compare the information you found with the information your partner found. Then combine your information. If your partner found the same information as you did, write it down once. Do not repeat the information. Only include the most important ideas.

Speak Out! With a small group, discuss some of the challenges involved in space travel. Consider the supplies and technology needed to travel in space. Think about what you found when you were researching and use that information to guide your discussion.

Vocabulary Strategy: Multiple-Meaning Words

Often when you're reading, you'll find a word that has more than one possible meaning. Words with one than more meaning are known as multiple-meaning words. We can often identify the intended definition of a multiple-meaning word by using context clues, or by looking up the word in a dictionary. Read the following sentence from "Neil Armstrong":

On May 25, 1961, President John F. Kennedy stood before Congress and asked the country to meet a huge challenge.

The word *before* can have more than one meaning. *Before* can mean "earlier than," but it can also mean "in front of." While it is possible that John F. Kennedy stood "earlier than" the members of Congress, it would make much more sense if the president stood "in front of" the members of Congress and asked them to meet a challenge. By using context clues, we can identify the intended definition of the multiple-meaning word *before*.

Practice and Apply   Read the following sentence from "Neil Armstrong":

But the ship had missed its original target, and had to land in a different site.

The word *land* is a multiple-meaning word. It can mean "part of the earth's surface not covered in water." It can also mean "to descend." Which meaning do you think makes the most sense? Use context clues to help you find the answer.

Performance Task

Writing Activity: Response to Literature

In this unit, you have read selections about different kinds of discoveries. Now it's time to write a response to literature.

Planning and Prewriting

Connect to the Theme

People have made discoveries throughout history. Sometimes, these people went looking for something on purpose. Other times, a discovery was accidental. Discoveries can have an effect on the person who makes the discovery, but occasionally a discovery will have an effect on many people or places. You can discover excitement in stories and historical accounts of events.

When you write a response to literature, you are letting readers know what you thought about something you read. Think about what you liked best about each selection in this unit. Think about what you disliked. Before you begin to write your response to literature, ask yourself if you enjoyed what you read. Would you recommend it to a friend? What would you change?

In this activity, you'll be writing a response to literature. First, decide what you want to write about. Which topic is the most interesting to you?

Choose Your Topic

Choose one selection from the unit. Then, answer the questions below. Cite text evidence in your response.

- Was the dialogue in "A Journey to the Center of the Earth" believable? Why or why not?

- Did the author's use of language add to your enjoyment of "The Bird Seeker?" Why or why not?

- Did the plot of "Neil Armstrong" hold your interest? Did you want to keep reading? Why or why not?

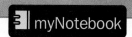

Decide the Basics

You have your topic. This topic will become your main idea. You will support your idea with examples and details from the selection. Ask yourself these questions:

Characters

- Are the characters believable?
- How are the characters described?
- What are the characters' relationships to one another?

Plot

- What are the important story events?
- What is the conflict?
- What is the resolution?

Style Elements

- How does the author express the theme?
- How is the setting important to the plot?
- What details suggest the mood and the tone of the story?
- How does the author use word choice and point of view to emphasize important ideas?

Point of View

Who tells the story? The point of view is how a writer chooses to tell a story. When a story is told from the first-person point of view, the narrator is a character in the story. In a story told from the third-person point of view, the narrator is not a character in the story.

Dialogue

- What do the characters think or say?
- Does the dialogue sound realistic?

Performance Task

Finalize Your Plan

You know what you want to say in your response to literature. Now it's time to plan the structure of your response.

Use the diagram in the Writing Toolbox to help you.

WRITING TOOLBOX

Elements of a Response to Literature

Introduction

Introduction Decide what to say about your topic to get the reader's attention. Be sure to include what you thought about the selection.

Detail

Detail

Main Ideas and Details State the main points you want to make. Include examples that reinforce those points.

Detail

Conclusion

Conclusion Restate your main idea. Using the details that you included in your response, give your opinion of the text.

Draft Your Response to Literature

You've got it all planned out. You've decided on your main idea and you have all the supporting evidence you need. You have a way to organize your ideas. Now it's time to start writing! As you write, think about:

- **Purpose and Audience** What do you want your readers to know?

- **Clarity** Make sure your ideas are clearly stated. Arrange your sentences in a logical order.

- **Support** Include examples that support your ideas.

- **Connecting Words** Use connecting words to show how one idea links to another.

Revise

Self Evaluation Use the checklist and rubric to guide your analysis.

Peer Review Exchange your response to literature with a classmate. Use the checklist to comment on your classmate's work.

Edit

Edit your response to literature to correct spelling, grammar, and punctuation errors.

Publish

Finalize your response to literature and choose a way to share it with your audience.

Student Resources

Grammar

Writing that has a lot of mistakes can confuse or even annoy a reader. Punctuation errors in a letter might lead to a miscommunication or delay a reply. A sentence fragment might lower your grade on an essay. Paying attention to grammar, punctuation, and capitalization rules can make your writing clearer and easier to read.

Quick Reference: Parts of Speech

Part of Speech	Function	Examples
Noun	names a person, a place, a thing, an idea, a quality, or an action	
Common	serves as a general name, or a name common to an entire group	subway, fog, puzzle, tollbooth
Proper	names a specific, one-of-a-kind person, place, or thing	Mrs. Price, Pompeii, China, Meg
Singular	refers to a single person, place, thing, or idea	onion, waterfall, lamb, sofa
Plural	refers to more than one person, place, thing, or idea	dreams, commercials, men, tortillas
Concrete	names something that can be perceived by the senses	jacket, teacher, caterpillar, aroma
Abstract	names something that cannot be perceived by the senses	friendship, opportunities, fear, stubbornness
Compound	expresses a single idea through a combination of two or more words	jump rope, paycheck, dragonfly, sandpaper
Collective	refers to a group of people or things	colony, family, clan, flock
Possessive	shows who or what owns something	Mama's, Tito's, children's, waitresses'
Pronoun	takes the place of a noun or another pronoun	
Personal	refers to the person making a statement, the person(s) being addressed, or the person(s) or thing(s) the statement is about	I, me, my, mine, we, us, our, ours, you, your, yours, she, he, it, her, him, hers, his, its, they, them, their, theirs
Reflexive	follows a verb or preposition and refers to a preceding noun or pronoun	myself, yourself, herself, himself, itself, ourselves, yourselves, themselves

continued

Part of Speech	Function	Examples
Intensive	emphasizes a noun or another pronoun	(same as reflexives)
Demonstrative	points to one or more specific persons or things	this, that, these, those
Interrogative	signals a question	who, whom, whose, which, what
Indefinite	refers to one or more persons or things not specifically mentioned	both, all, most, many, anyone, everybody, several, none, some
Relative	introduces an adjective clause by relating it to a word in the clause	who, whom, whose, which, that
Verb	expresses an action, a condition, or a state of being	
Action	tells what the subject does or did, physically or mentally	run, reaches, listened, consider, decides, dreamed
Linking	connects the subject to something that identifies or describes it	am, is, are, was, were, sound, taste, appear, feel, become, remain, seem
Auxiliary	precedes the main verb in a verb phrase	be, have, do, can, could, will, would, may, might
Transitive	directs the action toward someone or something; always has an object	The storm **sank** the ship.
Intransitive	does not direct the action toward someone or something; does not have an object	The ship **sank.**
Adjective	modifies a noun or pronoun	**strong** women, **two** epics, **enough** time
Adverb	modifies a verb, an adjective, or another adverb	walked **out, really** funny, **far** away
Preposition	relates one word to another word	at, by, for, from, in, of, on, to, with
Conjunction	joins words or word groups	
Coordinating	joins words or word groups used the same way	and, but, or, for, so, yet, nor
Correlative	used as a pair to join words or word groups used the same way	both . . . and, either . . . or, neither . . . nor
Subordinating	introduces a clause that cannot stand by itself as a complete sentence	although, after, as, before, because, when, if, unless
Interjection	expresses emotion	wow, ouch, hurrah

Quick Reference: The Sentence and Its Parts

The diagrams that follow will give you a brief review of the essentials of a sentence and some of its parts.

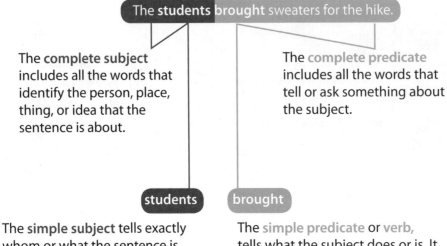

The students brought sweaters for the hike.

The **complete subject** includes all the words that identify the person, place, thing, or idea that the sentence is about.

The **complete predicate** includes all the words that tell or ask something about the subject.

students

brought

The **simple subject** tells exactly whom or what the sentence is about. It may be one word or a group of words, but it does not include modifiers.

The **simple predicate** or **verb,** tells what the subject does or is. It may be one word or several, but it does not include modifiers.

Every word in a sentence is part of a complete subject or a complete predicate.

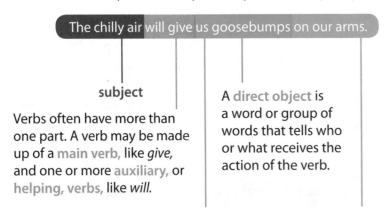

The chilly air will give us goosebumps on our arms.

subject

Verbs often have more than one part. A verb may be made up of a **main verb,** like *give,* and one or more **auxiliary,** or **helping, verbs,** like *will.*

A **direct object** is a word or group of words that tells who or what receives the action of the verb.

An **indirect object** is a word or group of words that tells to whom or for whom or to what or for what the verb's action is performed. A sentence can have an indirect object only if it has a direct object. The indirect object always comes before the direct object.

A **prepositional phrase** consists of a preposition, its object, and any modifiers of the object. In this phrase, *on* is the preposition, *arms* is the object, and *our* modifies *arms.*

Quick Reference: Punctuation

Mark	Function	Examples
End Marks period, question mark, exclamation point	ends a sentence	We can start now**.** When would you like to leave**?** What a fantastic hit**!**
period	follows an initial or abbreviation **Exception**: postal abbreviations of states	Mrs**.** Dorothy Parker, Apple Inc**.,** C**.** P**.** Cavafy, P.M**.,** lb**.,** oz**.,** Blvd**.,** Dr**.,** NE (Nebraska), NV (Nevada)
period	follows a number or letter in an outline or a list	I**.** Volcanoes A**.** Central-vent 1**.** Shield
Comma	separates parts of a compound sentence	I had never disliked poetry**,** but now I really love it.
	separates items in a series	She is brave**,** loyal**,** and kind.
	separates adjectives of equal rank that modify the same noun	The slow**,** easy route is best.
	sets off a term of address	Maria**,** how can I help you? You must do something**,** soldier.
	sets off a parenthetical expression	Hard workers**,** as you know**,** don't quit. I'm not a quitter**,** believe me.
	sets off an introductory word, phrase, or dependent clause	Yes**,** I forgot my key. At the beginning of the day**,** I feel fresh. While she was out**,** I was here. Having finished my chores**,** I went out.
	sets off a nonessential phrase or clause	Ed Pawn**,** the captain of the chess team**,** won. Ed Pawn**,** who is the captain**,** won. The two leading runners**,** sprinting toward the finish line**,** finished in a tie.
	sets off parts of dates and addresses	Mail it by May 14**,** 2010**,** to the Hauptman Company**,** 321 Market Street**,** Memphis**,** Tennessee.
	separates words to avoid confusion	By noon**,** time had run out. What the minister does**,** does matter. While cooking**,** Jim burned his hand.

continued

Mark	Function	Examples
Semicolon	separates items in a series that contain commas	We spent the first week of summer vacation in Chicago, Illinois; the second week in St. Louis, Missouri; and the third week in Albany, New York.
	separates parts of a compound sentence that are not joined by a coordinating conjunction	The last shall be first; the first shall be last. I read the Bible; however, I have not memorized it.
	separates parts of a compound sentence when the parts contain commas	After I ran out of money, I called my parents; but only my sister was home, unfortunately.
Colon	introduces a list	The names we wrote were the following: Dana, John, and Will.
	introduces a long quotation	Abraham Lincoln wrote: "Four score and seven years ago, our fathers brought forth on this continent a new nation. . . ."
	follows the salutation of a business letter	To Whom It May Concern: Dear Leonard Atole:
	separates certain numbers	1:28 P.M., Genesis 2:5
Dash	indicates an abrupt break in thought	I was thinking of my mother—who is arriving tomorrow— just as you walked in.
Parentheses	enclose less important material	It was so unlike him (John is always on time) that I began to worry. The last World Series game (did you see it?) was fun.
Ellipses	replace material omitted from a quotation	"Early one morning, Mrs. Bunnin wobbled into the classroom lugging a large cardboard box. . . . Robert was at his desk scribbling a ball-point tattoo . . . on the tops of his knuckles."
Italics	indicate the title of a book, a play, a magazine, a long poem, an opera, a film, or a TV series, or the name of a ship	*Colin Powell: Military Leader, The Prince and the Pauper, Time, After the Hurricane, The Marriage of Figaro, Hatchet, American Idol, Titanic*

continued

Mark	Function	Examples
Hyphen	joins parts of a compound adjective before a noun	That's a not-so-happy face.
	joins parts of a compound with *all-, ex-, self-,* or *-elect*	The ex-firefighter helped rescue him. Our president-elect is self-conscious.
	joins parts of a compound number (to ninety-nine)	My bicycle wheel has twenty-six spokes.
	joins parts of a fraction	My cup is one-third full.
	joins a prefix to a word beginning with a capital letter	Were your grandparents born post-World War II? The mid-April snow-storm surprised everyone.
	indicates that a word is divided at the end of a line	How could you have any reason-able expectations of getting a new computer?

Quick Reference: Capitalization

Category	Examples
People and Titles	
Names and initials of people	Maya Angelou, **W.E.B. DuBois**
Titles used before a name	Mrs. Price, Scoutmaster Brenkman
Deities and members of religious groups	Jesus, Allah, Buddha, Zeus, Baptists
Names of ethnic and national groups	Hispanics, Jews, African Americans
Geographical Names	
Cities, states, countries, continents	Philadelphia, Kansas, Japan, Europe
Regions, bodies of water, mountains	the South, Lake Baikal, Mount Everest
Geographic features, parks	Great Basin, Yellowstone National Park
Streets and roads, planets	318 East Sutton Drive, Charles Court, Jupiter, Mars
Organizations, Events, Etc.	
Companies, organizations, teams	Ford Motor Company, Boy Scouts of America, St. Louis Cardinals
Buildings, bridges, monuments	Empire State Building, Eads Bridge, Washington Monument
Documents, awards	Declaration of Independence, Stanley Cup
Special named events	Mardi Gras, World Series
Government bodies, historical periods and events	U.S. Senate, House of Representatives, Middle Ages, Vietnam War
Days and months, holidays	Thursday, March, Thanksgiving, Labor Day
Specific cars, boats, trains, planes	Porsche, *Carpathia*, *Southwest Chief*, Concorde
Proper Adjectives	
Adjectives formed from proper nouns	French cooking, Spanish omelet, Edwardian age

continued

First Words and the Pronoun *I*	
First word in a sentence or quotation	**T**his is it. **H**e said, "**L**et's go." **I** have it.
First word of a sentence in parentheses that is not within another sentence	The spelling rules are covered in another section. (**C**onsult that section for more information.)
First words in the salutation and closing of a letter	**D**ear Madam, **V**ery truly yours,
First word, last word, and all important words in a title	"**A**lone in the **N**ets," *Under the Royal Palms*

Grammar Handbook

1 Nouns

A **noun** is a word used to name a person, a place, a thing, an idea, a quality, or an action. Nouns can be classified in several ways.

For more information on different types of nouns, see **Quick Reference: Parts of Speech,** page R2.

1.1 COMMON NOUNS

Common nouns are general names, common to entire groups.

1.2 PROPER NOUNS

Proper nouns name specific, one-of-a-kind people, places, and things.

Common	Proper
volcano, student, country, president	Mount Vesuvius, June, China, President Cleveland

For more information, see **Quick Reference: Capitalization,** page R8.

1.3 SINGULAR AND PLURAL NOUNS

A noun may take a singular or a plural form, depending on whether it names a single person, place, thing, or idea or more than one. Make sure you use appropriate spellings when forming plurals.

Singular	Plural
walrus, bully, lagoon, goose	walruses, bullies, lagoons, geese

For more information, see **Forming Plural Nouns,** page R68.

1.4 POSSESSIVE NOUNS

A **possessive noun** shows who or what owns something.

For more information, see **Forming Possessives,** page R69.

2 Pronouns

A **pronoun** is a word that is used in place of a noun or another pronoun. The word or word group to which the pronoun refers is called its **antecedent.**

2.1 PERSONAL PRONOUNS

Personal pronouns change their form to express person, number, gender, and case. The forms of these pronouns are shown in the following chart.

	Nominative	Objective	Possessive
Singular			
First Person	I	me	my, mine
Second Person	you	you	your, yours
Third Person	she, he, it	her, him, it	her, hers, his, its
Plural			
First Person	we	us	our, ours
Second Person	you	you	your, yours
Third Person	they	them	their, theirs

2.2 AGREEMENT WITH ANTECEDENT

Pronouns should agree with their antecedents in number, gender, and person.

If an antecedent is singular, use a singular pronoun.

EXAMPLE: *That **poem** was fun to read. It rhymed.*

If an antecedent is plural, use a plural pronoun.

EXAMPLES: ***Poets** choose their words carefully. I like **poems**, but Mischa doesn't care for them.*

The gender of a pronoun must be the same as the gender of its antecedent.

EXAMPLE: ***Eve Merriam's** creativity makes her poems easy to remember.*

The person of the pronoun must be the same as the person of its antecedent. As the chart in Section 2.1 shows, a pronoun can be in first-person, second-person, or third-person form.

EXAMPLES: ***We** each have our favorite poets.*

Grammar Practice

Rewrite each sentence so that the underlined pronoun agrees with its antecedent.

1. The speaker in Maya Angelou's poem "Life Doesn't Frighten Me" talks about their fears.
2. When I read this poem, we felt braver already.
3. Scary things lose its power.
4. Even frogs and snakes don't seem as bad as you usually do.
5. I want to know how to be unafraid in her life.

2.3 PRONOUN FORMS

Personal pronouns change form to show how they function in sentences. The three forms are the subject form, the object form, and the possessive form. For examples of these pronouns, see the chart in Section 2.1.

A **subject pronoun** is used as a subject in a sentence.

EXAMPLES: *Steven is my brother. He is the best player on the team.*

Also use the subject form when the pronoun follows a linking verb.

EXAMPLE: *The girl in the closet was she.*

An **object pronoun** is used as a direct object, an indirect object, or the object of a preposition.

SUBJECT   OBJECT
They locked her in it.
OBJECT OF PREPOSITION

A **possessive pronoun** shows ownership. The pronouns *mine, yours, hers, his, its, ours,* and *theirs* can be used in place of nouns.

EXAMPLE: *The cat is mine.*

The pronouns *my, your, her, his, its, our,* and *their* are used before nouns.

EXAMPLE: *I found her keys on the floor.*

WATCH OUT! Many spelling errors can be avoided if you watch out for *its* and *their*. Don't confuse the possessive pronoun *its* with the contraction *it's*, meaning "it is" or "it has." The homonyms *they're* (a contraction of *they are*) and *there* ("in that place") are often mistakenly used for *their*.

TIP To decide which pronoun to use in a comparison, such as "He tells better tales than (*I* or *me*)," fill in the missing word(s): *He tells better tales than I tell.*

Grammar Practice

Write the correct pronoun form to complete each sentence.

1. When (he, him) is done with the book, I will give it to you.
2. Mary is going to invite (her, she) to go rollerskating.
3. My friends have lost (their, they) tickets.
4. (We, Us) can cook vegetables on the grill tonight, or we can make a salad.
5. (I, Me) sent an e-mail earlier today to my aunt.

2.4 REFLEXIVE AND INTENSIVE PRONOUNS

These pronouns are formed by adding *-self* or *-selves* to certain personal pronouns. Their forms are the same, and they differ only in how they are used.

A **reflexive pronoun** follows a verb or preposition and reflects back on an earlier noun or pronoun.

> EXAMPLES: *He likes himself too much. She is now herself again.*

Intensive pronouns intensify or emphasize the nouns or pronouns to which they refer.

> EXAMPLES: *They themselves will educate their children.*
> *You yourself did it.*

WATCH OUT! Avoid using *hisself* or *theirselves*. Standard English does not include these forms.

> NONSTANDARD: *The children congratulated theirselves.*

> STANDARD: *The children congratulated themselves.*

2.5 DEMONSTRATIVE PRONOUNS

Demonstrative pronouns point out things and persons near and far.

	Singular	Plural
Near	this	these
Far	that	those

2.6 INDEFINITE PRONOUNS

Indefinite pronouns do not refer to specific persons or things and usually have no antecedents. The chart shows some commonly used indefinite pronouns.

Singular	Plural	Singular or Plural	
another	both	all	none
anybody	few	any	some
no one	many	more	most
neither			

TIP Indefinite pronouns that end in **one, body,** or **thing** are always singular.

> INCORRECT: *Did everybody play their part well?*

If the indefinite pronoun might refer to either a male or a female, **his or her** may be used to refer to it, or the sentence may be rewritten.

> CORRECT: *Did everybody play his or her part well? Did all the students play their parts well?*

2.7 INTERROGATIVE PRONOUNS

An **interrogative pronoun** tells a reader or listener that a question is coming. The interrogative pronouns are **who, whom, whose, which,** and **what.**

> EXAMPLES: *Who is going to rehearse with you? From whom did you receive the script?*

TIP *Who* is used as a subject; *whom* is used as an object. To find out which pronoun you need to use in a question, change the question to a statement.

> QUESTION: *(Who/Whom) did you meet there?*
> STATEMENT: *You met (?) there.*

Since the verb has a subject (**you**), the needed word must be the object form, **whom.**

> EXAMPLE: *Whom did you meet there?*

WATCH OUT! A special problem arises when you use an interrupter, such as **do you think,** within a question.

> EXAMPLE: *(Who/Whom) do you think will win?*

If you eliminate the interrupter, it is clear that the word you need is **who.**

2.8 RELATIVE PRONOUNS

Relative pronouns relate, or connect, adjective clauses to the words they modify in sentences. The noun or pronoun that a relative clause modifies is the antecedent of the relative pronoun. Here are the relative pronouns and their uses.

	Subject	Object	Possessive
Person	who	whom	whose
Thing	which	which	whose
Thing/ Person	that	that	whose

Often, short sentences with related ideas can be combined by using a relative pronoun to create a more effective sentence.

SHORT SENTENCE: *Lucy is an accountant.*

RELATED SENTENCE: *She helped us do our taxes.*

COMBINED SENTENCE: *Lucy is an accountant who helped us do our taxes.*

Grammar Practice

Write the correct form of each incorrect pronoun.

1. John is a car salesman whom helped me buy a new automobile.
2. The pitcher threw the ball to I.
3. To who should I address this letter?
4. Us love the sea.
5. Betty is as smart as her is.

2.9 PRONOUN REFERENCE PROBLEMS

You should always be able to identify the word a pronoun refers to. Avoid problems by rewriting sentences.

An **indefinite reference** occurs when the pronoun *it, you,* or *they* does not clearly refer to a specific antecedent.

UNCLEAR: *They told me how the story ended, and it was annoying.*

CLEAR: *They told me how the story ended, and I was annoyed.*

A **general reference** occurs when the pronoun *it, this, that, which,* or *such* is used to refer to a general idea rather than a specific antecedent.

UNCLEAR: *I'd rather not know what happens. That keeps me interested.*

CLEAR: *I'd rather not know what happens. Not knowing keeps me interested.*

Ambiguous means "having more than one possible meaning." An **ambiguous reference** occurs when a pronoun could refer to two or more antecedents.

UNCLEAR: *Jan told Danielle that she would read her story aloud.*

CLEAR: *Jan told Danielle that she would read Danielle's story aloud.*

Grammar Practice

Rewrite the following sentences to correct indefinite, ambiguous, and general pronoun references.

1. The teacher was speaking to Maggie, and she looked unhappy.
2. High winds developed. This trapped mountain climbers in their tents.
3. Although Matt likes working at a donut shop, he doesn't eat them.
4. The pitcher was set on the glass-topped table and it broke.
5. They unloaded the clothes from the boxes and then threw them away.

3 Verbs

A **verb** is a word that expresses an action, a condition, or a state of being.

For more information, see **Quick Reference: Parts of Speech,** page R2.

3.1 ACTION VERBS

Action verbs express mental or physical activity.

EXAMPLE: *Lucy ran several miles every day.*

3.2 LINKING VERBS

Linking verbs join subjects with words or phrases that rename or describe them.

EXAMPLE: *After a few months, her shoes were worn out.*

3.3 PRINCIPAL PARTS

Action and linking verbs typically have four principal parts, which are used to form verb tenses. The principal parts are the **present,** the **present participle,** the **past,** and the **past participle.**

Action verbs and some linking verbs also fall into two categories: regular and irregular.
A **regular verb** is a verb that forms its past and past participle by adding *-ed* or *-d* to the present form.

Present	Present Participle	Past	Past Participle
jump	(is) jumping	jumped	(has) jumped
solve	(is) solving	solved	(has) solved
grab	(is) grabbing	grabbed	(has) grabbed
carry	(is) carrying	carried	(has) carried

An **irregular verb** is a verb that forms its past and past participle in some other way than by adding *–ed* or *–d* to the present form.

Present	Present Participle	Past	Past Participle
begin	(is) beginning	began	(has) begun
break	(is) breaking	broke	(has) broken
go	(is) going	went	(has) gone

3.4 VERB TENSE

The **tense** of a verb indicates the time of the action or the state of being. An action or state of being can occur in the present, the past, or the future. There are six tenses, each expressing a different range of time.

The **present tense** expresses an action or state that is happening at the present time, occurs regularly, or is constant or generally true. Use the present part.

NOW: *This apple is rotten.*

REGULAR: *I eat an apple every day.*

GENERAL: *Apples are round.*

The **past tense** expresses an action that began and ended in the past. Use the past part.

EXAMPLE: *They settled the argument.*

The **future tense** expresses an action or state that will occur. Use *shall* or *will* with the present part.

EXAMPLE: *You will understand someday.*

The **present perfect tense** expresses an action or state that (1) was completed at an indefinite time in the past or (2) began in the past and continues into the present. Use *have* or *has* with the past participle.

EXAMPLE: *These buildings have existed for centuries.*

The **past perfect tense** expresses an action in the past that came before another action in the past. Use *had* with the past participle.

EXAMPLE: *I had told you, but you forgot.*

The **future perfect tense** expresses an action in the future that will be completed before another action in the future. Use **shall have** or **will have** with the past participle.

> EXAMPLE: *She will have found the note by the time I get home.*

TIP A past-tense form of an irregular verb is not used with an auxiliary, or helping, verb, but a past-participle main irregular verb is always used with an auxiliary verb.

> INCORRECT: *He has did that too many times.* (*Did* is the past-tense form of an irregular verb and shouldn't be used with *has*.)
>
> INCORRECT: *He done that too many times.* (*Done* is the past participle of an irregular verb and shouldn't be used without an auxiliary verb.)
>
> CORRECT: *He has done that too many times.*

3.5 PROGRESSIVE FORMS

The progressive forms of the six tenses show ongoing actions. Use forms of **be** with the present participles of verbs.

> PRESENT PROGRESSIVE: *Angelo is taking the test.*
>
> PAST PROGRESSIVE: *Angelo was taking the test.*
>
> FUTURE PROGRESSIVE: *Angelo will be taking the test.*
>
> PRESENT PERFECT PROGRESSIVE: *Angelo has been taking the test.*
>
> PAST PERFECT PROGRESSIVE: *Angelo had been taking the test.*
>
> FUTURE PERFECT PROGRESSIVE: *Angelo will have been taking the test.*

WATCH OUT! Do not shift from tense to tense needlessly. Watch out for these special cases:

- In most compound sentences and in sentences with compound predicates, keep the tenses the same.

> INCORRECT: *She smiled and shake his hand.*
>
> CORRECT: *She smiled and shook his hand.*

- If one past action happens before another, do shift tenses.

> INCORRECT: *He remembered what he studied.*
>
> CORRECT: *He remembered what he had studied.*

Grammar Practice

Rewrite each sentence using a form of the verb(s) in parentheses. Identify each form that you use.

1. Helen Keller (become) blind and deaf before she (be) two.
2. A wonderful teacher (change) her life.
3. Anne Sullivan (be) almost blind before she (have) an operation.
4. Even now, Keller (be) an inspiration to everyone with a disability.
5. People (remember) both Helen and her teacher for years to come.

Rewrite each sentence to correct an error in tense.

1. Helen Keller writes a book about her life.
2. She described how she learns to understand language.
3. She felt like she knew it once and forgotten it.
4. Anne Sullivan was a determined teacher and does not give up.
5. Helen had began a life of learning.

3.6 ACTIVE AND PASSIVE VOICE

The voice of a verb tells whether its subject performs or receives the action expressed by the verb. When the subject performs the action, the verb is in the **active voice.** When the subject is the receiver of the action, the verb is in the **passive voice.**

Compare these two sentences:

> ACTIVE: *Nancy Wood wrote "Animal Wisdom."*
>
> PASSIVE: *"Animal Wisdom" was written by Nancy Wood.*

To form the passive voice, use a form of **be** with the past participle of the verb.

WATCH OUT! Use the passive voice sparingly. It can make writing awkward and less direct.

AWKWARD: *"Animal Wisdom" is a poem that was written by Nancy Wood.*

BETTER: *Nancy Wood wrote the poem "Animal Wisdom."*

There are occasions when you will choose to use the passive voice because:

• you want to emphasize the receiver: ***The king was shot.***
• the doer is unknown: ***My books were stolen.***
• the doer is unimportant: ***French is spoken here.***

4 Modifiers

Modifiers are words or groups of words that change or limit the meanings of other words. Adjectives and adverbs are common modifiers.

4.1 ADJECTIVES

Adjectives modify nouns and pronouns by telling which one, what kind, how many, or how much.

WHICH ONE: *this, that, these, those*
EXAMPLE: *This poem moves along quickly.*
WHAT KIND: *square, dirty, fast, regular*
EXAMPLE: *Fast runners make baseball exciting.*
HOW MANY: *some, few, both, thousands*
EXAMPLE: *Thousands of fans cheer in the stands.*
HOW MUCH: *more, less, enough, as much*
EXAMPLE: *I had more fun watching the game than I expected.*

4.2 PREDICATE ADJECTIVES

Most adjectives come before the nouns they modify, as in the examples above. A **predicate adjective,** however, follows a linking verb and describes the subject.

EXAMPLE: *Baseball players are strong.*

Be especially careful to use adjectives (not adverbs) after such linking verbs as *look, feel, grow, taste,* and *smell.*

EXAMPLE: *Exercising feels good.*

4.3 ADVERBS

Adverbs modify verbs, adjectives, and other adverbs by telling where, when, how, or to what extent.

WHERE: *The children played outside.*
WHEN: *The author spoke yesterday.*
HOW: *We walked slowly behind the leader.*
TO WHAT EXTENT: *He worked very hard.*

Adverbs may occur in many places in sentences, both before and after the words they modify.

EXAMPLE: *Suddenly the wind shifted.*
The wind suddenly shifted.
The wind shifted suddenly.

4.4 ADJECTIVE OR ADVERB?

Many adverbs are formed by adding *–ly* to adjectives.

EXAMPLES: *sweet, sweetly; gentle, gently*

However, *–ly* added to a noun will usually yield an adjective.

EXAMPLES: *friend, friendly; woman, womanly*

4.5 COMPARISON OF MODIFIERS

Modifiers can be used to compare two or more things. The form of a modifier shows the degree of comparison. Both adjectives and adverbs have **comparative** and **superlative forms.**

The **comparative form** is used to compare two things, groups, or actions.

EXAMPLES: *Today's weather is hotter than yesterday's.*

The boy got tired more quickly than his sister did.

The **superlative form** is used to compare more than two things, groups, or actions.

EXAMPLES: *This has been the hottest month ever recorded.*

Older people were most affected by the heat.

4.6 REGULAR COMPARISONS

Most one-syllable and some two-syllable adjectives and adverbs have comparatives and superlatives formed by adding *-er* and *-est*. All three-syllable and most two-syllable modifiers have comparatives and superlatives formed with *more* or *most.*

Modifier	Comparative	Superlative
messy	messier	messiest
quick	quicker	quickest
wild	wilder	wildest
tired	more tired	most tired
often	more often	most often

WATCH OUT! Note that spelling changes must sometimes be made to form the comparatives and superlatives of modifiers.

AWKWARD: *friendly, friendlier* (Change y to i and add the ending.)

sad, sadder (Double the final consonant and add the ending.)

4.7 IRREGULAR COMPARISONS

Some commonly used modifiers have irregular comparative and superlative forms. They are listed in the following chart. You may wish to memorize them.

Modifier	Comparative	Superlative
good	better	best
bad	worse	more
far	farther *or* further	farthest *or* furthest
little	less *or* lesser	least
many	more	most
well	better	best
much	more	most

4.8 PROBLEMS WITH MODIFIERS

Study the tips that follow to avoid common mistakes.

Farther* and *Further Use *farther* for distances; use *further* for everything else.

Double Comparisons Make a comparison by using *-er/-est* or by using *more/most.* Using *-er* with *more* or using *-est* with *most* is incorrect.

INCORRECT: *I like her more better than she likes me.*

CORRECT: *I like her better than she likes me.*

Illogical Comparisons An illogical or confusing comparison occurs when two unrelated things are compared or when something is compared with itself. The word *other* or the word *else* should be used when comparing an individual member to the rest of a group.

ILLOGICAL: *I like "A Voice" more than any poem.* (implies that "A Voice" isn't a poem)

LOGICAL: *I like "A Voice" more than any other poem.* (identifies that "A Voice" is a poem)

Bad* vs. *Badly *Bad,* always an adjective, is used before a noun or after a linking verb. *Badly,* always an adverb, never modifies a noun. Be sure to use the right form after a linking verb.

INCORRECT: *I felt badly that I missed the game.*

CORRECT: *I felt bad that I missed the game.*

Good vs. Well *Good* is always an adjective. It is used before a noun or after a linking verb. *Well* is often an adverb meaning "expertly" or "properly." *Well* can also be used as an adjective after a linking verb when it means "in good health."

INCORRECT: *I wrote my essay good.*

CORRECT: *I wrote my essay well.*

CORRECT: *I didn't feel well when I wrote it, though.*

Double Negatives If you add a negative word to a sentence that is already negative, the result will be an error known as a double negative. When using *not* or *-n't* with a verb, use *any-* words, such as *anybody* or *anything,* rather than *no-* words, such as *nobody* or *nothing,* later in the sentence.

INCORRECT: *The teacher didn't like nobody's paper.*

CORRECT: *The teacher didn't like anybody's paper.*

Using *hardly, barely,* or *scarcely* after a negative word is also incorrect.

INCORRECT: *My friends couldn't hardly catch up.*

CORRECT: *My friends could hardly catch up.*

Misplaced Modifiers Sometimes a modifier is placed so far away from the word it modifies that the intended meaning of the sentence is unclear. Prepositional phrases and participial phrases are often misplaced. Place modifiers as close as possible to the words they modify.

MISPLACED: *We found the child in the park who was missing.*

CLEARER: *We found the child who was missing in the park.* (The child was missing, not the park.)

Dangling Modifiers Sometimes a modifier doesn't appear to modify any word in a sentence. Most dangling modifiers are participial phrases or infinitive phrases.

DANGLING: *Looking out the window, his brother was seen driving by.*

CLEARER: *Looking out the window, Josh saw his brother driving by.*

Grammar Practice

Choose the correct word from each pair in parentheses.

1. According to my neighbor, squirrels are a (bad, badly) problem in the area.
2. The (worst, worse) time of the year to go to India is in the summer.
3. The boy didn't have (any, no) interest in playing baseball.
4. Molly sings really (good, well), though.
5. Tom was (more, most) daring than any other boy scout on the trip.

Grammar Practice

Rewrite each sentence that contains a misplaced or dangling modifier. Write "correct" if the sentence is written correctly.

1. Coyotes know how to survive in the wild.
2. Hunting their prey, we have seen them in the forest.
3. Looking out the window, a coyote was seen in the yard.
4. My brother and I found books about coyotes at the library.
5. We learned that wolves are their natural enemies reading about them.

5 The Sentence and Its Parts

A **sentence** is a group of words used to express a complete thought. A complete sentence has a subject and a predicate.

For more information, see **Quick Reference: The Sentence and Its Parts,** page R4.

5.1 KINDS OF SENTENCES

There are four basic types of sentences.

Type	Definition	Example
Declarative	states a fact, a wish, an intent, or a feeling	Salisbury writes about young people.
Interrogative	asks a question	Have you read "The Ravine"?
Imperative	gives a command or direction	Find a copy.
Exclamatory	expresses strong feeling or excitement	It's really suspenseful!

5.2 COMPOUND SUBJECTS AND PREDICATES

A compound subject consists of two or more subjects that share the same verb. They are typically joined by the coordinating conjunction *and* or *or.*

> EXAMPLE: *A short story or novel will keep you interested.*

A compound predicate consists of two or more predicates that share the same subject. They too are usually joined by a coordinating conjunction such as *and, but,* or *or.*

> EXAMPLE: *The class finished all the poetry but did not read the short stories.*

5.3 COMPLEMENTS

A **complement** is a word or group of words that completes the meaning of a sentence. Some sentences contain only a subject and a verb. Most sentences, however, require additional words placed after the verb to complete the meaning of the sentence. There are three kinds of complements: direct objects, indirect objects, and subject complements.

Direct objects are words or word groups that receive the action of action verbs. A direct object answers the question *what* or *who.*

> EXAMPLES: *Daria caught the ball.* (Caught what?)
> *She tagged the runner.* (Tagged who?)

Indirect objects tell to whom or what or for whom or what the actions of verbs are performed. Indirect objects come before direct objects. In the examples that follow, the indirect objects are highlighted.

> EXAMPLES: *The audience gave us a standing ovation.* (Gave to whom?)
> *We offered the newspaper an interview.*
> (Offered to what?)

Subject complements come after linking verbs and identify or describe the subjects. A subject complement that names or identifies a subject is called a **predicate nominative.** Predicate nominatives include **predicate nouns** and **predicate pronouns.**

> EXAMPLES: *The students were happy campers.*
> *The best actor in the play is he.*

A subject complement that describes a subject is called a **predicate adjective.**

> EXAMPLE: *The coach seemed thrilled.*

6 Phrases

A **phrase** is a group of related words that does not contain a subject and a predicate but functions in a sentence as a single part of speech.

6.1 PREPOSITIONAL PHRASES

A **prepositional phrase** is a phrase that consists of a preposition, its object, and any modifiers of the object. Prepositional phrases that modify nouns or pronouns are called **adjective phrases.** Prepositional phrases that modify verbs, adjectives, or adverbs are **adverb phrases.**

ADJECTIVE PHRASE: *The central character of the story is a villain.*

ADVERB PHRASE: *He reveals his nature in the first scene.*

6.2 APPOSITIVES AND APPOSITIVE PHRASES

An **appositive** is a noun or pronoun that identifies or renames another noun or pronoun. An **appositive phrase** includes an appositive and modifiers of it. An appositive usually follows the noun or pronoun it identifies.

An appositive can be either **essential** or **nonessential.** An **essential appositive** provides information that is needed to identify what is referred to by the preceding noun or pronoun.

EXAMPLE: *Longfellow's poem is about the American patriot Paul Revere.*

A **nonessential appositive** adds extra information about a noun or pronoun whose meaning is already clear. Nonessential appositives and appositive phrases are set off with commas.

EXAMPLE: *The story, a poem, has historical inaccuracies.*

7 Verbals and Verbal Phrases

A **verbal** is a verb form that is used as a noun, an adjective, or an adverb. A **verbal phrase** consists of a verbal along with its modifiers and complements. There are three kinds of verbals: infinitives, participles, and gerunds.

7.1 INFINITIVES AND INFINITIVE PHRASES

An **infinitive** is a verb form that usually begins with *to* and functions as a noun, an adjective, or an adverb. An **infinitive phrase** consists of an infinitive plus its modifiers and complements.

NOUN: *To be happy is not easy.* (subject) *I want to have fun.* (direct object)

My hope is to enjoy every day. (predicate nominative)

ADJECTIVE: *That's a goal to be proud of.* (adjective modifying goal)

ADVERB: *I'll work to achieve it.* (adverb modifying work)

Because *to,* the sign of the infinitive, precedes infinitives, it is usually easy to recognize them. However, sometimes *to* may be omitted.

EXAMPLE: *No one can help me [to] achieve my goal.*

7.2 PARTICIPLES AND PARTICIPIAL PHRASES

A **participle** is a verb form that functions as an adjective. Like adjectives, participles modify nouns and pronouns. Most participles are present-participle forms ending in -*ing,* or past-participle forms ending in -*ed* or -*en.* In the examples below, the participles are highlighted.

MODIFYING A NOUN: *The waxed floor was sticky.*

MODIFYING A PRONOUN: *Sighing, she mopped up the mess.*

Participial phrases are participles with all their modifiers and complements.

MODIFYING A NOUN: *The girls working on the project are very energetic.*

MODIFYING A PRONOUN: *Having finished his work, he took a nap.*

7.3 DANGLING AND MISPLACED PARTICIPLES

A participle or participial phrase should be placed as close as possible to the word that it modifies. Otherwise the meaning of the sentence may not be clear.

MISPLACED: *The boys were looking for squirrels searching the trees.*

CLEARER: *The boys searching the trees were looking for squirrels.*

A participle or participial phrase that does not clearly modify anything in a sentence is called a **dangling participle.** A dangling participle causes confusion because it appears to modify a word that it cannot sensibly modify. Correct a dangling participle by providing a word for the participle to modify.

DANGLING: *Waiting for the show to start, the phone rang.* (The phone wasn't waiting.)

CLEARER: *Waiting for the show to start, I heard the phone ring.*

7.4 GERUNDS AND GERUND PHRASES

A **gerund** is a verb form ending in *-ing* that functions as a noun. Gerunds may perform any function nouns perform.

SUBJECT: *Cooking is a good way to relax.*

DIRECT OBJECT: *I enjoy cooking.*

INDIRECT OBJECT: *They should give cooking a chance.*

SUBJECT COMPLEMENT: *My favorite pastime is cooking.*

OBJECT OF PREPOSITION: *A love of cooking runs in the family.*

Gerund phrases are gerunds with all their modifiers and complements.

SUBJECT: *Depending on luck never got me far.*

OBJECT OF PREPOSITION: *I will finish before leaving the office.*

APPOSITIVE: *Her hobby, training horses, finally led to a career.*

Grammar Practice

Rewrite each sentence, adding the type of phrase shown in parentheses.

1. "Fine?" is by Margaret Peterson Haddix. (appositive phrase)
2. Bailey suffered from a migraine headache. (infinitive phrase)
3. Bailey had an MRI. (prepositional phrase)
4. The pediatric wing is full. (gerund phrase)
5. Bailey's mom leaves the hospital. (participial phrase)

8 Clauses

A **clause** is a group of words that contains a subject and a predicate. A sentence may contain one clause or more than one. The sentence in the following example contains two clauses. The subject and verb in each clause are highlighted.

EXAMPLE: *Some students like to play sports, but others prefer to play music.*

There are two kinds of clauses: independent clauses and subordinate clauses.

8.1 INDEPENDENT AND SUBORDINATE CLAUSES

An independent clause expresses a complete thought and can stand alone as a sentence.

INDEPENDENT CLAUSE: *I read "The Banana Tree."*

A sentence may contain more than one independent clause.

EXAMPLE: *I read it once, and I liked it.*

In the preceding example, the coordinating conjunction *and* joins two independent clauses.

For more information, see **Coordinating Conjunctions,** page R3.

A **subordinate (dependent) clause** cannot stand alone as a sentence because it does not express a complete thought. By itself, a subordinate clause is a sentence fragment. It needs an independent clause to complete its meaning. Most subordinate clauses are introduced by words such as *after, although, because, if, that, when,* and *while.*

SUBORDINATE CLAUSE: *Because they worked hard.*

A subordinate clause can be joined to an independent clause to make a sentence that expresses a complete thought. In the following example, the subordinate clause explains why the students did well on the test.

EXAMPLE: *The students did well on the test because they worked hard.*

9 The Structure of Sentences

When classified by their structure, there are four kinds of sentences: simple, compound, complex, and compound-complex.

9.1 SIMPLE SENTENCES

A **simple sentence** is a sentence that has one independent clause and no subordinate clauses. Even a simple sentence can include many details.

EXAMPLES: *Chloe looked for the train.*
Seth drove to the station in an old red pickup truck.

A simple sentence may contain a compound subject or a compound verb. A compound subject is made up of two or more subjects that share the same verb. A compound verb is made up of two or more verbs that have the same subject.

EXAMPLES: *Seth and Chloe drove to the station.* (compound subject)
They waved and shouted as the train pulled in. (compound verb)

9.2 COMPOUND SENTENCES

A **compound sentence** consists of two or more independent clauses. The clauses in compound sentences are joined with commas and coordinating conjunctions (*and, but, or, nor, yet, for, so*) or with semicolons. Like simple sentences, compound sentences do not contain any subordinate clauses.

EXAMPLES: *We all get older, but not everyone gets wiser.*
Some young people don't want to grow up; others grow up too quickly.

WATCH OUT! Do not confuse compound sentences with simple sentences that have compound parts.

EXAMPLE: *Books and clothes were scattered all over her room.*

Here, the conjunction *and* is used to join the parts of a compound subject, not the clauses in a compound sentence.

9.3 COMPLEX SENTENCES

A **complex sentence** consists of one independent clause and one or more subordinate clauses. Most subordinate clauses start with words such as *when, until, who, where, because,* and *so that*.

EXAMPLES: *While I eat my breakfast, I often wonder what I'll be like in ten years. When I think about the future, I see a canvas that has nothing on it.*

Grammar Practice

Write these sentences on a sheet of paper. Underline each independent clause once and each subordinate clause twice.

1. Although the Foster Grandparent Program is more than 40 years old, many people do not know about it.
2. This program was established so that children with special needs could get extra attention.
3. Anyone can volunteer who is at least 60 years old and meets other requirements.
4. After a volunteer is trained, he or she works 15 to 40 hours a week.
5. Foster grandparents often help with homework so that the children can improve in school.
6. Since this program was founded in 1965, there have been foster grandparent projects in all 50 states.

9.4 COMPOUND-COMPLEX SENTENCES

A **compound-complex** sentence contains two or more independent clauses and one or more subordinate clauses. Compound-complex sentences are both compound and complex. If you start with a compound sentence, all you need to do to form a compound-complex sentence is add a subordinate clause.

COMPOUND: *All the students knew the answer, yet they were too shy to volunteer.*

COMPOUND–COMPLEX: *All the students knew the answer that their teacher expected, yet they were too shy to volunteer.*

Grammar Practice

Identify each sentence as compound (*CD*), complex (*C*), or compound-complex (*CC*).

1. In 1998, a hurricane swept through Central America, where it hit Honduras and Nicaragua especially hard.
2. Hurricane Mitch was one of the strongest storms ever in this region; it caused great destruction.
3. People on the coast tried to flee to higher ground, but flooding and mudslides made escape difficult.
4. More than 9,000 people were killed, and crops and roads were wiped out.
5. TV images of homeless and hungry people touched many Americans, who responded generously.
6. They donated money and supplies, which were flown to the region.
7. Volunteers helped clear roads so that supplies could get to villages that needed them.
8. Charity groups distributed food and safe drinking water, and they handed out sleeping bags and mosquito nets, which were needed in the tropical climate.
9. Medical volunteers treated people who desperately needed care.
10. Other volunteers rebuilt homes, and they helped restore the farm economy so that people could earn a living again.

10 Writing Complete Sentences

Remember, a sentence is a group of words that expresses a complete thought. In writing that you wish to share with a reader, try to avoid both sentence fragments and run-on sentences.

10.1 CORRECTING FRAGMENTS

A **sentence fragment** is a group of words that is only part of a sentence. It does not express a complete thought and may be confusing to a reader or listener. A sentence fragment may be lacking a subject, a predicate, or both.

> FRAGMENT: *Didn't care about sports.* (no subject)
>
> CORRECTED: *The lawyer didn't care about sports.*
>
> FRAGMENT: *Her middle-school son.* (no predicate)
>
> CORRECTED: *Her middle-school son played on the soccer team.*
>
> FRAGMENT: *Before every game.* (neither subject nor predicate)
>
> CORRECTED: *Before every game, he tried to teach his mom the rules.*

In your writing, fragments may be a result of haste or incorrect punctuation. Sometimes fixing a fragment will be a matter of attaching it to a preceding or following sentence.

> FRAGMENT: *She made an effort. But just couldn't make sense of the game.*
>
> CORRECTED: *She made an effort but just couldn't make sense of the game.*

10.2 CORRECTING RUN-ON SENTENCES

A **run-on sentence** is made up of two or more sentences written as though they were one. Some run-ons have no punctuation within them. Others may have only commas where conjunctions or stronger punctuation marks are necessary. Use your judgment in correcting run-on sentences, as you have choices. You can change a run-on to two sentences if the thoughts are not closely connected. If the thoughts are closely related, you can keep the run-on as one sentence by adding a semicolon or a conjunction.

> RUN–ON: *Most parents watched the game his mother read a book instead.*
>
> MAKE TWO SENTENCES: *Most parents watched the game. His mother read a book instead.*
>
> RUN–ON: *Most parents watched the game they played sports themselves.*
>
> USE A SEMICOLON: *Most parents watched the game; they played sports themselves.*
>
> ADD A CONJUNCTION: *Most parents watched the game since they played sports themselves.*

> **WATCH OUT!** When you form compound sentences, make sure you use appropriate punctuation: a comma before a coordinating conjunction, a semicolon when there is no coordinating conjunction. A very common mistake is to use a comma without a conjunction or instead of a semicolon. This error is called a **comma splice.**
>
> INCORRECT: *He finished the job, he left the village.*
>
> CORRECT: *He finished the job, and he left the village.*

11 Subject-Verb Agreement

The subject and verb in a clause must agree in number. Agreement means that if the subject is singular, the verb is also singular, and if the subject is plural, the verb is also plural.

11.1 BASIC AGREEMENT

Fortunately, agreement between subjects and verbs in English is simple. Most verbs show the difference between singular and plural only in the third person of the present tense. In the present tense, the third-person singular form ends in **-s.**

Present-Tense Verb Forms	
Singular	**Plural**
I sleep	we sleep
you sleep	you sleep
she, he, it sleeps	they sleep

11.2 AGREEMENT WITH *BE*

The verb *be* presents special problems in agreement, because this verb does not follow the usual verb patterns.

Forms of *Be*			
Present Tense		Past Tense	
Singular	Plural	Singular	Plural
I am	we are	I was	we were
you are	you are	you were	you were
she, he, it is	they are	she, he, it was	they were

11.3 WORDS BETWEEN SUBJECT AND VERB

A verb agrees only with its subject. When words come between a subject and a verb, ignore them when considering proper agreement. Identify the subject and make sure the verb agrees with it.

> EXAMPLES: *The poem I read describes a moose. The moose in the poem searches for a place where he belongs.*

11.4 AGREEMENT WITH COMPOUND SUBJECTS

Use plural verbs with most compound subjects joined by the word *and.*

> EXAMPLE: *My father and his friends play chess every day.*

To confirm that you need a plural verb, you could substitute the plural pronoun *they* for *my father and his friends.*

If a compound subject is thought of as a unit, use a singular verb. Test this by substituting the singular pronoun *it.*

> EXAMPLE: *A bagel and cream cheese [it] is my usual breakfast.*

Use a singular verb with a compound subject that is preceded by *each, every,* or *many a.*

> EXAMPLES: *Each novel and short story seems grounded in personal experience.*

When the parts of a compound subject are joined by *or, nor,* or the correlative conjunctions *either . . . or* or *neither . . . nor,* make the verb agree with the noun or pronoun nearest the verb.

> EXAMPLES: *Cookies or ice cream is my favorite dessert.*
> *Either Cheryl or her parents are being invited.*
> *Neither ice storms nor snow is predicted today.*

11.5 PERSONAL PRONOUNS AS SUBJECTS

When using a personal pronoun as a subject, make sure to match it with the correct form of the verb *be.* (See the chart in Section 11.2.) Note especially that the pronoun *you* takes the forms *are* and *were,* regardless of whether it is singular or plural.

WATCH OUT! *You is* and *you was* are nonstandard forms and should be avoided in writing and speaking. *We was* and *they was* are also forms to be avoided.

> INCORRECT: *You was a good student.*
> CORRECT: *You were a good student.*
> INCORRECT: *They was starting a new school.*
> CORRECT: *They were starting a new school.*

11.6 INDEFINITE PRONOUNS AS SUBJECTS

Some indefinite pronouns are always singular; some are always plural.

Singular Indefinite Pronouns			
another	either	neither	one
anybody	everybody	nobody	somebody
anyone	everyone	no one	someone
anything	everything	nothing	something
each	much		

EXAMPLES: *Each of the writers was given an award.*
Somebody in the room upstairs is sleeping.

Plural Indefinite Pronouns			
both	few	many	several

EXAMPLES: *Many of the books in our library are not in circulation.*
Few have been returned recently.

Still other indefinite pronouns may be either singular or plural.

Singular or Plural Indefinite Pronouns		
all	more	none
any	most	some

The number of the indefinite pronoun *any* or *none* often depends on the intended meaning.

EXAMPLES: *Any of these stories has an important message.* (any one story)
Any of these stories have important messages. (all of the many stories)

The indefinite pronouns *all, some, more, most,* and *none* are singular when they refer to quantities or parts of things. They are plural when they refer to numbers of individual things. Context will usually give a clue.

EXAMPLES: *All of the flour is gone.* (referring to a quantity)
All of the flowers are gone. (referring to individual items)

11.7 INVERTED SENTENCES

A sentence in which the subject follows the verb is called an **inverted sentence.** A subject can follow a verb or part of a verb phrase in a question; a sentence beginning with **here** or **there**; or a sentence in which an adjective, an adverb, or a phrase is placed first.

EXAMPLES: *Here comes the scariest part. There goes the hero with a flashlight.*
Then, into the room rushes a big black cat!

TIP To check subject-verb agreement in some inverted sentences, place the subject before the verb. For example, change **There are many people** to **Many people are there.**

11.8 SENTENCES WITH PREDICATE NOMINATIVES

In a sentence containing a predicate noun (nominative), the verb should agree with the subject, not the predicate noun.

EXAMPLES: *Josh's jokes are a source of laughter.* (*Jokes* is the subject—not *source*—and it takes the plural verb *are.*)
One source of laughter is Josh's jokes. (The subject is *source*—not *jokes*—and it takes the singular verb *is.*)

11.9 *DON'T* AND *DOESN'T* AS AUXILIARY VERBS

The auxiliary verb **doesn't** is used with singular subjects and with the personal pronouns **she, he,** and **it.** The auxiliary verb **don't** is used with plural subjects and with the personal pronouns **I, we, you,** and **they.**

SINGULAR: *The humor doesn't escape us.*
Doesn't the limerick about Dougal MacDougal make you laugh?

PLURAL: *We don't usually forget such funny images.*
Don't people like to recite limericks?

11.10 COLLECTIVE NOUNS AS SUBJECTS

Collective nouns are singular nouns that name groups of persons or things. *Team,* for example, is a collective name of a group of individuals. A collective noun takes a singular verb when the group acts as a single unit. It takes a plural verb when the members of the group act separately.

EXAMPLES: *The class creates a bulletin board of limericks.* (The class as a whole creates the board.)
The faculty enjoy teaching poetry. (The individual members enjoy teaching poetry.)

11.11 RELATIVE PRONOUNS AS SUBJECTS

When the relative pronoun *who, which,* or *that* is used as a subject in an adjective clause, the verb in the clause must agree in number with the antecedent of the pronoun.

SINGULAR: *The* **myth** *from ancient Greece that interests me most is "The Apple of Discord I."*

The antecedent of the relative pronoun *that* is the singular *myth*; therefore, *that* is singular and must take the singular verb *interests.*

PLURAL: *James Berry and Sandra Cisneros are writers who publish short stories.*

The antecedent of the relative pronoun *who* is the plural subject *writers.* Therefore *who* is plural, and it takes the plural verb *publish.*

Grammar Practice

Locate the subject of each verb in parentheses in the sentences below. Then choose the correct verb form.

1. George Graham Vest's "Tribute to a Dog" (describes, describe) the friendship and loyalty canines show humans.
2. Stories about a dog (is, are) touching.
3. Besides dogs, few animals (has, have) an innate desire to please humans.
4. Many traits specific to dogs (bring, brings) their owners happiness.
5. No matter if the owner is rich or poor, a dog, and all canines for that matter, (acts, act) with love and devotion.
6. There (is, are) countless reasons to own a dog.
7. A dog's unselfishness (endears, endear) it to its owner.
8. (Doesn't, Don't) a dog offer its owner constant affection and guardianship?
9. A man's dog (stands, stand) by him in prosperity and in poverty.
10. A dog (guards, guard) his master as if the owner was a prince.

Vocabulary and Spelling

The key to becoming an independent reader is to develop a tool kit of vocabulary strategies. By learning and practicing the strategies, you'll know what to do when you encounter unfamiliar words while reading. You'll also know how to refine the words you use for different situations—personal, school, and work.

Being a good speller is important when communicating your ideas in writing. Learning basic spelling rules and checking your spelling in a dictionary will help you spell words that you may not use frequently.

1 Using Context Clues

The context of a word is made up of the punctuation marks, words, sentences, and paragraphs that surround the word. A word's context can give you important clues about its meaning.

1.1 GENERAL CONTEXT

Sometimes you need to determine the meaning of an unfamiliar word by reading all the information in a passage.

Kevin set out the broom, a dustpan, and three trash bags before beginning the monumental task of cleaning his room.

You can figure out from the context that *monumental* means "huge."

1.2 SPECIFIC CONTEXT CLUES

Sometimes writers help you understand the meanings of words by providing specific clues such as those shown in the chart. When reading content area materials, use word, sentence, and paragraph clues to help you figure out meanings.

1.3 IDIOMS, SLANG, AND FIGURATIVE LANGUAGE

Use context clues to figure out the meanings of idioms, slang, and figurative language.

An **idiom** is an expression whose overall meaning differs from the meaning of the individual words.

The mosquitos drove us crazy on our hike. (Drove us crazy means "irritated.")

Slang is informal language that features made-up words and ordinary words that are used to mean something different from their meanings in formal English.

That's a really cool backpack you're wearing. (Cool means "excellent.")

Figurative language is language that communicates meaning beyond the literal meaning of the words.

Like a plunging horse, my car kicked up dirt, moved ahead quickly, and made a loud noise when I hit the gas. (Kicked up dirt, moved ahead, and made a loud noise describe a plunging horse.)

Specific Context Clues		
Type of Clue	**Key Words/ Phrases**	**Example**
Definition or restatement of the meaning of the word	or, which is, that is, in other words, also known as, also called	In 1909, a French inventor flew a *monoplane*, or a **single-winged plane**.

continued

Type of Clue	Key Words/ Phrases	Example
Example following an unfamiliar word	such as, like, as if, for example, especially, including	The stunt pilot performed *acrobatics,* such as **dives and wingwalking.**
Comparison with a more familiar word or concept	as, like, also, similar to, in the same way, likewise	The doctor prescribed a *bland* diet, similar to the **rice and potatoes** he was already eating.
Contrast with a familiar word or experience	unlike, but, however, although, on the other hand, on the contrary	The moon will *diminish* at the end of the month; however it will **grow** during the first part of the month.
Cause-and-effect relationship in which one term is familiar	because, since, when, conse-quently, as a result, therefore	Because their general was *valiant,* the soldiers **showed courage** in battle.

2 Analyzing Word Structure

Many words can be broken into smaller parts. These word parts include base words, roots, prefixes, and suffixes.

2.1 BASE WORDS

A **base word** is a word part that by itself is also a word. Other words or word parts can be added to base words to form new words.

2.2 ROOTS

A **root** is a word part that contains the core meaning of the word. Many English words contain roots that come from older languages such as Greek and Latin. Knowing the meanings of a word's root can help you determine the word's meaning.

Root	Meaning	Example
auto (Greek)	self, same	**auto**mobile
hydr (Greek)	water	**hydr**ant
cent (Latin)	hundred	**cent**ury
circ (Latin)	ring	**circ**le
port (Latin)	carry	**port**able

2.3 PREFIXES

A **prefix** is a word part attached to the beginning of a word. Most prefixes come from Greek, Latin, or Old English (OE).

Prefix	Meaning	Example
dis- (Latin)	not	**dis**honest
auto- (Greek)	self, same	**auto**biography
un- (OE)	the opposite of, not	**un**happy
re- (Latin)	carry, back	**re**pay

2.4 SUFFIXES

A **suffix** is a word part that appears at the end of a root or base word to form a new word.

Some suffixes do not change word meaning. These suffixes are:

- added to nouns to change the number of persons or objects
- added to verbs to change the tense
- added to modifiers to change the degree of comparison

Suffix	Meaning	Example
-s, -es	to change the number of a noun	lock + s = locks
-d, -ed, -ing	to change verb tense	stew + ed = stewed
-er, -est	to indicate comparison in modifiers	mild + er = milder soft + est = softest

Other suffixes can be added to the root or base to change the word's meaning. These suffixes can also determine a word's part of speech.

Suffix	Meaning	Example
-ion (Latin)	process of	operation
-able (Latin)	capable of	readable
-ize (Greek)	to cause or become	legalize

Strategies for Understanding New Words

- If you recognize elements—prefix, suffix, root, or base—of a word, you may be able to guess its meaning by analyzing one or two elements.
- Think about the way the word is used in the sentence. Use the context and the word parts to make a logical guess about the word's meaning.
- Look in a dictionary to see if you are correct.

3 Understanding Word Origins

3.1 ETYMOLOGIES

Etymologies show the origin and historical development of a word. When you study a word's history and origin, you can find out when, where, and how the word came to be.

em·per·or (ĕm′pər-ər) *n.* **1.** The male ruler of an empire. **2a.** The emperor butterfly. **b.** The emperor moth. [Middle English emperour, from Old French *empereor*, from Latin imperātor, from *imperāre*, to command: *in-, in*; see EN–[1] + *parāre*, to prepare.]

3.2 WORD FAMILIES

Words that have the same root make up a word family and have related meanings. The following chart shows a common Greek root and a common Latin root. Notice how the meanings of the example words are related to the meanings of their roots.

Latin Root	*man:* "hand"	
English	**manual** by hand **manage** handle **manuscript** document written by hand	
Greek Root	*phon:* "sound"	
English	**telephone** an instrument that transmits sound **phonograph** machine that reproduces sound **phonetic** representing sounds of speech	

3.3 FOREIGN WORDS IN ENGLISH

The English language includes words from other languages, such as French, Dutch, Spanish, Italian, and Chinese. Many words have stayed the way they were in their original language.

French	Dutch	Spanish	Italian
ballet	boss	canyon	diva
vague	caboose	rodeo	cupola
mirage	dock	bronco	spaghetti

Practice and Apply

Look up the origin and meaning of each word listed in the preceding chart. Then use each word in a sentence.

4 Synonyms and Antonyms

4.1 SYNONYMS

A **synonym** is a word with a meaning similar to that of another word. You can find synonyms in a thesaurus or a dictionary. In a dictionary, synonyms are often given as part of the definition of a word. The following word pairs are synonyms:

satisfy/please   occasionally/sometimes

rob/steal   schedule/agenda

4.2 ANTONYMS

An **antonym** is a word with a meaning opposite that of another word. The following word pairs are antonyms.

accurate/incorrect   similar/different

fresh/stale   unusual/ordinary

5 Denotation and Connotation

5.1 DENOTATION

A word's dictionary meaning is called its **denotation.** For example, the denotation of the word *thin* is "having little flesh; spare; lean."

5.2 CONNOTATION

The images or feelings you connect to a word add a finer shade of meaning, called **connotation.** The connation of a word goes beyond its basic dictionary definition. Writers use connotations of words to communicate positive or negative feelings.

Positive	Negative
slender	scrawny
thrifty	cheap
young	immature

Make sure you understand the denotation and connotation of a word when you read it or use it in your writing.

6 Analogies

An **analogy** is a comparison between two things that are similar in some way but are otherwise not alike. Analogies are sometimes used in writing when unfamiliar subjects or ideas are explained in terms of familiar ones. Analogies often appear on tests as well. In an analogy problem, the analogy is expressed using two groups of words. The relationship between the first pair of words is the same as the relationship between the second pair of words. Some analogy problems are expressed like this:

in love **:** hate **::** war **:** _____

a. soldier   **b.** peace   **c.** battle   **d.** argument

Follow these steps to determine the correct answer:

- Read the problem as "*Love* is to *hate* as *war* is to . . . ."
- Ask yourself how the words *love* and *hate* are related. (*Love* and *hate* are antonyms.)
- Ask yourself which answer choice is an antonym of *war*. (*Peace* is an antonym of *war*, therefore *peace* is the best answer.)

7 Homonyms, Homographs, and Homophones

7.1 HOMONYMS

Homonyms are words that have the same spelling and sound but have different meanings.

The snake shed its skin in the shed behind the house.

Shed can mean "to lose by natural process," but an identically spelled word means "a small structure."

Sometimes only one of the meanings of a homonym may be familiar to you. Use context clues to help you figure out the meaning of an unfamiliar word.

7.2 HOMOGRAPHS

Homographs are words that are spelled the same but have different meanings and origins. Some are also pronounced differently, as in these examples:

Please close the door. (klōz)

That was a close call. (klōs)

If you see a word used in a way that is unfamiliar to you, check a dictionary to see if it is a homograph.

7.3 HOMOPHONES

Homophones are words that sound alike but have different meanings and spellings. The following homophones are frequently misused:

it's/its	they're/their/there
to/too/two	stationary/stationery

Many misused homophones are pronouns and contractions. Whenever you are unsure whether to write *your* or *you're* and *who's* or *whose,* ask yourself if you mean *you are* and *who is/has.* If you do, write the contraction. For other homophones, such as *fair* and *fare,* use the meaning of the word to help you decide which one to use.

8 Words with Multiple Meanings

Over time, some words have acquired additional meanings that are based on the original meaning.

I had to be replaced in the cast of the play because of the cast on my arm.

These two uses of cast have different meanings, but both of them have the same origin. You will find all the meanings of cast listed in one entry in the dictionary. Context can also help you figure out the meaning of the word.

9 Specialized Vocabulary

Specialized vocabulary is a group of terms suited to a particular field of study or work. For example, science, mathematics, and history all have their own technical or specialized vocabularies. To figure out specialized terms, you can use context clues and reference sources, such as dictionaries on specific subjects, atlases, or manuals.

10 Using Reference Sources

10.1 DICTIONARIES

A **general dictionary** will tell you not only a word's definitions but also its pronunciation, syllabication, parts of speech, history, and origin.

tan·gi·ble (tăn′jə-bəl) *adj.*
1a. Discernible by the touch; palpable. **b.** Possible to touch. **c.** Possible to be treated as fact; real or concrete. **2.** Possible to understand or realize. **3.** *Law* That can be valued monetarily. [Late Latin *tangibilis*, from Latin *tangere*, to touch.]

① Entry word syllabication
② Pronunciation
③ Part of speech
④ Definitions
⑤ Etymology

A **specialized dictionary** focuses on terms related to a particular field of study or work. Use a dictionary to check the spelling of any word you are unsure of in your reading.

10.2 THESAURI

A **thesaurus** (plural, *thesauri*) is a dictionary of synonyms. A thesaurus can be especially helpful when you find yourself using the same modifiers over and over again.

10.3 SYNONYM FINDERS

A **synonym finder** is often included in wordprocessing software. It enables you to highlight a word and be shown a display of its synonyms.

10.4 GLOSSARIES

A **glossary** is a list of specialized terms and their definitions. It is often found in the back of a book and sometimes includes pronunciations. Many textbooks contain glossaries. In fact, this textbook has three glossaries: the **Glossary of Literary and Informational Terms,** the **Glossary of Academic Vocabulary,** and the **Glossary of Critical Vocabulary.** Use these glossaries to help you understand how terms are used in this textbook.

11 Spelling Rules

11.1 WORDS ENDING IN A SILENT *E*

Before adding a suffix beginning with a vowel or *y* to a word ending in a silent *e,* drop the *e* (with some exceptions).

amaze + -ing = amazing
love + -able = lovable
create + -ed = created
nerve + -ous = nervous

Exceptions: *change + -able = changeable; courage + -ous = courageous*

When adding a suffix beginning with a consonant to a word ending in a silent *e,* keep the *e* (with some exceptions).

late + -ly = lately
spite + -ful = spiteful
noise + -less = noiseless
state + -ment = statement

Exceptions: *truly, argument, ninth, wholly, awful,* and *others*

When a suffix beginning with *a* or *o* is added to a word with a final silent *e,* the final *e* is usually retained if it is preceded by a soft *c* or a soft *g.*

bridge + -able = bridgeable
peace + -able = peaceable
outrage + -ous = outrageous
advantage + -ous = advantageous

When a suffix beginning with a vowel is added to words ending in *ee* or *oe,* the final, silent *e* is retained.

agree + -ing = agreeing
free + -ing = freeing
hoe + -ing = hoeing
see + -ing = seeing

11.2 WORDS ENDING IN *Y*

Before adding most suffixes to a word that ends in *y* preceded by a consonant, change the *y* to *i.*

easy + -est = easiest

crazy + -est = craziest
silly + -ness = silliness
marry + -age = marriage

Exceptions: *dryness, shyness,* and *slyness*

However, when you add *-ing,* the **y** does not change.

empty + -ed = emptied   but
empty + -ing = emptying

When adding a suffix to a word that ends in **y** preceded by a vowel, the **y** usually does not change.

play + -er = player
employ + -ed = employed
coy + -ness = coyness
pay + -able = payable

11.3 WORDS ENDING IN A CONSONANT

In one-syllable words that end in one consonant preceded by one short vowel, double the final consonant before adding a suffix beginning with a vowel, such as *-ed* or *-ing.* These are sometimes called 1+1+1 words.

dip + -ed = dipped
set + -ing = setting
slim + -est = slimmest
fit + -er = fitter

The rule does not apply to words of one syllable that end in a consonant preceded by two vowels.

feel + -ing = feeling
peel + -ed = peeled
reap + -ed = reaped
loot + -ed = looted

In words of more than one syllable, double the final consonant when (1) the word ends with one consonant preceded by one vowel and (2) when the word is accented on the last syllable.

be•gin′   per•mit′   re•fer′

In the following examples, note that in the new words formed with suffixes, the accent remains on the same syllable.

be•gin′ + -ing = be•gin′ning = beginning

per•mit′ + -ed = per•mit′ted = permitted

Exceptions: In some words with more than one syllable, though the accent remains on the same syllable when a suffix is added, the final consonant is nevertheless not doubled, as in the following examples.

tra′vel + er = tra′vel•er = traveler
mar′ket + er = mar′ket•er = marketer

In the following examples, the accent does not remain on the same syllable; thus, the final consonant is not doubled:

re•fer′ + -ence = ref′er•ence = reference
con•fer′ + -ence = con′fer•ence = conference

11.4 PREFIXES AND SUFFIXES

When adding a prefix to a word, do not change the spelling of the base word. When a prefix creates a double letter, keep both letters.

dis- + approve = disapprove
re- + build = rebuild
ir- + regular = irregular
mis- + spell = misspell
anti- + trust = antitrust
il- + logical = illogical

When adding *-ly* to a word ending in **l,** keep both **l**'s. When adding *-ness* to a word ending in **n,** keep both **n**'s.

careful + -ly = carefully
sudden + -ness = suddenness
final + -ly = finally
thin + -ness = thinness

11.5 FORMING PLURAL NOUNS

To form the plural of most nouns, just add *-s.*

prizes   dreams   circles   stations

For most singular nouns ending in **o,** add *-s.*

solos   halos   studios   photos   pianos

For a few nouns ending in **o,** add *-es.*

heroes   tomatoes   potatoes   echoes

When a singular noun ends in **s, sh, ch, x,** or **z,** add *-es.*

waitresses	brushes	ditches
axes	buzzes	

When a singular noun ends in **y** with a consonant before it, change the **y** to **i** and add **-es.**

army—armies   candy—candies
baby—babies   diary—diaries
ferry—ferries   conspiracy—conspiracies

When a vowel (**a, e, i, o, u**) comes before the **y,** just add **-s.**

boy—boys   way—ways
array—arrays   alloy—alloys
weekday—weekdays jockey—jockeys

For most nouns ending in **f** or **fe,** change the **f** to **v** and add **-es** or **-s.**

life—lives   loaf—loaves
calf—calves   knife—knives
thief—thieves   shelf—shelves

For some nouns ending in **f,** add **-s** to make the plural.

roofs   chiefs   reefs   beliefs

Some nouns have the same form for both singular and plural.

deer   sheep   moose   salmon   trout

For some nouns, the plural is formed in a special way.

man—men   goose—geese
ox—oxen   woman—women
mouse—mice   child—children

For a compound noun written as one word, form the plural by changing the last word in the compound to its plural form.

stepchild—stepchildren firefly—fireflies

If a compound noun is written as a hyphenated word or as two separate words, change the most important word to the plural form.

brother-in-law—brothers-in-law
life jacket—life jackets

11.6 FORMING POSSESSIVES

If a noun is singular, add **'s.**

mother—my mother's car
Ross—Ross's desk

Exception: An apostrophe alone is used to indicate the possessive case with the names Jesus and Moses and with certain names in classical mythology (such as Zeus).

If a noun is plural and ends with **s,** add an apostrophe.

parents—my parents' car
the Santinis—the Santinis' house

If a noun is plural but does not end in **s,** add **'s.**

people—the people's choice
women—the women's coats

11.7 SPECIAL SPELLING PROBLEMS

Only one English word ends in **-sede:** supersede. Three words end in **-ceed: exceed, proceed,** and **succeed.** All other verbs ending in the sound "seed" are spelled with **-cede.**

concede   precede   recede   secede

In words with **ie** or **ei,** when the sound is long **e** (as in **she**), the word is spelled **ie** except after **c** (with some exceptions).

i before *e*	thief	relieve	field
piece	grieve	pier	
except	conceit	perceive	ceiling
after *c*	receive	receipt	
Exceptions: either	neither	weird	
leisure	seize		

11.8 USING A SPELL CHECKER

Most computer word processing programs have spell checkers to catch misspellings. Most computer spell checkers do not correct errors automatically. Instead, they stop at a word and highlight it. Sometimes the highlighted word may not be misspelled; it may be that the program's dictionary does not include the word. Keep in mind that spell checkers will identify only misspelled words, not misused words. For example, if you used **their** when you meant to use **there,** a spelling checker will not catch the error.

12 Commonly Confused Words

Words	Definitions	Examples
accept/except	The verb *accept* means "to receive" or "to believe." *Except* is usually a preposition meaning "excluding."	Did the teacher **accept** your report? Everyone smiled for the photographer **except** Jody.
advice/advise	*Advise* is a verb. *Advice* is a noun naming that which an *adviser* gives.	I **advise** you to take that job. Whom should I ask for **advice**?
affect/effect	As a verb, *affect* means "to influence." *Effect* as a verb means "to cause." If you want a noun, you will almost always want *effect*.	How deeply did the news **affect** him? The students tried to **effect** a change in school policy. What **effect** did the acidic soil produce in the plants?
all ready/already	*All ready* is an adjective meaning "fully ready." *Already* is an adverb meaning "before" or "by this time."	He was **all ready** to go at noon. I have **already** seen that movie.
desert/dessert	*Desert* (dĕz´ərt) means "a dry, sandy, barren region." *Desert* (dĭ-zûrt´) means "to abandon." *Dessert* (dĭ-zûrt´) is a sweet, such as cake.	The Sahara, in North Africa, is the world's largest **desert.** The night guard did not **desert** his post. Alison's favorite **dessert** is chocolate cake.
among/between	*Between* is used when you are speaking of only two things. *Among* is used for three or more.	**Between** ice cream and sherbet, I prefer the latter. Gary Soto is **among** my favorite authors.
bring/take	*Bring* is used to denote motion toward a speaker or place. *Take* is used to denote motion away from such a person or place.	**Bring** the books over here, and I will **take** them to the library.
fewer/less	*Fewer* refers to the number of separate, countable units. *Less* refers to bulk quantity.	We have **less** literature and **fewer** selections in this year's curriculum.

continued

Words	Definitions	Examples
leave/let	*Leave* means "to allow something to remain behind." *Let* means "to permit."	The librarian will **leave** some books on display but will not **let** us borrow any.
lie/lay	To *lie* is "to rest or recline." It does not take an object. *Lay* always takes an object.	Rover loves to **lie** in the sun. We always **lay** some bones next to him.
loose/lose	*Loose* (lo͞os) means "free, not restrained." *Lose* (lo͞oz) means "to misplace" or "to fail to find."	Who turned the horses **loose**? I hope we won't **lose** any of them.
passed/past	*Passed* is the past tense of *pass* and means "went by." *Past* is an adjective that means "of a former time." *Past* is also a noun that means "time gone by."	We **passed** through the Florida Keys during our vacation. My **past** experiences have taught me to set my alarm. Ebenezer Scrooge is a character who relives his **past**.
than/then	Use *than* in making comparisons. Use *then* on all other occasions.	Ramon is stronger **than** Mark. Cut the grass and **then** trim the hedges.
two/too/to	*Two* is the number. *Too* is an adverb meaning "also" or "very." Use *to* before a verb or as a preposition.	Meg had **to** go **to** town, **too**. We had **too** much reading **to** do. **Two** chapters is **too** many.
their/there/ they're	*Their* means "belonging to them." *There* means "in that place." *They're* is the contraction for "they are."	**There** is a movie playing at 9 P.M. **They're** going to see it with me. Sakara and Jessica drove away in **their** car after the movie.

Using the Glossary

This glossary is an alphabetical list of vocabulary words found in the selections in this book. Use this glossary just as you would a dictionary—to determine the meanings, parts of speech, pronunciation, and syllabication of words. (Some technical, foreign, and more obscure words in this book are not listed here but are defined for you in the footnotes that accompany many of the selections.)

Many words in the English language have more than one meaning. This glossary gives the meanings that apply to the words as they are used in the selections in this book. Words closely related in form and meaning are listed together in one entry (for instance, *consumption* and *consume*), and the definition is given for the first form.

The following abbreviations are used to identify parts of speech of words:

adj. adjective *adv.* adverb *n.* noun *v.* verb

Each word's pronunciation is given in parentheses. A guide to the pronunciation symbols appears in the Pronunciation Key below. The stress marks in the Pronunciation Key are used to indicate the force given to each syllable in a word. They can also help you determine where words are divided into syllables.

For more information about the words in this glossary or for information about words not listed here, consult a dictionary.

Pronunciation Key

Symbol	Examples	Symbol	Examples	Symbol	Examples	Sounds in Foreign Words	
ă	pat	l	lid, needle* (nēd'l)	sh	ship, dish	KH	German ich, ach; Scottish loch
ā	pay			t	tight, stopped		
ä	father	m	mum	th	thin	N	French, bon (bôn)
âr	care	n	no, sudden* (sud'n)	th	this	œ	French feu, œuf; German schön
b	bib			ŭ	cut		
ch	church	ng	thing	ûr	urge, term, firm, word, heard	ü	French tu; German uber
d	deed, milled	ŏ	pot				
ě	pet	ō	toe	v	valve		
ē	bee	ô	caught, paw	w	with		
f	fife, phase, rough	oi	noise	y	yes		
g	gag	ŏŏ	took	z	zebra, xylem		
h	hat	ōō	boot	zh	vision, pleasure, garage		
hw	which	ŏŏr	lure				
ĭ	pit	ôr	core	ə	about, item, edible, gallop, circus		
ī	pie, by	ou	out				
îr	pier	p	pop	ər	butter		
j	judge	r	roar				
k	kick, cat, pique	s	sauce				

*In English the consonants *l* and *n* often constitute complete syllables by themselves.

Stress Marks

The relevant emphasis with which the syllables of a word or phrase are spoken, called stress, is indicated in three different ways. The strongest, or primary, stress is marked with a bold mark (´). An intermediate, or secondary, level of stress is marked with a similar but lighter mark (´). The weakest stress is unmarked. Words of one syllable show no stress mark.

Glossary of Literary and Informational Terms

Act An act is a major division within a play, similar to a chapter in a book. Each act may be further divided into smaller sections, called scenes. Plays can have as many as five acts, or as few as one.

Adventure Story An adventure story is a literary work in which action is the main element. An **adventure novel** usually focuses on a main character who is on a mission and faces many challenges and choices.

Alliteration Alliteration is the repetition of consonant sounds at the beginning of words. Note the repetition of the **d** sound in this line: The **d**aring boy **d**ove into the **d**eep sea.

Allusion An allusion is a reference to a famous person, place, event, or work of literature.

Almanac See Reference Works.

Analogy An analogy is a comparison between two things that are alike in some way. Often, writers use analogies to explain unfamiliar subjects or ideas in terms of familiar ones.
See also **Metaphor; Simile.**

Anecdote An anecdote is a short account of an event that is usually intended to entertain or make a point.

Antagonist The antagonist is a force working against the protagonist, or main character, in a story, play, or novel. The antagonist is usually another character but can be a force of nature, society itself, or an internal force within the main character.
See also Protagonist.

Appeal to Authority An appeal to authority is an attempt to persuade an audience by making reference to people who are experts on a subject.

Argument An argument is speaking or writing that expresses a position on a problem and supports it with reasons and evidence. An argument often anticipates and answers objections that opponents might raise.
See also Claim; Counterargument; Evidence.

Assonance Assonance is the repetition of vowel sounds within nonrhyming words. An example of assonance is the repetition of the o͞o sound in the following line: Do you like blue?

Assumption An assumption is an opinion or belief that is taken for granted. It can be about a specific situation, a person, or the world in general. Assumptions are often unstated.

Audience The audience of a piece of writing is the group of readers that the writer is addressing. A writer considers his or her audience when deciding on a subject, a purpose, a tone, and a style in which to write.

Author's Message An author's message is the main idea or theme of a particular work.
See also Main Idea; Theme.

Author's Perspective An author's perspective is the combination of ideas, values, feelings, and beliefs that influences the way the writer looks at a topic. **Tone,** or attitude, often reveals an author's perspective.
See also Author's Purpose; Tone.

Author's Position An author's position is his or her opinion on an issue or topic.
See also Claim.

Author's Purpose A writer usually writes for one or more of these purposes: to express thoughts or feelings, to inform or explain, to persuade, or to entertain.
See also Author's Perspective.

Autobiography An autobiography is a writer's account of his or her own life. In almost every case, it is told from the first-person point of view. An autobiography focuses on the most important events and people in the writer's life over a period of time.
See also Memoir; Personal Narrative.

Ballad A ballad is a type of narrative poem that tells a story and was originally meant to be sung or recited. Because it tells a story, a ballad has a setting, a plot, and characters. **Folk ballads** were composed orally and handed down by word of mouth from generation to generation.

Bias In a piece of writing, the author's bias is the side of an issue that he or she favors. Words with extremely positive or negative connotations are often a signal of an author's bias.

Bibliography A bibliography is a list of related books and other materials used to write a text. Bibliographies can be good sources for further study on a subject.
See also Works Consulted.

Biography A biography is the true account of a person's life, written by another person. As such, biographies are usually told from a third-person point of view. The writer of a biography—a **biographer**—usually researches his or her subject in order to present accurate information. The best biographers strive for honesty and balance in their accounts of their subjects' lives.

Business Correspondence Business correspondence is written business communications such as business letters, e-mails, and memos. In general, business correspondence is brief, to the point, clear, courteous, and professional.

Cast of Characters In the script of a play, a cast of characters is a list of all the characters in the play, usually in order of appearance. It may include a brief description of each character.

Cause and Effect Two events are related by cause and effect when one event brings about, or causes, the other. The event that happens first is the **cause**; the one that follows is the **effect.** Cause and effect is also a way of organizing an entire piece of writing. It helps writers show the relationships between events or ideas.

Character Characters are the people, animals, or imaginary creatures who take part in the action of a work of literature. Like real people, characters display certain qualities, or **character traits,** that develop and change over time, and they usually have **motivations,** or reasons, for their behaviors.

> **Main character:** Main characters are the most important characters in literary works. Generally, the plot of a short story focuses on one main character, but a novel may have several main characters.
>
> **Minor characters:** The less important characters in a literary work are known as minor characters. The story is not centered on them, but they help carry out the action of the story and help the reader learn more about the main character.
>
> **Dynamic character:** A dynamic character is one who undergoes important changes as a plot unfolds. The changes occur because of the character's actions and experiences in the story. The changes are usually internal and may be good or bad. Main characters are usually, though not always, dynamic.
>
> **Static character:** A static character is one who remains the same throughout a story. The character may experience events and interact with other characters, but he or she is not changed because of them.

See also Characterization; Character Traits.

Character Development Characters that change during a story are said to undergo character development. Any character can change, but main characters usually develop the most.

See also Character: Dynamic Character.

Characterization The way a writer creates and develops characters is known as characterization. There are four basic methods of characterization.

- The writer may make direct comments about a character through the voice of the narrator.
- The writer may describe the character's physical appearance.
- The writer may present the character's own thoughts, speech, and actions.
- The writer may present the thoughts, speech, and actions of other characters.

See also Character; Character Traits.

Character Traits Character traits are the qualities shown by a character. Traits may be physical (tall) or expressions of personality (confidence). Writers reveal the traits of their characters through methods of characterization. Sometimes writers directly state a character's traits, but more often readers need to infer traits from a character's words, actions, thoughts, appearance, and relationships. Examples of words that describe traits include ***brave, considerate,*** and ***rude.***

Chronological Order Chronological order is the arrangement of events in their order of occurrence. This type of organization is used in fictional narratives and in historical writing, biography, and autobiography.

Claim In an argument, a claim is the writer's position on an issue or problem. Although an argument focuses on supporting one claim, a writer may make more than one claim in a text.

Clarify Clarifying is a reading strategy that helps readers understand or make clear what they are reading. Readers usually clarify by rereading, reading aloud, or discussing.

Classification Classification is a pattern of organization in which objects, ideas, and/or information are presented in groups, or classes, based on common characteristics.

Cliché A cliché is an overused expression. "Better late than never" and "hard as nails" are common examples. Good writers generally avoid clichés unless they are using them in dialogue to indicate something about a character's personality.

Climax The climax stage is the point of greatest interest in a story or play. The climax usually occurs toward the end of a story, after the reader has understood the **conflict** and become emotionally involved with the characters. At the climax, the conflict is resolved and the outcome of the plot usually becomes clear.

See also Plot.

Comedy A comedy is a dramatic work that is light and often humorous in tone, usually ending happily with a peaceful resolution of the main conflict.

Compare and Contrast To compare and contrast is to identify the similarities and differences of two or more subjects. Compare and contrast is also a pattern of organizing an entire piece of writing.

See also Pattern of Organization.

Conclusion A conclusion is a statement of belief based on evidence, experience, and reasoning. A valid conclusion is one that logically follows from the facts or statements upon which it is based.

Conflict A conflict is a struggle between opposing forces. Almost every story has a main conflict—a conflict that is the story's focus. An **external conflict** involves a character who struggles against a force outside him- or herself, such as nature, a physical obstacle, or another character. An **internal conflict** is one that occurs within a character. For example, a character with an internal conflict might struggle with fear.

See also Plot.

Connect Connecting is a reader's process of relating the content of a text to his or her own knowledge and experience.

Connotation A word's connotations are the ideas and feelings associated with the word, as opposed to its dictionary definition. For example, the word *bread,* in addition to its basic meaning ("a baked food made from flour and other ingredients"), has connotations of life and general nourishment.

See also Denotation.

Consumer Documents Consumer documents are printed materials that accompany products and services. They usually provide information about the use, care, operation, or assembly of the product or service they accompany. Some common consumer documents are applications, contracts, warranties, manuals, instructions, labels, brochures, and schedules.

Context Clues When you encounter an unfamiliar word, you can often use context clues to understand it. Context clues are the words or phrases surrounding the word that provide hints about the word's meaning.

Counterargument A counterargument is an argument made to oppose another argument. A good argument anticipates opposing viewpoints and provides counterarguments to disprove them.

Couplet A couplet is a rhymed pair of lines. A couplet may be written in any rhythmic pattern. For example, Follow your heart's desire/And good things may transpire.

See also Rhyme; Stanza.

Credibility Credibility is the believability or trustworthiness of a source and the information it provides.

Critical Essay *See* Essay.

Critical Review A critical review is an evaluation or critique by a reviewer, or critic. Types of reviews include film reviews, book reviews, music reviews, and art show reviews.

Cultural Values Cultural values are the behaviors that a society expects from its people.

Database A database is a collection of information that can be quickly and easily accessed and searched and from which information can be easily retrieved. It is frequently presented in an electronic format.

Debate A debate is an organized exchange of opinions on an issue. In school settings, debate is usually a formal contest in which two opposing teams defend and attack a proposition.

See also Argument.

Deductive Reasoning Deductive reasoning is a way of thinking that begins with a generalization, presents a specific situation, and then moves forward with facts and evidence toward a logical conclusion. The following passage has a deductive argument embedded in it: "All students in the math class must take the quiz on Friday. Since Lana is in the class, she had better show up." This deductive argument can be broken down as follows: generalization—All students in the math class must take the quiz on Friday; specific situation—Lana is a student in the math class; conclusion—Therefore, Lana must take the math quiz.

Denotation A word's denotation is its dictionary definition.

See also **Connotation.**

Description Description is writing that helps a reader to picture events, objects, and characters. To create descriptions, writers often use **imagery**—words and phrases that appeal to the reader's senses.

Dialect A dialect is a form of a language that is spoken in a particular place or by a particular group of people. Dialects may feature unique pronunciations, vocabulary, and grammar.

Dialogue Dialogue is written conversation between two or more characters. Writers use dialogue to bring characters to life and to give readers insights into the characters' qualities, traits, and reactions to other characters. In fiction, dialogue is usually set off with quotation marks. In drama, stories are told primarily through dialogue.

Diary A diary is a daily record of a writer's thoughts, experiences, and feelings. As such, it is a type of autobiographical writing. A **journal** is another term for a diary.

Dictionary *See* **Reference Works.**

Drama A drama, or play, is a form of literature meant to be performed by actors in front of an audience. In a drama, the characters' dialogue and actions tell the story. The written form of a drama is called a script. A script usually includes dialogue, a cast of characters, and stage directions that give instructions about performing the drama. The person who writes the drama is known as the playwright or dramatist.

Draw Conclusions To draw a conclusion is to make a judgment or arrive at a belief based on evidence, experience, and reasoning.

Editorial An editorial is an opinion piece that usually appears on the editorial page of a newspaper or as part of a news broadcast. The editorial section of the newspaper presents opinions rather than objective news reports.

See also Op/Ed Piece.

Either/Or Fallacy An either/or fallacy is a statement that suggests that there are only two choices available in a situation when in fact there are more than two.

Emotional Appeal An emotional appeal is a message that creates strong feelings in order to make a point.

An appeal to fear is a message that taps into people's fear of losing their safety or security. An appeal to pity is a message that taps into people's sympathy and compassion for others to build support for an idea, a cause, or a proposed action. An appeal to vanity is a message that attempts to persuade by tapping into people's desire to feel good about themselves.

Encyclopedia *See* Reference Works.

Epic Poem An epic poem is a long narrative poem about the adventures of a hero whose actions reflect the ideals and values of a nation or a group of people.

Essay An essay is a short work of nonfiction that deals with a single subject. There are many types of essays. An **expository essay** presents or explains information and ideas. A **persuasive essay** attempts to convince the reader to adopt a certain viewpoint. A **critical essay** evaluates a situation or a work of art. A **personal essay** usually reflects the writer's experiences, feelings, and personality.

Ethical Appeal In an ethical appeal, a writer links a claim to a widely accepted value in order to gain moral support for the claim. The appeal also creates an image of the writer as a trustworthy, moral person.

Evaluate To evaluate is to examine something carefully and to judge its value or worth. A reader can evaluate the actions of a particular character, for example. A reader can also form opinions about the value of an entire work.

Evidence Evidence is a specific piece of information that supports a claim. Evidence can take the form of a fact, a quotation, an example, a statistic, or a personal experience, among other things.

Exaggeration An extreme overstatement of an idea is called an exaggeration. It is often used for purposes of emphasis or humor.

Exposition Exposition is the first stage of a typical story plot. The exposition provides important background information and introduces the setting and the important characters. The conflict the characters face may also be introduced in the exposition, or it may be introduced later, in the rising action.

See also Plot.

Expository Essay *See* Essay.

External Conflict *See* Conflict.

Fable A fable is a brief tale told to illustrate a moral or teach a lesson. Often the moral of a fable appears in a distinct and memorable statement near the tale's beginning or end.

See also Moral.

Fact Versus Opinion   A **fact** is a statement that can be proved, or verified. An opinion, on the other hand, is a statement that cannot be proved because it expresses a person's beliefs, feelings, or thoughts.

See also Generalization; Inference.

Fallacious Reasoning   Reasoning that includes errors in logic or fallacies.

Fallacy   A fallacy is an error of reasoning. Typically, a fallacy is based on an incorrect inference or a misuse of evidence.

See also Either/Or Fallacy; Logical Appeal; Overgeneralization.

Falling Action   The falling action is the stage of the plot in which the story begins to draw to a close. The falling action comes after the **climax** and before the **resolution,** also called denouement. Events in the falling action show the results of the important decision or action that happened at the climax. Tension eases as the falling action begins; however, the final outcome of the story is not yet fully worked out at this stage.

See also Climax; Plot.

Fantasy   Fantasy is a type of fiction that is highly imaginative and portrays events, settings, or characters that are unrealistic. The setting might be a nonexistent world, the plot might involve magic or the supernatural, and the characters might have superhuman powers.

Faulty Reasoning   *See* Fallacy.

Feature Article   A feature article is an article in a newspaper or magazine about a topic of human interest or lifestyles.

Fiction   Fiction is prose writing that tells an imaginary story. The writer of a short story or novel might invent all the events and characters or might base parts of the story on real people and events. The basic elements of fiction are plot, character, setting, and theme. Different types of fiction include realistic fiction, historical fiction, science fiction, and fantasy.

See also Novel; Novella; Short Story.

Figurative Language   In figurative language, words are used in an imaginative way to express ideas that are not literally true. "Megan has a bee in her bonnet" is an example of figurative language. The sentence does not mean that Megan is wearing a bonnet, nor that there is an actual bee in it. Instead, it means that Megan is angry or upset about something. Figurative language is used for comparison, emphasis, and emotional effect.

See also Metaphor; Onomatopoeia; Personification; Simile.

First-Person Point of View   *See* **Point of View.**

Flashback   In a literary work, a flashback is an interruption of the action to present events that took place at an earlier time. A flashback provides information that can help a reader better understand a character's current situation.

Folklore   The traditions, customs, and stories that are passed down within a culture are known as its folklore. Folklore includes various types of literature, such as legends, folk tales, myths, trickster tales, and fables.

See also Fable; Folk Tale; Myth.

Folk Tale   A folk tale is a story that has been passed down from generation to generation by word of mouth. Folk tales may be set in the distant past and involve supernatural events. The characters in them may be animals, people, or superhuman beings.

Foreshadowing   Foreshadowing occurs when a writer provides hints that suggest future events in a story. Foreshadowing creates suspense and makes readers eager to find out what will happen.

Form   The structure or organization of a written work is often called its form. The form of a poem includes the arrangement of its words and lines on the page.

Free Verse   Poetry without regular patterns of rhyme and rhythm is called free verse. Some poets use free verse to capture the sounds and rhythms of ordinary speech.

See also Rhyme, Rhythm.

Generalization   A generalization is a broad statement about a class or category of people, ideas, or things based on a study of, or a belief about, only some of its members.

See also Overgeneralization; Stereotyping.

Genre   The term *genre* refers to a category in which a work of literature is classified. The major genres in literature are fiction, nonfiction, poetry, and drama.

Government Publications   Government publications are documents produced by government organizations. Pamphlets, brochures, and reports are just some of the many forms these publications take. Government publications can be good resources for a wide variety of topics.

Graphic Aid A graphic aid is a visual tool that is printed, handwritten, or drawn. Charts, diagrams, graphs, photographs, and maps are examples of graphic aids.

Graphic Organizer A graphic organizer is a "word picture"—a visual illustration of a verbal statement—that helps a reader understand a text. Charts, tables, webs, and diagrams can all be graphic organizers. Graphic organizers and graphic aids can look the same. However, graphic organizers and graphic aids do differ in how they are used. Graphic aids help deliver important information to students using a text. Graphic organizers are actually created by students themselves. They help students understand the text or organize information.

Haiku Haiku is a form of Japanese poetry in which 17 syllables are arranged in three lines of 5, 7, and 5 syllables. The rules of haiku are strict. In addition to following the syllabic count, the poet must create a clear picture that will evoke a strong emotional response in the reader. Nature is a particularly important source of inspiration for Japanese haiku poets, and details from nature are often the subjects of their poems.

Hero A hero is a main character or protagonist in a story. They are typically courageous, strong, honorable, and intelligent. They are protectors of society who hold back the forces of evil and fight to make the world a better place. In modern literature, a hero may simply be the most important character in a story. Such a hero is often an ordinary person with ordinary problems.

Historical Document Historical documents are writings that have played a significant role in human events. The Declaration of Independence, for example, is a historical document.

Historical Fiction A short story or a novel can be called historical fiction when it is set in the past and includes real places and real events of historical importance.

How-To Book A how-to book explains how to do something—usually an activity, a sport, or a household project.

Humor Humor is a quality that provokes laughter or amusement. Writers create humor through exaggeration, amusing descriptions, irony, and witty and insightful dialogue.

Idiom An idiom is an expression that has a meaning different from the meaning of its individual words.

For example, "to let the cat out of the bag" is an idiom meaning "to reveal a secret or surprise."

Imagery Imagery consists of words and phrases that appeal to a reader's five senses. Writers use sensory details to help the reader imagine how things look, feel, smell, sound, and taste.

Implied Main Idea *See* Main Idea.

Index The index of a book is an alphabetized list of important topics covered in the book and the page numbers on which they can be found. An index can be used to quickly find specific information about a topic.

Inductive Reasoning Inductive reasoning is the process of logical reasoning that starts with observations, examples, and facts and moves on to a general conclusion or principle.

Inference An inference is a logical guess that is made based on facts and one's own knowledge and experience.

Informational Text Informational text is writing that provides factual information. Examples include news reports, a science textbook, and lab reports. Informational text also includes literary nonfiction, such as personal essays, opinion pieces, speeches, biographies, and historical accounts.

Internal Conflict *See* Conflict.

Internet The Internet is a global, interconnected system of computer networks that allows for communication through e-mail, listservs, and the World Wide Web. The Internet connects computers and computer users throughout the world.

Interview An interview is a conversation conducted by a writer or reporter in which facts or statements are elicited from another person, recorded, and then broadcast or published.

Irony Irony is a contrast between what is expected and what actually exists or happens. Exaggeration and sarcasm are techniques writers use to express irony.

Journal A journal is a periodical publication used by legal, medical, and other professional organizations. The term may also be used to refer to a diary or daily record. *See* **Diary.**

Legend A legend is a story handed down from the past about a specific person, usually someone of heroic accomplishments. Legends usually have some basis in historical fact.

Limerick A limerick is a short, humorous poem made up of five lines. It usually has the rhyme scheme *aabba,* created by two rhyming couplets followed by a fifth line that rhymes with the first couplet. A limerick typically has a sing-song rhythm.

Literary Nonfiction *See* Narrative Nonfiction.

Loaded Language Loaded language consists of words with strongly positive or negative connotations intended to influence a reader's or listener's attitude.

Logical Appeal A logical appeal is a way of writing or speaking that relies on logic and facts. It appeals to people's reasoning or intellect rather than to their values or emotions. Flawed logical appeals—that is, errors in reasoning—are called logical fallacies.
See also **Fallacy.**

Logical Argument A logical argument is an argument in which the logical relationship between the support and claim is sound.

Lyric Poetry Lyric poetry is poetry that presents the personal thoughts and feelings of a single speaker. Most poems, other than narrative poems, are lyric poems. Lyric poetry can be in a variety of forms and cover many subjects, from love and death to everyday experiences.

Main Character *See* Character.

Main Idea The main idea, or central idea, is the most important idea about a topic that a writer or speaker conveys. It can be the central idea of an entire work or of just a paragraph. Often, the main idea of a paragraph is expressed in a topic sentence. However, a main idea may just be implied, or suggested, by details. A main idea is typically supported by details.

Make Inferences *See* **Inference.**

Memoir A memoir is a form of autobiographical writing in which a writer shares his or her personal experiences and observations of important events or people. Often informal in tone, memoirs usually give readers information about a particular person or period of time in the writer's life. In contrast, autobiographies focus on many important people and events in the writer's life over a long period of time.
See also Autobiography; Personal Narrative.

Metaphor A metaphor is a comparison of two things that are basically unlike but have some qualities in common. Unlike a simile, a metaphor does not contain the words *like* or *as.*
See also Figurative Language; Simile.

Meter In poetry, meter is the regular pattern of stressed (ˊ) and unstressed (˘) syllables. Although poems have rhythm, not all poems have regular meter. Each unit of meter is known as a **foot** and is made up of one stressed syllable and one or two unstressed syllables.
See also Rhythm.

Minor Character *See* **Character.**

Monitor Monitoring is the strategy of checking your comprehension as you read and modifying the strategies you are using to suit your needs. Monitoring often includes the following strategies: questioning, clarifying, visualizing, predicting, connecting, and rereading.

Mood Mood is the feeling or atmosphere that a writer creates for the reader. Descriptive words, imagery, and figurative language all influence the mood of a work.

Moral A moral is a lesson that a story teaches. A moral is often stated at the end of a fable.
See also Fable.

Motivation Motivation is the reason why a character acts, feels, or thinks in a certain way. A character may have more than one motivation for his or her actions. Understanding these motivations helps readers get to know the character.

Myth A myth is a traditional story that attempts to answer basic questions about human nature, origins of the world, mysteries of nature, and social customs.

Narrative Writing that tells a story is called a narrative. The events in a narrative may be real or imagined. Autobiographies and biographies are narratives that deal with real people or events. Fictional narratives include short stories, fables, myths, and novels. A narrative may also be in the form of a poem.
See also Autobiography; Biography; Personal Narrative.

Narrative Nonfiction Narrative nonfiction is writing that reads much like fiction, except that the characters, setting, and plot are real rather than imaginary. Narrative nonfiction includes autobiographies, biographies, and memoirs.

Narrative Poetry Poetry that tells a story is called narrative poetry. Like fiction, a narrative poem contains characters, a setting, and a plot. It might also contain such elements of poetry as rhyme, rhythm, imagery, and figurative language.

Narrator The narrator is the voice that tells a story. Sometimes the narrator is a character in the story. At other times, the narrator is an outside voice created by the writer. The narrator is not the same as the writer.

See also Point of View.

News Article A news article is writing that reports on a recent event. In newspapers, news articles are usually brief and to the point, presenting the most important facts first, followed by more detailed information.

Nonfiction Nonfiction is writing that tells about real people, places, and events. Unlike fiction, nonfiction is mainly written to convey factual information. Nonfiction includes a wide range of writing—newspaper articles, letters, essays, biographies, movie reviews, speeches, true-life adventure stories, advertising, and more.

Novel A novel is a long work of fiction. Like a short story, a novel is the product of a writer's imagination. Because a novel is considerably longer than a short story, a novelist can develop the characters and story line more thoroughly.

See also Fiction.

Novella A novella is a work of fiction that is longer than a short story but shorter than a novel. Due to its shorter length, a novella generally includes fewer characters and a less complex plot than a novel.

See also Fiction; Novel; Short Story.

Ode An ode is a type of lyric poem that deals with serious themes, such as justice, truth, or beauty.

Onomatopoeia Onomatopoeia is the use of words whose sounds echo their meanings, such as *buzz, whisper, gargle,* and *murmur.*

Op/Ed Piece An op/ed piece is an opinion piece that typically appears opposite ("op") the editorial page of a newspaper. Unlike editorials, op/ed pieces are written and submitted by readers.

Oral Literature Oral literature, or the oral tradition, consists of stories that have been passed down by word of mouth from generation to generation. Oral literature includes folk tales, legends, and myths. In more recent times, some examples of oral literature have been written down or recorded so that the stories can be preserved.

Organization *See* Pattern of Organization.

Overgeneralization An overgeneralization is a statement that is too broad to be accurate. You can often recognize overgeneralizations by the appearance of words and phrases such as *all, everyone, every time, any, anything, no one,* or *none.* An example is

"None of the city's workers really cares about keeping the environment clean." In all probability, there are many exceptions. The writer can't possibly know the feelings of every city worker.

Overview An overview is a short summary of a story, a speech, or an essay.

Paraphrase Paraphrasing is the restating of information in one's own words.

See also **Summarize.**

Parody A parody is a humorous imitation of another writer's work. Parodies can take the form of fiction, drama, or poetry. Jon Scieszka's "The True Story of the Three Little Pigs" is an example of a parody.

Pattern of Organization The term *pattern of organization* refers to the way ideas and information are arranged and organized. Patterns of organization include cause and effect, chronological, compare and contrast, classification, and problem-solution, among others.

See also Cause and Effect; Chronological Order; Classification; Compare and Contrast; Problem-Solution Order; Sequential Order.

Periodical A periodical is a magazine or another type of publication that is issued on a regular basis.

Personal Narrative A short essay told as a story in the first-person point of view. A personal narrative usually reflects the writer's experiences, feelings, and personality.

See also Autobiography; Memoir.

Personification The giving of human qualities to an animal, object, or idea is known as personification.

See also Figurative Language.

Persuasion Persuasion is the art of swaying others' feelings, beliefs, or actions. Persuasion normally appeals to both the mind and the emotions of readers.

See also Appeal to Authority; Emotional Appeal; Ethical Appeal; Loaded Language; Logical Appeal.

Persuasive Essay *See* Essay.

Play *See* Drama.

Playwright *See* Drama.

Plot The series of events in a story is called the plot. The plot usually centers on a **conflict,** or struggle, faced by the main character. The action that the characters take to solve the problem builds toward a **climax** in the story. At this point, or shortly afterward, the problem is solved and the story ends. Most story plots have five stages: exposition, rising action, climax, falling action, and resolution.

See also Climax; Conflict; Exposition; Falling Action; Rising Action.

Poetry Poetry is a type of literature in which words are carefully chosen and arranged to create certain effects. Poets use a variety of sound devices, imagery, and figurative language to express emotions and ideas.

See also Alliteration; Assonance; Ballad; Free Verse; Imagery; Meter; Narrative Poetry; Rhyme; Rhythm; Stanza.

Point of View Point of view refers to how a writer chooses to narrate a story. When a story is told from the **first-person** point of view, the narrator is a character in the story and uses first-person pronouns, such as *I, me,* and *we.* In a story told from the **third-person** point of view, the narrator is not a character in the story. A writer's choice of narrator affects the information readers receive.

See also Narrator.

Predict Predicting is a reading strategy that involves using text clues to make a reasonable guess about what will happen next in a story.

Primary Source *See* Sources.

Prior Knowledge Prior knowledge is the knowledge a reader already possesses about a topic. This information might come from personal experiences, expert accounts, books, films, or other sources.

Problem-Solution Order Problem-solution order is a pattern of organization in which a problem is stated and analyzed and then one or more solutions are proposed and examined.

Prop The word *prop,* originally an abbreviation of the word *property,* refers to any physical object that is used in a drama.

Propaganda Propaganda is any form of communication that is so distorted that it conveys false or misleading information to advance a specific belief or cause.

Prose The word *prose* refers to all forms of writing that are not in verse form. The term may be used to describe very different forms of writing, such as short stories and essays.

Protagonist A protagonist is the main character in a story, play, or novel. The protagonist is involved in the main conflict of the story. Usually, the protagonist undergoes changes as the plot runs its course.

Public Document Public documents are documents that were written for the public to provide information that is of public interest or concern. They include government documents, speeches, signs, and rules and regulations.

See also Government Publications.

Pun A pun is a play on words based on similar senses of two or more words, or on various meanings of the same word. A pun is usually made for humorous effect. For example, the fisherman was fired for playing hooky.

Radio Play A radio play is a drama that is written specifically to be broadcast over the radio. Because the audience is not meant to see a radio play, sound effects are often used to help listeners imagine the setting and the action. The stage directions in the play's script indicate the sound effects.

Realistic Fiction Realistic fiction is fiction that is set in the real, modern world. The characters behave like real people and use human abilities to cope with modern life's problems and conflicts.

Recurring Theme *See* Theme.

Reference Work Reference works are sources that contain facts and background information on a wide range of subjects. Most reference works are good sources of reliable information because they have been reviewed by experts. The following are some common reference works: encyclopedias, dictionaries, thesauri, almanacs, atlases, and directories.

Refrain A refrain is one or more lines repeated in each stanza of a poem.

Repetition Repetition is a technique in which a sound, word, phrase, or line is repeated for emphasis or unity. Repetition often helps to reinforce meaning and create an appealing rhythm.

See also Alliteration; Refrain; Sound Devices.

Resolution *See* Falling Action.

Review *See* Critical Review.

Rhetorical Question Rhetorical questions are those that have such obvious answers that they do not require a reply. Writers often use them to suggest that their claim is so obvious that everyone should agree with it.

Rhyme Rhyme is the repetition of sounds at the end of words. Words rhyme when their accented vowels and the letters that follow have identical sounds. *Pig* and *dig* rhyme, as do *reaching* and *teaching.* The most common type of rhyme in poetry is called **end**

rhyme, in which rhyming words come at the ends of lines. Rhyme that occurs within a line of poetry is called **internal rhyme.**

Rhyme Scheme A rhyme scheme is a pattern of end rhymes in a poem. A rhyme scheme is noted by assigning a letter of the alphabet, beginning with **a,** to each line. Lines that rhyme are given the same letter.

Rhythm Rhythm is the musical quality created by the alternation of stressed and unstressed syllables in a line of poetry. Poets use rhythm to emphasize ideas and to create moods. Devices such as alliteration, rhyme, and assonance often contribute to creating rhythm.

See also Meter.

Rising Action The rising action is the stage of the plot that develops the **conflict,** or struggle. During this stage, events occur that make the conflict more complicated. The events in the rising action build toward a **climax,** or turning point.

See also Plot.

Scanning Scanning is the process used to search through a text for a particular fact or piece of information. When you scan, you sweep your eyes across a page, looking for key words that may lead you to the information you want.

Scene In drama, the action is often divided into acts and scenes. Each scene presents an episode of the play's plot and typically occurs at a single place and time.

See also Act.

Scenery Scenery is a painted backdrop or other structures used to create the setting for a play.

Science Fiction Science fiction is fiction in which a writer explores unexpected possibilities of the past or the future, combining scientific information with his or her creative imagination. Most science fiction writers create believable worlds, although some create fantasy worlds that have familiar elements.

See also Fantasy.

Scope Scope refers to a work's focus. For example, an article about Austin, Texas, that focuses on the city's history, economy, and residents has a broad scope. An article that focuses only on the restaurants in Austin has a narrower scope.

Script The text of a play, film, or broadcast is called a script.

Secondary Source *See* Source.

Sensory Details Sensory details are words and phrases that appeal to the reader's senses of sight, hearing, touch, smell, and taste.

See also Imagery.

Sequential Order Sequential order is a pattern of organization that shows the order of steps or stages in a process.

Setting The setting of a story, poem, or play is the time and place of the action. Sometimes the setting is clear and well-defined. At other times, it is left to the reader's imagination. Elements of setting include geographic location, historical period (past, present, or future), season, time of day, and culture.

Setting a Purpose The process of establishing specific reasons for reading a text is called setting a purpose. Readers can look at a text's title, headings, and illustrations to guess what it might be about. They can then use these guesses to figure out what they want to learn from reading the text.

Short Story A short story is a work of fiction that centers on a single idea and can be read in one sitting. Generally, a short story has one main conflict that involves the characters and keeps the story moving.

See also Fiction.

Sidebar A sidebar is additional information set in a box alongside or within a news or feature article. Popular magazines often make use of sidebars.

Signal Words In a text, signal words are words and phrases that help show how events or ideas are related. Some common examples of signal words are **and, but, however, nevertheless, therefore,** and **in addition.**

Simile A simile is a figure of speech that makes a comparison between two unlike things using the words **like** or **as.**

See also Figurative Language; Metaphor.

Sound Devices Sound devices are ways of using words for the sound qualities they create. Sound devices can help convey meaning and mood in a writer's work. Some common sound devices include **alliteration, assonance, meter, onomatopoeia, repetition, rhyme,** and **rhythm.**

See also Alliteration; Assonance; Meter; Onomatopoeia; Repetition; Rhyme; Rhythm.

Source A source is anything that supplies information. **Primary sources** are materials created by people who witnessed or took part in the event they supply information about. Letters, diaries, autobiographies, and eyewitness accounts are primary sources. **Secondary sources** are those made by people who were not directly involved in the event or even present when it occurred. Encyclopedias, textbooks, biographies, and most news articles are secondary sources.

Speaker In poetry the speaker is the voice that "talks" to the reader, similar to the narrator in fiction. The speaker is not necessarily the poet.

Speech A speech is a talk or public address. The purpose of a speech may be to entertain, to explain, to persuade, to inspire, or any combination of these purposes.

Stage Directions In the script of a play, the instructions to the actors, director, and stage crew are called the stage directions. Stage directions might suggest scenery, lighting, sound effects, and ways for actors to move and speak. Stage directions often appear in parentheses and in italic type.

Stanza A stanza is a group of two or more lines that form a unit in a poem. Each stanza may have the same number of lines, or the number of lines may vary.

See also Couplet; Form; Poetry.

Stereotype In literature, characters who are defined by a single trait are known as stereotypes. Such characters do not usually demonstrate the complexities of real people. Familiar stereotypes in popular literature include the absent-minded professor and the busybody.

Stereotyping Stereotyping is a dangerous type of overgeneralization. It can lead to unfair judgments of people based on their ethnic background, beliefs, practices, or physical appearance.

Structure The structure of a work of literature is the way in which it is put together. In poetry, structure involves the arrangement of words and lines to produce a desired effect. One structural unit in poetry is the stanza. In prose, structure involves the arrangement of such elements as sentences, paragraphs, and events. **Sentence structure** refers to the length and types of sentences used in a work.

Style A style is a manner of writing. It involves how something is said rather than what is said.

Subject The subject of a literary work is its focus or topic. In an autobiography, for example, the subject is the life of the person telling the story. Subject differs from

theme in that theme is a deeper meaning, whereas the subject is the main situation or set of facts described by the text.

Summarize To summarize is to briefly retell the main ideas of a piece of writing in one's own words.

See also Paraphrase.

Support Support is any information that helps to prove a claim.

Supporting Detail *See* Main Idea.

Surprise Ending A surprise ending is an unexpected plot twist at the end of a story. The surprise may be a sudden turn in the action or a piece of information that gives a different perspective to the entire story.

Suspense Suspense is a feeling of growing tension and excitement experienced by a reader. Suspense makes a reader curious about the outcome of a story or an event within a story. A writer creates suspense by raising questions in the reader's mind. The use of **foreshadowing** is one way that writers create suspense.

See also Foreshadowing.

Symbol A symbol is a person, a place, an object, an animal, or an activity that stands for something beyond itself. For example, a flag is a colored piece of cloth that stands for a country. A white dove is a bird that represents peace.

Synthesize To synthesize information means to take individual pieces of information and combine them in order to gain a better understanding of a subject.

Tall Tale A tall tale is a humorously exaggerated story about impossible events, often involving the supernatural abilities of the main character. Stories about folk heroes such as Pecos Bill and Paul Bunyan are typical tall tales.

Teleplay A teleplay is a play written for television. In a teleplay, scenes can change quickly and dramatically. The camera can focus the viewer's attention on specific actions. The camera directions in teleplays are much like the stage directions in stage plays.

Text Feature Text features are elements of a text, such as boldface type, headings, and subheadings, that help organize and call attention to important information. Italic type, bulleted or numbered lists, sidebars, and graphic aids such as charts, tables, timelines, illustrations, and photographs are also considered text features.

Theme A theme is a message about life or human nature that the writer shares with the reader. In many cases, readers must infer the writer's message. One way to infer a theme is to note the lessons learned by the main characters.

    Recurring themes: Themes found in a variety of works. For example, authors from different backgrounds might express similar themes having to do with the importance of family values.

    Universal themes: Themes that are found throughout the literature of all time periods. For example, Cinderella stories contain a universal theme relating to goodness being rewarded.

See also Moral.

Thesaurus *See* Reference Works.

Thesis Statement A thesis statement, or controlling idea, is the main proposition that a writer attempts to support in a piece of writing.

Third-Person Point of View *See* Point of View.

Title The title of a piece of writing is the name that is attached to it. A title often refers to an important aspect of the work.

Tone The tone of a literary work expresses the writer's attitude toward his or her subject. Words such as *angry,* *sad,* and *humorous* can be used to describe different tones.

See also Author's Perspective.

Topic Sentence The topic sentence of a paragraph states the paragraph's main idea. All other sentences in the paragraph provide supporting details.

Tragedy A tragedy is a dramatic work that presents the downfall of a character or characters. The events in a tragic plot are set in motion by a decision that is often an error in judgment on the part of the hero. Events are linked in a cause-and-effect relationship and lead to a disastrous conclusion, usually death.

Traits *See* Character.

Treatment The way a topic is handled in a work is referred to as its treatment. Treatment includes the form the writing takes as well as the writer's purpose and tone.

Turning Point *See* Climax.

Universal Theme *See* Theme.

Unsupported Inference A guess that may seem logical but that is not supported by facts.

Visualize Visualizing is the process of forming a mental picture based on written or spoken information.

Voice The term *voice* refers to a writer's unique use of language that allows a reader to "hear" a human personality in the writer's work. Elements of style that contribute to a writer's voice can reveal much about the author's personality, beliefs, and attitudes.

Website A website is a collection of "pages" on the World Wide Web that usually covers a specific subject. Linked pages are accessed by clicking hyperlinks or menus, which send the user from page to page within a website. Websites are created by companies, organizations, educational institutions, government agencies, the military, and individuals.

Word Choice The success of any writing depends on the writer's choice of words. Words not only communicate ideas but also help describe events, characters, settings, and so on. Word choice can make a writer's work sound formal or informal, serious or humorous. A writer must choose words carefully depending on the goal of the piece of writing. For example, a writer working on a science article would probably use technical, formal words; a writer trying to establish the setting in a short story would probably use more descriptive words. Word choice is sometimes referred to as diction.

See also Style.

Workplace Document Workplace documents are materials that are produced or used within a work setting, usually to aid in the functioning of the workplace. They include job applications, office memos, training manuals, job descriptions, and sales reports.

Works Cited The term *works cited* refers to a list of all the works a writer has referred to in his or her text. This list often includes not only books and articles but also Internet sources.

Works Consulted The term *works consulted* refers to a list of all the works a writer consulted in order to create his or her text. It is not limited just to those works cited in the text.

See also Bibliography.

Glossary of Academic Vocabulary

adapted (ə-dăp′təd) *adj.* changed for a new place or situation

advantages (ăd-văn′tĭj-əz) *n.* reasons that make one person more likely to succeed than others; qualities of something that make it better or more useful than something else

available (ə-vā′lə-bəl) *adj.* possible or easy to get

collected (kə-lĕk′tĭd) *adj.* brought together into a group

competition (kŏm′pĭ-tĭsh′ən) *n.* a contest or challenge; another person or group who is also trying to win

contrary (kŏn′trĕr′ē) *adj.* completely different or opposite

dependent (dĭ-pĕn′dənt) *adj.* needing something or someone for help or support

deserted (dĭ-zûr′tĭd) *adj.* empty of people

developed (dĭ-vĕl′əpt) *adj.* improved or advanced

effective (ĭ-fĕk′tĭv) *adj.* working very well

efficient (ĭ-fĭsh′ənt) *adj.* done without wasting time, money or energy

embarrassed (ĕm-băr′əst) *adj.* uncomfortable or ashamed in front of other people

endangered (ĕn-dān′jərd) *adj.* at risk

extending (ĭk-stĕn′dĭng) *v.* covering a certain area; making longer or wider

gradually (grăj′ōō-əl′ lē) *adv.* little by little

hostile (hŏs′təl, -tīl′) *adj.* very unfriendly

incredibly (ĭn-krĕd′ə-blē) *adj.* amazingly

intimidated (ĭn-tĭm′ĭ-dāt′ əd) *adj.* afraid or not confident

personally (pûr′sə-nə-lē) *adv.* done by a particular person; in one's own opinion

persuade (pər-swād′) *v.* to make someone do or believe something by giving them good reasons

presence (prĕz′əns) *n.* being somewhere at a certain time

primitive (prĭm′ĭ-tĭv) *adj.* from an earlier time; in an early stage of development

range (rānj) *n.* the area where something can operate; open land that farm animals live on; a row of mountains

residents (rĕz′ĭ-dənts, -dĕnts′) *n.* people who live in a particular place

responsibility (rĭ-spŏn′sə-bĭl′ĭ-tē) *n.* something you should or must do

rhythmic (rĭth′mĭk) *adj.* having a regular pattern of sounds or movements

specialty (spĕsh′əl-tē) *n.* special skill or knowledge

uniform (yōō′nə-fôrm′) *adj.* the same; *n.* a special outfit that everyone in a group wears

unique (yōō-nēk′) *adj.* different from everything else

viewpoint (vyōō′point′) *n.* a way of looking at or thinking about something

Index of Titles and Authors

Acknowledgments

Arabian Nights retold by Dina McClellan. Copyright © 2014 by Escletxa. Reprinted by permission of Escletxa.

Around the World in 80 Days retold by Jessica Cohn. Copyright © 2014 by Escletxa. Reprinted by permission of Escletxa.

Excerpt from *Athlete vs. Mathlete* by W.C. Mack. Text copyright © 2013 by W.C. Mack. Reprinted by permission of Bloomsbury Publishing and Scholastic Canada Ltd.

Excerpt from *Island of the Blue Dolphins* by Scott O'Dell. Text copyright © 1969, renewed © 1988 by Scott O'Dell. Reprinted by permission of Dunow, Carlson, and Lerner Literary Agency and Houghton Mifflin Harcourt Publishing Company.

Jane Goodall by Mercedes Roffé. Copyright © 2014 by Escletxa. Reprinted by permission of Escletxa.

Excerpt from *The Land of Stories: The Wishing Spell* by Chris Colfer. Text copyright © 2012 by Christopher Colfer. Reprinted by permission of Little, Brown and Company, a division of Hachette Book Group, Inc.

Neil Armstrong by Meredith Mann. Copyright © 2014 by Escletxa. Reprinted by permission of Escletxa.

"Ode to Family Photographs" from *Neighborhood Odes: A Poetry Collection* by Gary Soto. Text copyright © 1992 by Gary Soto. Reprinted by permission of Houghton Mifflin Harcourt Publishing Company.

Excerpt from *Princess Academy: Palace of Stone* by Shannon Hale. Text copyright © 2012 by Shannon Hale. Reprinted by permission of Bloomsbury Publishing.

The Quillworker Girl by Eden Foster. Copyright © 2014 by Escletxa. Reprinted by permission of Escletxa.

Excerpt from *Rachel's Journal: The Story of a Pioneer Girl* by Marissa Moss. Copyright © 1998 by Marissa Moss. Reprinted by permission of Houghton Mifflin Harcourt Publishing Company and Marissa Moss.

The Legend of Robin Hood by Jessica Cohn. Copyright © 2014 by Escletxa. Reprinted by permission of Escletxa.

Podcast Acknowledgments